For the Healing of the Nations: Essays on Creation, Redemption, and Neo-Calvinism

Proceedings of the 2nd Annual Convivium Irenicum

Presented June 4–7, 2014

Edited by Peter Escalante and W. Bradford Littlejohn

Copyright © 2014 The Davenant Trust

All rights reserved.

ISBN: 0692322183
ISBN-13: 9780692322185

Front cover image taken from Edward Hicks (1780–1849), *The Peaceable Kingdom* (de Young Museum, San Francisco).

"And he shewed me a pure river of water of life, clear as crystal, proceeding out of the throne of God and of the Lamb. In the midst of the street of it, and on either side of the river, was there the tree of life, which bare twelve manner of fruits, and yielded her fruit every month: and the leaves of the tree were for the healing of the nations."
—Rev. 22:1–2

LIST OF CONTRIBUTORS

Brian J. Auten currently serves as an intelligence analyst with the United States government and teaches counter-terrorism as an adjunct professor of government at Patrick Henry College. He is the author of *Carter's Conversion: The Hardening of American Defense Policy* (2008), and occasionally writes for a number of evangelical outlets. All non-attributed views, opinions, conclusions and/or errors in his chapter are solely the author's and not those of the US intelligence community.

James Bratt is professor of history at Calvin College in Grand Rapids, Michigan. A graduate of Calvin (1971) he took his PhD in American Intellectual and Religious History at Yale University (1978) under the direction of Sydney Ahlstrom. His first book was *Dutch Calvinism in Modern America* (1984); his most recent, *Abraham Kuyper: Modern Calvinist, Christian Democrat* (2013). He is currently working on a study of American religion in the generation before the Civil War.

Andrew Fulford is currently pursuing a PhD at McGill University on the subject of Richard Hooker; previously he received a MA in Theology from the University of St. Michael's College, and a BA in Religious Studies from Tyndale University College. He is a regular contributor to *The Calvinist International*.

E.J. Hutchinson is Assistant Professor of Classics at Hillsdale College (Hillsdale, Mich.), where he has taught since 2007. His research interests focus on the literature of Late Antiquity and the Neo-Latin literature of the Renaissance and Reformation. He is a member of the Orthodox Presbyterian Church.

Benjamin W. Miller is a church planter for the Orthodox Presbyterian Church in central Long Island, and organizing pastor of Trinity Church. In 1999, he received his *juris doctor* from Oak Brook College of Law, and was subsequently admitted to the California bar. Thereafter, he attended Greenville Presbyterian Theological Seminary, earning his master of divinity in 2005. He served as associate pastor of the OPC in Franklin Square from 2005 to 2011. He and his wife Sarah are blessed with four children.

Joseph Minich is a graduate of The Catholic University of America (BA) and Reformed Theological Seminary (MAR) in Washington D.C. He currently resides in Garland, Texas and is pursuing a Ph.D in intellectual history at the University of Texas at Dallas. He is a regular contributor to *The Calvinist International*.

Laurence O'Donnell (MDiv, 2008 RTS Orlando; ThM, 2010 Calvin Seminary) is a PhD student in systematic theology at Calvin Seminary and a licentiate in the Orthodox Presbyterian Church. He serves as associate editor of *The Bavinck Review* and has published articles in the *Mid-America Journal of Theology*, the *Puritan Reformed Journal*, and *The Outlook*.

Matthew J. Tuininga holds a PhD in Religion, Ethics and Society from Emory University, and an MDiv from Westminster Seminary California. He teaches at Oglethorpe University in Atlanta, Georgia.

CONTENTS

Introduction   vii
Peter Escalante

1   Abraham Kuyper: A Compact Introduction   1
Dr. James D. Bratt

2   Sphere Sovereignty among Abraham Kuyper's Other Political Theories   21
Dr. James D. Bratt

3   And Zeus Shall Have No Dominion, or, How, When, Where, and Why to "Plunder the Egyptians": The Case of Jerome   49
Dr. E. J. Hutchinson

4   "The Kingdom of Christ is Spiritual": John Calvin's Concept of the Restoration of the World   81
Dr. Matthew J. Tuininga

5   Participating in Political Providence: The Theological Foundations of Resistance in Calvin   105
Andrew Fulford

6   "Bavinck's bug" or "Van Tilian" hypochondria?: An analysis of Prof. Oliphint's assertion that cognitive realism and Reformed theology are incompatible   139
Laurence O'Donnell

7   De-Klining From Chalcedon: Exegetical Roots Of The "R2k" Project   173
Rev. Benjamin Miller

8   Narrating Christian Transformationalism: Rousas J. Rushdoony and Christian Reconstructionism in Current Histories of American Religion and Politics   209
Dr. Brian J. Auten

9   Nature and Grace, Visible and Invisible: A New Look at the Question of Infant Baptism   241
Joseph Minich

Introduction

Peter Escalante
The Davenant Trust

The Convivium Irenicum

We could just as easily have called our annual meeting a conference rather than a convivium; we chose convivium, however, to indicate its difference from the academic conference, that difference being that the formal presentations at our gathering occur within a within a wider conversation amongst a circle of friends.

But like all things human, that wider conversation is a work of art. To our minds, the new media, inclusive of social media, offered ground and opportunity to reconstitute the old republic of letters, which had by the later middle 20th century shrunk like late Byzantium to a mere remnant of its former extent due to the rise of corporate mass media on the one hand and highly restrictive gatekeeping on the other. While all acknowledged that religious and philosophical fora on the internet were a mix of gems and dross, what was generally assumed all around was that this was all merely virtual, a sort of second world, from which one might take some wisdom the way one does from books but which otherwise offered only simulated neighborhood.

But we saw other opportunities, and looked to use such mediated encounters as means of going further into actual friendship and collaboration in matters of common care, despite initial difference; what mattered was not so much the particular position being expounded but the mind expounding it. In fact, a number of the men gathered at our yearly symposium first met in musketeer skirmishes online which, as soon as the good faith and character of the momentary opponent was seen, gave way at once to truce and then to earnest conversation in nascent friendship.

So we built circles of likeminded friends through social media, using the possibilities of those media to their maximum good effect, and we sought to make those circles little cities in the republic of letters, which, like the old salons, meet as much or more by correspondence as in person but which always regard meeting in person as the ideal. And like some of the

INTRODUCTION

old salons, we have looked to make our circles of conversation seminars of civic and philosophical education with a close relation to the practice of academic scholarship, though independent of its institutions.

Thus at our convivia the topics of conversation are primarily presentations of academic quality, offered largely by academic scholars (though this is no requirement) but which are discussed in— what word might I use besides convivium?—close fellowship, for lack of any single synonym. In most modern academic conferences, the Q and A and panel discussions are very different things from the free time festivities at the bar or the restaurant or around town; but we have united these, and under the aegis of daily prayer, since we close and end each day with matins and evensong, circumscribing with divinity our conviviality and conversation.

The Convivium of the summer of 2014 was a very great success by all accounts. All the ways in which that was so would be best recounted in person by the participants; for the purposes of this introduction, however, I will simply say that I think the success of the papers will be evident to all who read them. And so now I will introduce them, and the theme on which they all played.

The Theme of Creation

The theme of the 2014 national Convivium was "Creation, Redemption, and Neo-Calvinism." As it turned out, the participants decided to take this primarily as a noun rather than a verb; thus in the sense of "cosmos" or "nature." The lectures given at our symposium of this year all revolved around this theme in some way or another, and they dealt with widely various aspects of it. This topic is obviously one of the first things, but it is also one of the last things since the world to come is also, by definition, creation. The simple truth that it is so is incontestable since the neither the world to come nor those whose dwelling it is built to be are God. But the way in which this is so is the subject of a long, long debate in Christendom, with the question of whether and in what degree the life to come is continuous with this one. How common is the "thing" in "first thing" and "last thing"? Obviously the world to come cannot be continuous with this one with respect to its sin or the flaws which follow from that. But if it cannot succeed it in defect, will it yet succeed it in substance? And how much? And in the meanwhile, what is our nature, and what can it, and what ought it, do with the world with which it is, of course, one flesh? The verbal sense of "creation" reappears here as the question of what Dr Tolkien called "sub-creation," the participation of mankind in God's providential development of his world.

Although the Lord wouldn't suffer the (badly-intended) question of the Pharisees regarding which of her several husbands a woman would be married to in the world to come, we are fools if we do not suffer the earnest inquiry of countless children from the beginning of Christendom: Papa, will my dog be in Heaven? Like many childish inquiries, is not at all mere child's play as a doctrinal question. It is simply one of many naturally arising instances of a wider and very difficult topic, the answer to which will necessarily be much the same as that to the question Dr Schaeffer left us and which our circles have taken up again: *how then shall we live*? Eschatology is protology and vice versa, and in the stars of the revealed Word stretching between the the Alpha and Omega horizons, the divine directives for our our dwelling—even if that be just be for the night, in what is always a pilgrimage and sometimes perhaps even a flight—must be faithfully read and followed.

So the question is a very ancient one. Is the world, at its heart, Eden or Egypt? Are we in exodus, or do we dwell in the Land? Or is exodus the only way to genuinely dwell—is the world only a land of promise, an extended Eden, for those who know they are pilgrims in transit toward God? Do we till the world or flee it? And if we flee it as Egypt, what of the golden spoils? And to which land are we taking them? Is the City of Man always a Tower of Babel, or can it be a tabernacle city?

In the 19th century, this sense of opposition would be figured, primarily by the unhelpful Matthew Arnold, as Hellenism and Hebraism, a false dichotomy which is still unfortunately with us and whose victims, once having a chosen a side, all too often do their best to impersonate the other's caricature of them.

The ancients seem to have worked with a similar rhetorical opposition, but things are not with them quite as they seem. For one thing, they did not oppose Hellenism to Hebraism, though they sometimes sound as though they do. But Hellenism and Hebraism are modern categories. In fact, they consistently range against each other not Hebraism and Hellenism, but rather, *Christian Scriptures and religion* against *pagan scriptures and religion*, that is, they oppose two different integral and architectonic claims, not two cultural legacies.

INTRODUCTION

A famous example of this is considered by Dr Eric Hutchinson of Hillsdale College, who in his "And Zeus Shall Have No Dominion: Literary 'Transformationalism' and the Plundering of the Egyptians in Christian Late Antiquity" turns a trained eye to the case of Jerome's dream in which he was castigated for his study and use of the classics and, under divine duress, made a spectacular renunciation. Dr Hutchinson discovers that a closer look at Jerome's famous renunciation reveals that what Jerome really renounced was not the texts of Plato and Aristotle altogether, but rather a certain kind of *studium,* which is to say, disproportion of place given the classics relative to the divine wisdom of the sacred scriptures.[1]

Given the antiquity and centrality of the question, the status of creation was unsurprisingly one of the great debates of the Reformation time. Very broadly speaking, the evangelicals of the Reform asserted the goodness of original nature in principle, and took redemption to be about getting nature back on track toward its primally intended maturation, whereas the Papalists stood for the primacy of supernature in principle, and took redemption to be about the restoration of the gift of supernature. Decidedly different ideas about the pattern of Christian life in this world followed from these different from principles.

Along with the "political Hebraism" of the Reformation, lately noticed by academics, we might speak too of a project of "cultural Hebraism," a Lutheran and finally pan-Protestant embrace of precisely the "carnality" of creation which in the two-tier Roman schema had and has, despite its empty propaganda about sacramentality and "incarnation," a decidedly inferior and dangerous character compared to "supernature."[2] But the dis-

---

[1] This is a conclusion reached also by Dr Paul Russell in his brilliant and unfortunately almost unknown little essay "A Note on Ephraim the Syrian and 'The Poison of the Greeks' in *Hymns of Faith* 2," *The Harp* 10.3 (Dec. 1997): 45–54.

[2] Here, despite their inevitably critical and too often sinfully ignorant and maligning view of Judaism, the Reformers, especially Luther, actually embraced the "carnality" accusingly ascribed by many semi-gnostic Church Fathers to Judaism, and thus embraced a Jewish (because Biblical) stance regarding the gritty goodness of creation and the task of *tikkun ha olam.* Although Dr Daniel Boyarin makes the ancient Christian witness much more (negatively) uniform than it really was, and in my view gets Paul wrong, his *Carnal Israel: Reading Sex in Talmudic Culture* (Berkeley: University of California Press, 1995) is still in many ways an excellent history of the tropes and strategies involved in this long history, and gives very useful background necessary to understanding the really radical character of the Lutheran and Calvinian revolution. It was not for nothing that Papalist apologists called Protestantism,

putes were not entirely between Papalism and the Reform. There were disputes within Papalism about first and last things, and disputes among Protestants about them too.

And there still are. Quite recently, the American Reformed world, already riven and weary by the early 20th disputes over orthodoxy, liberalism, and neo-orthodoxy, found itself divided between two very vocal schools.

The first was "Reconstructionism", or "Dominionism", which was a peculiar Cold War-era twist on certain old but marginal tendencies among the Reformed. Its thesis was that the Kingship of Christ is of universal extent, and that it has vicars—heads of Christian households—and signally, a thesis unique to them, that this Kingdom has a law, the Mosaic law, but with the specifically sacrificial elements of course subtracted. One can question whether the sacrificial elements really were in fact subtracted; although the rubrics of the temple cultus certainly were in their account, it seems clear that the civil-punitive machinery of the Law functioned in Reconstructionist thought as a cathartic rite, constantly propitiating God by purifying the land of evil; a very marked departure from normal Protestant thinking about law. Be that as it may, its theme was comprehensive consecration and cultivation; here, it claimed to stand on the same Reformed commonplace as did the teachers of what we know to be the mainstream tradition, the most notable among them in our time being Dr Abraham Kuyper, who was the father of modern "transformationalism," the idea that Christians are called to orient all things to God through an art of cultivation whose first principles are derived from the Bible.

Our plenary speaker, Dr James Bratt, in his "Abraham Kuyper: A Compact Introduction," recounts the life of Dr Abraham Kuyper who perhaps more than anyone turned the mind of the modern Reformed to the wider world beyond chapel walls, inspired by Kuyper's vision of a world crafted to reflect the glory of God, in which the original end of creation would be approximated. Dr Bratt further traces the development of Kuyper's doctrine of creational and political order in his "Sphere Sovereignty Among Among Abraham Kuyper's Other Political Theories," outlining

---

especially Calvinism, "Judaizing." They were right in a way about the fact, but wrong about it being an insult.

INTRODUCTION

the structure of Kuyper's schema and noting too some of the unresolved tensions between aspects of his outlook.

The legacy of Abraham Kuyper was claimed, more or less fervently, by a large section of the American Reformed in the 20th century. But there were several profound differences between the mainstream tradition, inclusive of Kuyper despite his own idiosyncrasies, and "Reconstructionism." However, due to the shared central commonplace, and the political circumstances in which Reconstructionism became momentarily popular, these grave differences often went altogether unremarked and Reconstructionism became confused with the Reformed tradition in the minds of many uninformed men.

Dr Brian Auten of Patrick Henry College discusses the peculiarly Californian and Cold War origins of the Reconstructionist movement in his meticulously researched and deeply illuminating paper "Narrating Christian Transformationalism: Rousas J. Rushdoony and Christian Reconstructionism in Current Histories of American Religion and Politics," in which he also recounts the perception of the movement by critical observers from the outside, perceptions which, due to the loud and oft-credited claim by Reconstructionists to be *the* Reformed tradition, led many more classically-minded Reformed to reasonably fear being found guilty by association. But it was not only "theocratic extremism" (and the fear of being associated with it) against which they understandably reacted, it was also against the related notion that the order and adornments of the human world need to be completely replaced by specifically Christian substitutes, a supposition much more widespread than Reconstructionism in the strict sense ever was. Here, they applied Kuyper's idea of "common grace"—more or less consonant with older Christian ideas of "nature"—against what might be better called substitutionalism than transformationalism.

The Reconstructionists were interested primarily in substituting an ahistoric "Biblical law" with no real precedent in Christendom for historic Christian jurisprudence, but the wider "substitutionalist" principle from which they argued was shared even by many of their critics, insofar as the latter were dependent upon the extremely curious novelties of Dr Cornelius Van Til, who monotonously inveighed against classical Reformed scholasticism and its categories of natural reason, natural law, and natural theology, and would have had to inveigh against Calvin himself but deftly avoided this by hardly ever discussing him in any depth. Here, the warrior children of Machen misstepped themselves right into Barth's NEIN! stance, and thus became Barthians of a sort themselves. Mr Laurence O' Donnell of Calvin College, in his brilliant "'Bavinck's Bug' or VanTilian Hypochondria? An Analysis of Professor Oliphint's Assertion That Cognitive Realism and Reformed Theology Are Incompatible," relentlessly dissects the claims of a representative modern Van Tilian and shows that Bavinck, so far from being an inconsistent Van Tilian, was in fact a completely consistent Calvinist, and that Reformed scholasticism was no more a departure from the Reformers in epistemology than it was in sacred doctrine.

In reaction to the theses of the Reconstructionists, a group of Reformed pastors and scholars began to insist not only on the demonstrable differences between "dominionism" and the mainstream Reformed tradition, but went even further. The whole history of this affair, which was inextricably intertwined with disputes about justification, has not yet been written and perhaps cannot yet be. But in rejecting, with perfect justice, the errors of their opponents, this second school was inclined and it seems sometimes even determined to step away from the old Reformed commonplace of consecrated cultivation of the world upon which their opponents had attempted to build their case. This second school asserted a doctrine of "two kingdoms," a theme which was certainly crucial for both Luther and Calvin, and it is by that name that they have become known, the so-called "Reformed Two-Kingdoms" school, associated largely with Westminster West Seminary and, preeminently, Dr David VanDrunen. It very deliberately echoes many leading themes of the Reformers, Aquinas, and Augustine; whether it repeats the substance of those, especially the themes of the Reformers, is a hotly contested question. Are they simply correctly reacting against Reconstructionism, or overreacting such that they depart from the mainstream Reformed tradition?

For this school, there can be no transformation of Egypt into an extended Eden, not simply because the consummation of all things is "not yet," but rather because the cosmos itself has a merely provisional function until the life to come. Hence Christians can participate as fellow travelers in civic life, but there can be no consecrating cultivation of it. The members of the school conceive their doctrine as a Biblical, humane, and wise *modus vivendi* of pilgrim life in the City of Man. Their critics conceive it as a Nestorian-sounding, and possibly even Manichaean-sounding, justification of withdrawal from civic life. In any case, the principles of this view are taken

INTRODUCTION

almost entirely from the work of Meredith Kline, and these are subjected to very precise examination and critique by the Rev Mr Benjamin Miller in his really masterful "De-Klining From Chalcedon: Exegetical Roots of the "R-2K" Project."

The "Reformed Two Kingdoms" school does not base itself exclusively on the Biblical exegesis of Dr Kline, however; it also claims precedent among the fathers of the Reformed churches, preeminently (it seems his fate to be ever preeminent among them) John Calvin. The degree to which the school can base itself largely or even wholly on Calvin as distinct from (some might say, as opposed to) Kline is an open question, but Dr Matthew Tuininga of Emory University, in his "John Calvin and the Redemption of the Cosmos" makes a winsome case for a moderate and Calvinist (as opposed to distinctively Klinean) version of the doctrine as being very much what it advertises itself to be: as said above, a Biblical, humane, and wise *modus vivendi* for citizens of the Kingdom of God passing through the City of Man. Questions remain, of course, for Dr Tuininga's position, especially about the role of religion in the commonwealth—is it formal public principle, or merely private influence? And *are* the two kingdoms, in the doctrine of the Reformers, actually organized magistracy and organized ministerium (as Dr VanDrunen would have it), or are they actually the invisible and visible churches, as many—including myself—have argued? Nevertheless, Dr Tuininga's careful essay marks a fascinating development and clarification of one version at least of the retrieval of two-kingdoms language.

Obviously all these positions have direct practical consequences not just in general, but even with regard to particular practices. From the side of those who hold that the two kingdoms actually refer to the invisible, *ecclesia mystica veraque*, and the visible, *ecclesia permixta*, and to the realms of grace and law respectively, Mr Joseph Minich of the University of Texas at Dallas, in his "Nature and Grace, Visible and Invisible: A New Look at the Question of Infant Baptism," considers the way in which a Reformed doctrine of "nature" and "grace" warrants the practice of infant baptism—but also underscores the theological tensions therein. In reviewing the several ways in which the Reformed community has sought to alleviate these tensions, he finds them wanting, and proposes to creatively re-appropriate the classic "visible/invisible" church distinction as a way forward in this debate—particularly when coordinated with an orthodox doctrine of God.

And beyond the walls of the temple, the question of Christian politics, which is to say, the question of whether Christians are called to serve as God's stewards of the goodness of the world not just privately but in public life, is a question of whether we are dwelling here (in however relative a way) or not. Mr Andrew Fulford of McGill University, in his "Participating in Political Providence: Theological Foundations of Calvin's Doctrine of Resistance," considers this question obliquely but deeply while directly addressing the question of whether Calvin's doctrine of politics implies a right to resistance against tyranny. He finds it does, despite Calvin's own hesitations. But tyrannomachy is not monarchomachy; it rather presupposes monarchy, in the sense of public office of direction toward the common good, because the classical Reformed doctrine of resistance hinges upon the idea of the lesser magistrate, who in a moment of complete crisis might find himself completely μόνος in his stand for justice and the good, in which stand he is, at least potentially, ἀρχή of public order. In doing this, he is participating in Providence subcreatively, as it were, reinstating God's political order of justice-shaped love.

I have alluded throughout to a mainstream, classical Reformed tradition distinct from either Reconstructionism or the so-called "Reformed Two Kingdoms." It will doubtless be obvious to the reader that the founders of our Convivium consider themselves disciples of this classical tradition, which entails fidelity to its central propositions. But part of our fidelity to the tradition, a very important part, has to do with method prior to propositions, a method made as much of intellectual hospitality and irenic conversation as of intellectual rigor and clarity. We hope that the essays in this first publication of the proceedings of our annual Convivium, besides illuminating the reader regarding the matters of which they treat, will bear very clear witness to that fidelity.

Acknowledgments

Both of the editors would like to particularly thank our plenary speakers of these first two years for elevating what might have seemed only a gathering of friends into a serious (and yet still very convivial) scholarly conversation. Our first Convivium was something of a leap of faith, but Prof. Torrance Kirby's willingness to participate and encouragement confirmed us in our hopes to make it an annual event; it was his suggestion, too, to begin publishing proceedings as of this year. Likewise, we are grateful to Prof. Bratt, no doubt the leading authority on the thought of Abraham Kuyper, for taking the time to share his profound knowledge on the subject this year, and for his friendship and support of this endeavor. With such fine participants as these, as well as the other men whose papers are included below, we have high hopes that this volume will be the first of many important contributions to contemporary historical and theological discourse. We would also like to thank Mr. Jake Meador for applying his sharp eyes to the final stages of proofreading this text, thus saving us from many embarrassments.

Lastly, we want to thank a pair of private benefactors without whom none of this would have been possible; they know who they are. Our gratitude to them here is very great, and their reward in Heaven will be even greater.

Abraham Kuyper: A Compact Introduction

James D. Bratt
Dept of History, Calvin College

Part I: A Compact Introduction

In the first part of this paper, I will outline the life of Abraham Kuyper as the backdrop to the development of his thought and initiatives. Most people are interested in Kuyper today because of his enduring ideas in theology and politics. While sharing that concern, as a historian I'm interested as well in the context out of which those ideas arose, the perceived needs and dynamics which drove them. The goal of this sort of inquiry is to open a line of reflection on the uses of Kuyper today, to promote not a copying of what he did but a search for what the dynamic equivalent of Kuyper's work in his time would come to in our own.

Kuyper's Life
Youth & Education

Kuyper was born on 29 October 1837 in the manse of the Dutch Reformed Church (Nederlandse Hervormde Kerk, or NHK) at Maassluis in the province of South Holland. His pastor father was ecumenically conservative by conviction and inclination, the first in his family to attend university, and quite solicitous of his career in the church. He moved his family to Middelburg (the provincial capital of Zeeland), then later to Leiden for young Bram's educational advantage. The Netherlands in the first decade of young Kuyper's life was at the trough of its national fortunes, having declined steadily—even more by morale than by material measure—for a century after 1740 to a level far below its 17th century "golden age." Kuyper was reared amid widespread yearnings for national revival, and an ongoing conversation about what such a renewal would entail and who was best suited to lead it. He would eventually offer himself and his program as the answer to those questions.

In 1858 Kuyper completed his BA at Leiden and entered straightaway into its doctoral program in theology. He showed extraordinary promise by winning a gold medal in a national scholarship competition, researching and writing (in Latin) a 300-page essay comparing the ecclesiology of

John Calvin to that of Johannes á Lasco. He found decidedly for the latter. Theologically he left behind his father's position as flaccid and outdated, preferring instead the rigor of his professor J. H. Scholten, the Netherlands' pioneering Modernist theologian. Letters from the time to his fiancée, Johanna Schaay, show a highly ethical and idealist Unitarianism, wedded to intense ambition. The anxiety and overwork of his prize essay on top of preparation for his qualifying exams led to the first of what would become a series of breakdowns in Kuyper's health. After some time off he completed his doctorate in 1862; at the same time he experienced something of an evangelical conversion through reading *The Heir of Redclyffe* by Charlotte Yonge, a novel written out of the Oxford movement in the Church of England and given to Kuyper as a gift by Jo. The couple married in 1863 and moved to the small town of Beesd (near Utrecht), where Kuyper had taken a pastorate, though he still harbored plans to carry on his á Lasco scholarship. During his tenure there (1863–67) the railroad finally came to town, a sign of the government's massive investment in infrastructure which, along with mercantile exploitation of the East Indies, revived the national economy. Kuyper's career, then, was launched under a rising star, with a shadow side detectable for those who cared to see.

Pastor

Beesd was the first of three parishes that Kuyper would serve. He began there as a pastor of evangelical sentiment but unsettled theological convictions; he left firmly committed to strict confessional orthodoxy. Two dynamics account for the shift—a series of conversations with dissenting parishioners of radically predestinarian views, and his own alarm about the way that Modernism, which had thought to salvage Christianity against the challenges of science, seemed to be succumbing to the latter instead. Reading European culture in the mid-1860s Kuyper was—and would remain for the rest of his life—deeply disturbed at the rise of philosophical materialism, particularly at the specter of social and ethical desolation which he saw as its certain consequence. In 1867 he took to popular print for the first time by issuing a pamphlet espousing democratization in the selection of church officers, mixing theological and political concerns against the reigning liberalism and stolid bureaucracy in church affairs.

As a consequence Kuyper received a call to Utrecht, the capital of "God and Country" conservatism in the NHK. He soon alienated other leaders there, however, by advocating a religiously pluralistic public school system. The canopy of generic Protestantism which Utrecht traditionalists wanted to extend over the entire nation, he thought, both eclipsed the rights of religious minorities (including the Netherlands' 40% Catholic population) while simultaneously thinning out real religion into insignificance. This position, along with his continued agitations against NHK officialdom, prompted his departure to Amsterdam in 1870. There Kuyper proved to be a radical conservative or conservative radical, popular with orthodox lower-middle and working-class audiences, and a skilled faction leader in local church councils.

Political organizer

Kuyper's involvement in the controversies around public schools stemmed from the theological-cultural trigger of his conversion to strong Calvinism—the specter of philosophical naturalism and the need to array effective spiritual resources against it. Education constituted an obvious theater for that operation. At the same time education was a key political issue across the entire north Atlantic world. The newly consolidated nation-states (Italy, Germany, the USA) forged in the 1860s' wars of national unification, along with the reformist regimes (e.g., France and Japan) that had been crystallized at the same time, looked to public education as a key venue for forming national identity and securing their citizens' loyalties. In the wake of newly passed laws democratizing (i.e., introducing mass) communications, newspapers became the best way to address political issues, and Kuyper was quick to seize on their potential. In 1872 he assumed the editorship of *De Standaard*, a political daily, and *De Heraut*, a Sunday weekly dedicated to ecclesiastical matters. This was another form of education or consciousness formation, and became his perennial pulpit and power base. His other roles might come and go, but Kuyper held on to these editorships the rest of his life. By this means he shaped an audience and a cause, both of which would ever identify with him as a person.

Kuyper's move toward politics became full-fledged in 1873 when he accepted election to Parliament. This required him to resign the ministry, although he remained active in the city-wide consistory of Amsterdam. Politics had long been an elite game in the Netherlands, so a populist like Kuyper represented a new and shocking phenomenon on the floor of Parliament, as much by the style as by the substance of his speeches. A bit beaten down by the swirl of polemics this generated, he attended the 1875 revival meetings at Brighton, England led by Robert Pearsall Smith. A precursor to what became the Keswick Holiness movement, the sessions taught the necessity of an experience of personal "consecration" to perfect the soul. Kuyper professed the same and took to proselytizing for the cause in the Netherlands. This potential third conversion proved abortive, however, as he succumbed in February 1876 to another breakdown. He resigned his seat in Parliament and repaired to Nice, Lake Como, and the Swiss Alps for more than a year of recuperation.

During Kuyper's absence—and perhaps one prospect that had worsened his anxiety—a bill reforming the Dutch universities passed through Parliament. The effect was to secularize higher education, transforming theology departments into programs for religious studies. The next year, 1877, came the turn for lower education. Having bolstered the nation's physical capital, the government was now determined to develop human capital in the increasingly competitive and technologically innovative international economy amid which the Netherlands had to find its way. The need was signaled, coincidentally, by the beginning of a twenty-year depression in Dutch agriculture which floundered in a flood of imported American and Ukrainian grain. The times thus augured double badly for Kuyper's clientele: material stress on their traditional livelihood and spiritual stress from the rigorous new demands that were mandated for elementary education and that threatened to drive faith-based schools (Reformed and Catholic) out of business.

At this juncture Kuyper displayed his organizational genius. Returning home in spring 1877, he undertook a three-year campaign that crystallized three national networks which lastingly defined the ideology, clientele, and program of his movement. He took leadership of a national "People's Petition" against the lower-education bill, then used those lists and zeal to form the Antirevolutionary Party (ARP) and a Christian school association. To that he added the Free University (VU) to produce leaders for those enterprises and for further initiatives to come. All three were the Netherlands' first in their field. Occupationally, Kuyper foreswore political office and settled into running the party's central committee (until World War I) and teaching theology at the VU (through 1901), besides carrying on with his daily journalism. His 1880 address at the opening of the VU, "Sphere

Sovereignty," became the signature oration defining the rationale, ideology, and spirit of his movement.

Church Reformer

Having launched his political and educational ventures, Kuyper returned to his original quest for church reform. His principal target was the administrative hierarchy of the NHK, which he believed would simply wither away if the faithful resisted its supervision; bereft of its artificial support, Modernist clergy would disappear along with it. The result would be a reinvigorated, genuinely "free church," full of committed, dedicated members, and from that a rejuvenated nation would necessarily follow. Kuyper's agitation swelled from 1883 to 1886, when the decisive steps were taken by his allies on the consistory of Amsterdam. For once he misread popular sentiment and was out-maneuvered. The result of the "Doleantie," the protest of the "aggrieved" by the usurpation of their church, was the withdrawal from the NHK of only a fraction of its orthodox members, quite less than Kuyper had hoped. He turned instead to helping unite his followers with most of the churches descended from an earlier protest, the Secession of 1834; together they formed the Gereformeerde Kerken in Nederland (GKN).

Politics & Scholarship

One reason the Doleantie was so controversial was its splitting of what many took to be the dearest icon of the nation's moral solidarity. Another was that it coincided with the harshest economic climate in fifty years, as a depression in the Netherlands' incipient industrial sector now compounded continuing hardship in the countryside. Kuyper had opportunity as well as need to turn back to politics in 1887, then, as the heretofore highly restrictive Dutch franchise was doubled in that year, as it would be again in 1897. The intervening decade would be his "red" period, as he revived a longstanding concern with the "social question" and pushed a populist agenda in political economy as he earlier had in the church. In 1891 he delivered his famous address on "The Social Question and the Christian Religion," with pointed attacks on "laissez-faire" capitalist orthodoxy alongside citations of Christ and the prophets' preferential option for the poor. He encouraged a Christian labor federation, "Patrimonium," which soon became the nation's largest. In 1894–95 his support for further franchise extension split the ARP, driving conservatives into their own party, the Christian Historical Union (CHU). While Kuyper thus consolidated his control over the ARP, the conflict precipitated his third breakdown, which took him out of action for six months in Tunisia and the south of France.

Meanwhile he was also hitting his high tide as a scholar, symbolized by the honorary degree he received and the Stone Lectures he delivered at Princeton on a trip to the USA (1898). These *Lectures on Calvinism* would become his best known book in English. Simultaneously he published his scholarly *magnum opus*, the *Encyclopedia of Sacred Theology*, and began a six-year series in his newspaper that would come out in book form as *Common Grace*. In it he stressed the ongoing divine sustenance of creation and the social order, legitimating Christian participation in public life with people of other convictions.

Kuyper's political career climaxed with his election to the prime ministership of the Netherlands, 1901–05. His principal goal for this term, educational reform, did make it through, but he ran into acute controversy over his handling of an anarchist-driven general strike on the heels of a Socialist-engineered railroad strike in 1903. The Liberals, having been displaced from their customary leadership by Kuyper's election, joined with the Left whom they otherwise disparaged in defeating him for reelection in 1905. Kuyper was embittered by the personal polemics exchanged in the campaign and also deeply disappointed at not having a chance to push through his agenda for his second term, social and labor reform. He left the country in something of a huff on an extended trip around the Mediterranean Sea. The resulting travel account, *Around the Old World Sea*, stands as a remarkable commentary in popular anthropology, but his long rude absence from the country cost him future electoral leadership of ARP.

'Retirement'

Kuyper remained active in politics from 1907 through 1915. Most of his energies went into intra-party squabbling as he used his chairmanship of the ARP central committee to maneuver, unsuccessfully, for another term as prime minister. His principal publication of this period was *Pro Rege*, a remarkable reconnoitering of the conditions of high modernity and a reassertion of the kingly—not just the priestly—claims of Christ therein. Seeing less salience in the traditional loci of church and family, Kuyper emphasized the importance of Christian cultural organization hand in hand with his perennial insistence upon the cultivation of distinctive consciousness.

By the dawn of World War I Kuyper had taken to the (semi-honorific) upper house of Parliament alongside of his party chairmanship and editorial functions. The war itself deeply disturbed him not only for its material but also its collective moral toll on the nations involved. Still aggrieved by British imperialism in the South African War (1899-1902), he took the German side though he hoped more for a negotiated settlement. Tellingly, his last theological series concerned eschatology against the backdrop of the lowering catastrophe of Western civilization. His health turned fitful, then entered into protracted decline in 1919. He died on November 8, 1920.

Essential Purpose & Ideas

Through all these twists, turns, and variations, Kuyper consistently pursued a matched pair of ideals: to revitalize the pious faithful to reclaim the full scope of their Calvinistic heritage, especially its public compass, and to direct the ensuing force against liberal hegemony in politics and culture, thus bringing the full influence of Christian witness upon the Dutch nation. His chief distinction from contemporary and preceding movements of this sort was twofold. On the one hand, over against traditional establishmentarian types, Kuyper did not seek to push his initiative through official ecclesiastical institutions or to press a Christian pattern on everyone regardless of conviction. On the other hand, vis á vis sectarian revivalists, he was not content with proceeding by "spiritual" change via interpersonal relations. That is, in a modern society ideological pluralism had to be respected, but the individualization and privatization of faith had to be avoided. Kuyper's margin of excellence therefore was calling Christians to attend to the structural, institutional, and philosophical dimensions of their witness, both for the welfare of the cause and for the responsibility of their public performance.

His chief ideas fall along the following chain:

1. <u>Principial psychology</u>: Applying his training in German idealist philosophy, Kuyper held that everything an individual thinks or an institution does comes out of a "root principle," a set of presuppositions built on a fundamental commitment. Thence proceed all ideas, emotions, structures,

actions. There is nothing in culture or society that is value free or—in this sense—non-religious.

2. <u>Antithesis</u>: The basic loyalties of Christians and non-Christians are opposed. Hence Christian action in culture and society must proceed from and ever be informed by a conscious, distinctive, and comprehensive worldview; must proceed through (in situations, like the Netherlands, of hegemonic secular liberalism) separate, self-sustaining Christian organizations; and must necessarily be combative and uncompromising.

3. <u>Common grace</u>: Once well-wdefined and stabilized, the Calvinist movement can play a responsible part in public life by cooperating—critically and ad hoc—with other groups for the achievement of mutually agreeable, middle-range policies and programs. This is possible because God's grace in creation has not been fully extinguished by sin, allowing non-Christians to attain a measure of truth and virtue outside of salvation.

4. <u>Sphere sovereignty</u>: Scripture and creation both testify to the overall intention God has for society and culture; namely, that every distinct mode of existence (or "sphere") be encouraged to develop on its own terms and its own ground without undue interference from other spheres. The state might not overly intrude in business, business in the family, the church in education, the schools in the arts, etc.

5. <u>Ideological pluralism</u> (= implicit sphere sovereignty II). Each confessional community (including those of secular persuasions) must be granted its full legitimate proportion of access to and participation in all sectors of public life: political representation, educational funding, communications media, etc. Let a dozen flowers bloom, let their relative beauty compete for attention, and let the Lord at the last day take care of those which turn out to be tares.

6. <u>Democratic populism</u>: According to Kuyper, the reactionary reflex of orthodox Calvinists on public issues had brought shame on the group—and had undercut its sources of power. Liberalism is inherently elitist, Calvinism popular. A broadened franchise and a check on economic oligarchy will therefore bring both credit and benefit to the orthodox Christian cause.

7. <u>The Kingdom of God</u> divides into two themes. First, God's sovereign gives assurance and consolation for a long struggle. It raises Calvinists above the temptation of compromising for immediate success, and it bolsters commitment to their real calling, which is faithfulness in the times and circumstances in which providence has placed them. Second, Christ is not

just savior of souls but king over the earth and all it contains. Hence Christians are called to the comprehensive socio-cultural witness which was Kuyper's starting point in the first place. His chain of ideas thus forms a self-perpetuating circle.

By comparison to 19th - and 20th-century conservative Reformed streams in the United States, Kuyper's distinctives can be articulated as follows:

1. His theology proceeds from a robust view of creation and toward a vision of cosmic redemption. While still holding the forensic, imputational, and substitutionary understanding of personal salvation characteristic of traditionalist Baptists and Presbyterians, Kuyper cast personal salvation as a means within God's greater design to redeem all things created and yet to come.

2. This implied a pointed calling to Christian public activism that was all the more urgent in light of the dramatic changes in the world of his time, when a whole new global order of industrialization, democratization, and rapid communication was unfolding. With magnified possibilities for good and ill, the promise that God will redeem all of life drew added existential weight, and so added urgency to believers' vocation to be witnesses to that redemption in all spheres of life.

3. Kuyper's emphasis on "worldview" is a means of bridging or elaborating abstract theology into concrete theorizing for every domain in a critical holistic system. Continental patterns of negotiation between the Enlightenment and Christian tradition had marked differences from the prevailing British one that so deeply shaped American Protestant culture. Kuyper's German Idealist background was suspicious of dualist or complementarian strategies that segmented theology and religious claims off from those propounded by a some "neutral" reason and science. Rather, he taught, all our thinking is—and therefore ought to be consistently—conducted within a framework rooted in pre-rational commitments. Thus, the Christian intellectual enterprise must go well beyond a supposedly purely rational defense of a supposedly timeless and rationally inducted set of theological claims as the Baconian, Common Sense regime at Old Princeton liked to mount.

4. Kuyper was as good at organizing and mobilizing laity as any American evangelical revivalist, but more than they, he knew that building

and sustaining institutions was essential to perpetuating a movement. Moreover, he saw a whole phalanx of institutions mirroring the full spectrum of social and cultural development as a necessary part of the Christian purpose—not just those answering the concerns of "spiritual ministries."

5. First and last, Kuyper showed a savvy grasp of the emerging problems and possibilities of his time, with a strategic vision of how to harvest and apply Christian resources in that situation. Keeping a tradition alive, which he certainly aimed to do, necessitated updating it via fresh activism in the context of new times, not cocooning it or seeking to serve as a custodian of its traditional formulations.

Salient quotations

Too often Kuyper is encapsulated in one classic quotation, namely, "that there is not a square inch in the whole domain of human existence over which Christ, who is Lord over *all*, does not exclaim, 'Mine!'" To reflexively repeat this one mantra is to escape, not engage, Kuyper's thinking, however. It is to preserve him in amber. Instead, or in addition, we should remember three other capsule statements of his vision and purpose:

- "God's entire counsel may be reduced to one thought, that in the end of the ages he may have a Church which shall understand His love and return it." *The Work of the Holy Spirit* (Grand Rapids: Eerdmans, 1956 [1888-89]), 205.

- Kuyper sought to build a body "of spiritually mature, sober-living, serious people who, consciously assuming God's promises and in the tradition of the historic Reformed church, sought to make visible in their personal lives and the life of the nation something of the kingdom of God." C. Augustijn, "De spiritualiteit van de dolerenden," in C. Augustijn and J. Vree, eds., *Abraham Kuyper; vast en veranderlijk* (Zoetermeer: Meinema, 1998), 195.

- "The world after the fall is no lost planet, only destined now to afford the Church a place in which to continue her combats; and humanity is no aimless mass of people which only serves the purpose of giving birth to the elect. On the contrary, the world now, as well as in the beginning, is the theater for the mighty works of God, and humanity remains a creation of His hand, which, apart from salvation, completes under this present dispensation, here on earth, a mighty process, and in its historical development is to glorify the name of Almighty God." *Lectures on Calvinism* (Grand Rapids: Eerdmans, 1931 [1899]), 162.

Part II: Kuyper's Theology: Personal, Public, Cosmic

"Kuyperian" theology has become a code word for all sorts of ideas cherished, or abhorred, by the person invoking it. This paper seeks to pull back from that impulse. It intends not to praise or criticize Kuyper's theological system but to describe its main points in brief compass. Kuyper never published a dogmatics, though he once hoped to do so, but left it to his students to compile and distribute the outlines of his lectures on theology at the Free University. He did publish a great deal of theological work, however, on the popular as well as the scholarly level, and from those sources we can draw a fair system of his thought. The outline below (1) presents that thought according to the traditional format of creation, fall, redemption, and consummation, then (2) delves into the theological themes and rationale for Kuyper's legendary emphasis upon Christian public activism, before (3) reflecting on how possible tensions between (1) and (2) can be resolved.

Kuyper's Classic Theology

Running first through Kuyper's theology is a robust doctrine of *creation*. This entailed a strong critique of Darwinian natural selection theory as that was understood in his day, although Kuyper was quite open to—in fact, affirmative of—a very old earth and a thoroughly developmental ("evolutionary") understanding of natural history. Indeed, he espoused a theory of "evolutionary creation" in so many words. More important to him was the picture of the original creation as a set of divinely endowed potentials possessed of inherent principles that would propel their 'unfolding' along lines defined by divinely decreed norms or 'creation ordinances.' Unbroken by sin, this original endowment would have increasingly flourished over time to its appointed (and from our point of view, unimaginable) glory. Even with the fall and all the destruction and disorder it spawned, the end of time will still show a cosmos full of perfectly realized potential, well beyond the original creation in richness, glory, and sophistication.

Accordingly, Kuyper placed a high value on history and evolution, and pushed against static or nostalgic mindsets. No doubt his thinking on this point owed considerably to his immersion in Hegelian concepts at university, but equally to the striking gains against poverty and disease evident in the Netherlands and Europe over the course of his life-time. Not incidentally, this was the era when European hegemony over the rest of the globe reached its peak, at the same time that its science delved seemingly without stint into the secrets of nature. Tropes of progress saturated the air during Kuyper's life, and he voiced his fair share of them. He was also, however, among the witnesses who raised a critical, and anxious, voice concerning the costs and dangers of this ascendancy. That had much to do with the next point in his theology.

Kuyper was second to no Calvinist in his estimate of the breadth, depth, and severity of *sin* and its consequences. Quite simply, the Fall corrupted and corroded everything. The damage in creation fell on nature as well as humanity; within human beings it was noetic as well as moral and physical. After Eden our operating equipment and capacity—intellectual as well as material—are damaged, broken, and distorted. Our grasp of reality is diminished and corrupted, just as the motivation of all our actions, great and small, is turned, in each and all, toward self-advancement instead of thankful praise to the glory of God and love for our neighbor.

Redemption for Kuyper was as cosmic, God-mandated, and God-driven as the original creation. Indeed, in Kuyper's supralapsarian understanding of things, election to redemption was the font of God's sovereign wisdom from before creation itself. That is, the Fall did not turn or reduce God's purposes but brought these out in their full measure. Redemption was not God's Plan B but Plan A, suffused start to finish with the intent to display the divine majesty. To us that majesty is defined above all by grace and love, and so it ought to elicit from us awe and unending praise. Redemption like creation, then, remains as from the start the theater of God's glory.

Kuyper honored traditional Reformed usages regarding the salvation of the individual elect via the imputation to them of Christ's merits as wrought upon the cross. But he immersed the forensic transaction in a broader picture. When God implanted the elect in Christ from all eternity, he planted in them the seed of regeneration. From birth the elect thus grow as something of a double person—the natural self, fallen in sin, alongside a graft of Christ fed by the Holy Spirit. At some point in time, early or late, the Spirit effects the calling inherent in regeneration so that the person becomes aware of her new Christ self and accepts it. This is conversion, a grace-enabled act of our own will. There follows a life-long process of sanctification, which for Calvinists amounts to a persistent pattern of reconversions. Yet though we experience this process as gradual and never finished, in Christ it, like justification, is complete.

As precious as this process is to each of the faithful, our personal salvation is not the ultimate point, Kuyper repeated. The redemption of the cosmos is the point, and our salvation is a means to that end. But how is that cosmic redemption unfolding, and what do the elect and their actions have to do with it? On the broadest level, this remained an open question—better, a matter properly left to the transcendent purposes and mysterious workings of our unfathomable God. In our own times and circumstances, Kuyper thought, our clear duties were clear enough. He himself took these to be the program of Christian public activism to which we will return below. Yet in that enterprise as in all else we are to do our part and leave the rest to God. Kuyper's distinctive lay in re-conceptualizing what "our part" might be.

Kuyper's emphasis on organizing and mobilizing collective Christian action should not obscure the real *eschatological* horizon that he always envisioned. The last series of articles he wrote in his Sunday paper treated this theme—and did so in the context of World War I. Just as strikingly, it avoided all the end-times calculations so characteristic of Anglo-American evangelical and proto-Fundamentalist commentaries of the day. Even amid the world's catastrophe unfolding around him, Kuyper kept his eye on the renewed cosmos populated by those elect in Christ that will emerge at the end of time. The contrast with the grim state of contemporary affairs was all the more testimony to the surpassing glory of God, who works as God wills, beyond our imagining. The exact means of that enterprise, and likewise the exact meanings of the signs of the times, are not for us finally to stipulate, Kuyper said. It is enough for us to hold to the promise that in the new heavens and the new earth, God will dwell with man and woman in a perfect city through which runs a river of life nourishing trees whose leaves will be for the healing of the nations.

If Kuyper delved explicitly into eschatology only at the end of his life, *ecclesiology* was his passion all along. In fact, it was the topic of his first formal writing as an undergraduate and of the last article that emerged from his death bed. The concept for which he is best known on this front is his distinction between the church as institute and the church as organism, with favor shown to the latter. But in fact Kuyper's concept of the church was complex and evolved over his career. During his pastorates (1863-73) he showed an increasingly high view of the church as the extension of the incarnation. This brought along a robust sacramentology. Baptism was the authoritative church standard upon which he staked out his battle against perceived corruption in the national church, just as weekly celebration of the Lord's Supper was the key liturgical reform he proposed in his final pastorate, at Amsterdam. His turn to the church organic came after his campaign for church reform (the *Doleantie* of 1886) met only limited success at the same time as Christian political prospects brightened. Here, in political and cultural witness, the cause of Christ apparently could best shine under the providential unfolding of God's will. That witness still amounted to the work of the church but by the church as organism: the prolix, holistic activity of the laity in their weekday roles and vocations, seeking to bear forth witness to the Kingdom of God.

The Purpose and Character of Christian Public Activism

Along with creation and cosmic redemption, the other, equally famous bookend of Kuyper's thought is Christian engagement with the world. Casual commentary on Kuyper tends to merge these two tenets—to see the latter, the activism, as designed to bring about the former, the cosmic redemption. "Kuyperianism" is thus associated with "transformationalism" and decried by critics of the same as worldly, arrogant, delusional, and triumphalistic. Yet Kuyper only rarely talked about any "Christian transformation of culture." When working this vein he used the term "metamorphosis," an organic metaphor (the sort he always favored) denoting a process that unfolds beyond our particular origination or intent. "Transformationalism" as such was a concept made famous by H. Richard Niebuhr in his *Christ and Culture* (1950) as one—and his somewhat preferred—model of the relationship between the two terms in his title. The term might have carried some triumphalism, emerging as it did at the peak of mainline Protestantism's influence on the American scene, but a close reading of Niebuhr's text would make this more an inference than his own implication. In any case, it was not Kuyper's.

If not "transformation," what did Kuyper have in mind? What was the purpose, and what the proper means, of Christian activism in the present world? The logical warrant for that activism was obvious. Just as God's creation valorized "every sphere" of life, and just as God's purpose was to redeem and perfect the same, so our redemption, personally and as the body of believers, is not only of the soul or "spiritual things" for some supernatural end or otherworldly destiny. Rather our vocations match up with God's purposes, so that we in our everyday capacities as laypeople work in every sphere for the glory of God. Strong classic Calvinist themes here manifest unmistakable here: divine sovereignty and providence, God's glory, the believer's calling, etc.

The crucial part of this grand abstraction lies in the details. Specifically, Kuyper taught, Christians have a threefold vocation in the world:

(1) to bear witness to and to work as best they can to approximate, where possible to instantiate, the implications and applications of creation ordinances in their particular sphere of activity.

(2) To promote the normative development of that sphere toward its ultimate goal.

(3) To stand for God's justice and mercy, especially for the weak and oppressed, the suffering and neglected.

In Kuyper's reading, this work would sustain some historic effects of God's gracious providence. By that instrument Christianity has had a marvelous impact on the Netherlands in particular, on Europe and the West more generally. True, the church has also sometimes comported with, even promoted abuses, leading to revolutionary attacks on Christendom. One result has been the separation of church and state, which, Kuyper said, is a good—and authentically Calvinistic—thing. But separation of church and state cannot mean separation of society, culture, or politics from religion. There, Christianity continues as a leaven, restraining sin, preserving the best of the past, and fostering good developments going forward.

This understanding frames the goals of Christian politics. As Kuyper once put it as prime minister during question time in Parliament, "the powerful work of the church" effects an alteration in hearts and homes; via political action "a precipitate of the life of faith [can seep] down deeply into the life of the nation."[1] From his wide range of political pronouncements and commentary, we can extract three persistent, overriding ends that he had in mind: (1) to preserve and promote the ethical consequences of the gospel in our common human life; (2) to quell violence and enforce justice

---

[1] See Bratt, *Abraham Kuyper: Modern Calvinist, Christian Democrat* (Grand Rapids: Eerdmans, 2013), 306.

in human relations; and (3) to lay the groundwork for human flourishing via free social development and the cultural instantiation of biblical values.

It is worth pulling out a few implications of these themes.

(1) Kuyper more than once explicitly decried any notion of enforcing specific Old Testament laws, much less the entire theocratic regime, on the present scene. He was anti-"theonomist" in the Christian Reconstructionist sense associated with Rousas Rushdoony and his school.

(2) While Kuyper sometimes used nostalgic tones, particularly in invoking the Netherlands' seventeenth-century "golden age" as a Calvinist product, he was devotedly anti-reactionary or restorationist. In his evolutionary historiography and enthusiastic encounter with the contemporary scene, as well as in policy prescriptions, he was consistently progressive, only believing that genuine progress can be secured by salting it with the best of tradition, including Christian tradition.

(3) At the same time, he was wary of the cost to human relationships and the temptations to human pride present in the emerging mastery of the world by science and technology and the putative triumph of human will in politics and society. More than once he pronounced modern technical and moral development to be on diverging trajectories. Thus Kuyper never believed—rather, regularly decried—any notion that human progress will bring in the Kingdom of God, by marked contrast with the mindset of liberal Protestant postmillennialism.

(4) Nevertheless Kuyper was anti-premillenarian and especially anti-dispensationalist. His commentary on eschatology, written during World War I, gave him a perfect opportunity to take that track; he did not.

(5) At bottom Kuyper was not a triumphalistic transformationalist. That human endeavor will never bring in the Kingdom of God means organized Christian endeavor will not do so either. God's redemptive transformation will accomplish that end by its own mysterious means, in its own hidden time. Our efforts here bear witness to that end, in gratitude for its first fruits already present in our lives as redeemed sinners and in witness to the glory of God.

Reconciliation

If there is no fundamental disjunction between Kuyper's call to activism and his classic Refomred theology, many observers certainly perceive one. Put another way, why do Kuyperians so often have the reputation of being triumphalistic transformationalists? Maybe the charge has served as an uninformed shorthand, or as a cheap shot negating the obligation for critics to deal more thoroughly with a system they fear as alien and threatening. But the objection is too persistent, and has come from inside loyalists as well as outside critics, for these explanations to be enough. Several factors from Kuyper's movement itself might help solve the conundrum.

(1) Kuyper was an activist and organizer as well as a thinker. That is, he conjoined to theory real passion—manifest in his rhetoric and his behavior—so as to mobilize, energize, and sustain a movement. Kuyper was a fighter, and fighters want to win, to triumph. Their tropes will, must, bear some aspect of triumphalism.

(2) Kuyper had no limit in himself to the work ethic that his late contemporary Max Weber associated with Calvinism. Neither did his followers. He and they went all out, for ultimate ends under ultimate suasions. This can, will, sound triumphalistic.

(3) Kuyper's followers were often responding with the enthusiasm of the convert to the great liberation they felt from the confines of their native pietistic quietism or dualism. They had to remind their former associates—and perhaps themselves—of the need for and joy upon this salvation.

(4) Kuyper often conveyed great confidence in the accuracy, sufficiency, and necessity of his theory. This was characteristic of his era but no less influential upon his followers.

Yet we should give the last word to Kuyper's own considered view of the matter. At the start and the close of his great decade of theological formulations on this question, he issued several different metaphors for the Christian role in public life. In 1887, under eclipsed hopes for church reform but dawning hopes for political action, he urged his followers to see themselves as "a colony of the heavenly fatherland" working in their "earthly fatherland" by calling rulers and people back to the testimony of God's ordinances for human life. In *Common Grace*, from the late 1890s, he rehearsed Jesus' three metaphors from the Sermon on the Mount, in rising order of preference. Christians were to be the salt of the earth, for the work of preservation. They were to be a light to the world, from a tower high on a hill, their beams radiating out to enlighten and guide the surrounding peoples on the landscape of their lives. Best of all, they could aspire to be a leaven that gradually comes to pervade their environment, working as an agent of marvelous transformation.

We understand Kuyper correctly only by remembering *all* of these metaphors.

Bibliography

Kuyper, Abraham. *Dat de Genade Particulier Is*. Amsterdam: J. H. Kruyt, 1884. *Uit de Woord*, Second series, volume I.

———. *De Leer der Verbonden*. Amsterdam: J. H. Kruyt, 1885. *Uit de Woord*, Second series, volume II.

———. *The Work of the Holy Spirit*. Grand Rapids: Eerdmans, 1956 [1888–89].

———. *Encyclopedia of Sacred Theology*. 3 vols. New York: Scribners, 1898 [1894].

———. *De Gemeene Gratie*. 3 vols. Leiden: D. Donner 1902.

———. *Pro Rege, of het Koningschap van Christus*. 3 vols. Kampen: J. H. Kok, 1911.

Bratt, James D. *Abraham Kuyper: Modern Calvinist, Christian Democrat*. Grand Rapids: Eerdmans, 2013.

Koch, Jeroen. *Abraham Kuyper: een biografie*. Amsterdam: Boom, 2006.

Kossmann, Ernst H. *The Low Countries, 1780-1940*. Oxford: Oxford University Press, 1978.

Kuipers, Tjitze. *Abraham Kuyper: An Annotated Bibliography*. Leiden: Brill, 2011.

Mouw, Richard. *Abraham Kuyper: A Short and Personal Introduction*. Grand Rapids: Eerdmans, 2011.

Sphere Sovereignty among Abraham Kuyper's Other Political Theories[1]

James D. Bratt
Dept of History, Calvin College

Ask people who have heard of Abraham Kuyper what his political philosophy might have been and you will likely get two answers: "sphere sovereignty" and/or "principled pluralism." Principled pluralism we'll return to below; let's start with his better known concept of sphere sovereignty.

The familiar version is this. According to Kuyper, human life has unfolded out of God's original creation along lines governed by inherent principles of development. The pattern is one of diversification, so that life manifestly falls into distinctive domains of activity, realms of being, "spheres" of reality. Development in each of these spheres is propelled by an innate principle, and they thrive when they are left to follow their own logic free from encroachment by other spheres, that is, by the imposition of a principle foreign to their purpose. To use some familiar examples, the arts should not be subordinated to the dictates of the church, universities should not be run as businesses, the state should not be expected to show the attributes of a family. The crucial applications in Kuyper's own career were to liberate education from dictates of church or state (hence, his "Free University" of Amsterdam) and to raise alarums about undue government interference in the economy.

Kuyper adumbrated the concept of sphere sovereignty in a famous speech by that title which he gave at the founding of the Free University. It would be hard to imagine a more august occasion for him. The university was to be the linchpin of his life's work. Here would be formed a leadership class to give his movement a permanent presence on the national scene; from here would flow a coherent body of distinctively Christian scholarship to defend and advance the claims of faith on the cultural high ground where so much of modem life was shaped. And so it happened. It was to "sphere sovereignty" that his activist followers would regularly appeal in warranting

---

[1] This paper is adapted in part from an article by the same title in *The Kuyper Review* (Abraham Kuyper Center for Public Theology, Princeton Theological Seminary) 1 (September 2009).

their policy proposals, and it was in the exploration of the spheres that the academics in his train would find an agenda for research as well as a charter for creative innovation.[2]

It is remarkable, then, to note how very brief is the allusion to the spheres themselves in Kuyper's speech: little more than one page of the nineteen that the modern English text entails. The picture was imprecise as well. For instance, as to the number of spheres, Kuyper says that "there are as many . . . as there are constellations in the sky." He names "a domain of the personal, a domain of nature, of the household, of science, of social and ecclesiastical life," but then lists another seven and yet another three before and after this enumeration. As for how we should pictures these domains, they might be "'spheres,' each animated with its own spirit," Kuyper says, but they also might be "cogwheels" in a "great machine . . . spring-driven on their own axles. . . ." The image doesn't matter, he hurries on, so long as we remember that "the circumference of each has been drawn on a fixed radius from the center of a unique principle. . . ."[3] In short, just as his evocation of the spheres is not a major part of Kuyper's speech, it is only the barest beginnings of a social philosophy.

Herman Dooyeweerd fifty years later would elaborate Kuyper's suggestions into a complete, precise, systematic philosophy, an ontology of being and human action.[4] For the moment, and by quantitative measure, "Sphere Sovereignty" worked more as a piece of political philosophy. But it is political philosophy told as historical narrative, a heroic saga of world his-

---

[2] The speech was originally published on the date of its delivery, 20 October 1880, as *Souvereiniteit in Eigen Kring* (Amsterdam: J. H. Kruyt, 1880). The full text (except for its extensive ceremonial postscript) is available in English as "Sphere Sovereignty," in James D. Bratt, ed., *Abraham Kuyper: A Centennial Reader* (Grand Rapids: Eerdmans, 1998), 461–90. The fullest study of sphere sovereignty as a theory is J. D. Dengerink, *Critisch-historisch onderzoek naar de sociologische ontwikkeling van het beginsel der "souvereiniteit in eigen kring" in de 19e en 20e eeuw* (Kampen: Kok, 1948). For shorter, English-language analyses, see Bob Goudzwaard, "Christian Social Thought in the Dutch Neo-Calvinist Tradition," in Walter Block and Irving Hexham, eds., *Religion, Economics, and Social Thought* (Vancouver: Fraser Institute, 1986), and James W. Skillen and Rockne M. McCarthy, eds., *Political Order and the Plural Structure of Society* (Atlanta: Scholars Press, 1991).

[3] Kuyper, "Sphere Sovereignty," 467.

[4] Herman Dooyeweerd, *De Wijsbegeerte der Wetsidee*, 3 vols. (Amsterdam: H. J. Paris, 1935-), translated into English as *A New Critique of Theoretical Thought*, 4 vols. (Philadelphia: Presbyterian and Reformed Publishers, 1953–58).

tory in which ultimate values were at stake and in whose culminating act the small band of believers whom Kuyper was addressing were to play a vital role. The speech also has a third, epistemological focus, where Kuyper sketches out an alternative model of perception and interpretation.[5] We will bypass that aspect here to concentrate on "Sphere Sovereignty's" political theory, but then supplement that with other key pieces of Kuyper's political thinking. He laid out them out on two other seminal occasions, one earlier and one much later in his career. Further, he translated theory into a concrete political program which, on the date of his oration, he had just finished elaborating in a long run of articles in his daily newspaper. Can we add up these four sources—the three orations and the political program—into a coherent unity?

I. Constitution and Revolution

The first oration in question Kuyper delivered when he went out on the Dutch university lecture circuit late in the election season of 1873 (thus seven years before "Sphere Sovereignty") to recruit young leaders for the budding political party he hoped to build. Such a purpose required some theoretical, or at least rhetorical, fireworks. On the other hand, the public could expect some reference to that year's being the twenty-fifth anniversary of the Dutch Constitution of 1848, but for that monument Kuyper's constituency had little affection. His solution was to ignore the Constitution altogether and concentrate on constitutionalism instead; that he located, as his title indicates, in "Calvinism, the Source and Stronghold of Our Constitutional Liberties."[6] Kuyper took pains to spell out that this "Calvinism" included its theological particulars, not just the generic Reformation that his mentor Guillaume Groen van Prinsterer favored for political grounding. But then he broadened out beyond the Netherlands to range across the international scene and in the bargain contradicted his audience's reflex antipathy for political revolution. Kuyper's speech does deliver an argument for stability and order but it gets there through a history of resistance, rebellion, and revolution—good, Christian revolution.

The Calvinist particulars at the bottom of Kuyper's speech were the

---

[5] Kuyper, "Sphere Sovereignty," 481–88.

[6] Most of the text is available in English in Bratt, *Kuyper Centennial Reader*, 279–317. It was originally published as *Het Calvinisme, oorsprong en waarborg onzer constitutioneele vrijheden* (Amsterdam: B. van der Land, 1874).

absolute sovereignty of God and the pervasiveness of human sin.[7] Far from warranting monarchy, as Restoration Catholic and Lutheran theorists had argued, Kuyper insisted that these tenets pointed toward a republic. On the first point, divine majesty brooked no human imitation; republicanism was the political counterpart of iconoclasm, both being rooted in the Calvinist horror of idolatry. On the second point, of human depravity, Kuyper jibed explicitly (invoking Calvin's words) that while monarchs did seem particularly prone to that condition, "he [Calvin] also knows that the same sin pervades the masses and that, as a result, there will be no end to resistance and rebellion, mutiny and troubles, except for a just constitution that restrains abuse of authority, sets limits, and offers the people a natural protection against lust for power and arbitrariness." Quite contrary to Groen, then, who deemed Calvin a monarchist that had reluctantly accommodated to Geneva's republicanism, Kuyper insisted that, "given a free choice, Calvin certainly prefers the republic."[8] Even more, it was the Genevan's notorious doctrine of divine election, which Groen typically skirted lest it arouse dissension in Dutch Protestant ranks, that Kuyper invoked as the charter for democracy.[9] With its leveling effect upon all human pretension, the doctrine of election made democracy safe for Calvinism; with the moral discipline against self-seeking it bred in the believer, it made Calvinists safe for democracy.

It was not theology but historical narrative that did most of the work in this speech, however, so the case studies Kuyper chose were telling. He took them up in reverse chronological order, beginning with the United States as the paragon of liberty and of Christian sobriety, moving back thence to English Puritanism, before hopping back across the Channel to the French Huguenots and then over the Swiss border to Geneva. There Calvin in his generation connected predestination to democracy while Theodore Beza, in the next, justified Huguenot armed resistance during the French wars of religion. Theirs was a *constitutional* resistance to *tyrants,* Kuyper reminded his hearers, but it entailed a violent defiance that Groen, for one, could never endorse. Groen had supplied Kuyper with the writings of Edmund Burke to help him prepare this lecture, but when Kuyper came

---

[7] He spells them out on pp. 307–10 in the text.

[8] Kuyper, "Calvinism and Constitutional Liberties," 304–06; quotations, 310, 305

[9] Ibid., 309–10; quotation, 310.

back and asked for the Huguenot sources as well, Groen revealingly replied that he did not have them in his library.[10] In the lecture itself Kuyper emphasized that the authors in question—Beza, Francois Hotman, and Hubert Languet (probably Philippe du Plessis-Mornay)—limited the right of resistance to duly constituted leaders, the "lesser magistrates," and subsequent historians have confirmed the significance of their concept for the development of modern political theory.[11] Yet, in chronicling the French case, Kuyper had to refer to a rebellion persistent, systematic, bloody, and radicalizing enough to count as a revolution, save for its lack of success. The case of seventeenth-century English Puritanism was not thus limited. That the Puritan Revolution involved violent insurrection, regicide, destruction of church properties, terror in the (Irish) countryside, instability eventuating in military dictatorship, and any number of other features resembling the French Revolution Kuyper did not mention. For him the Puritans' was a permissible, even commendable, revolution as attested to by its official documents and the good discipline of Cromwell's New Model army.[12]

Kuyper could bypass these uncomfortable parts of this story because in both the Huguenot and Puritan cases his first focus was ecclesiastical rather than civil politics. This reflected the centrality for him of religious freedom among other "constitutional liberties," but it also served his current polemical agenda; when he gave his talk, his proposals for reforming church arrangements in Amsterdam, where he still served as a parish pastor, had just been rejected.[13] Thus his lecture attributed the synodical hierarchy

---

[10] See Groen's letter to Kuyper of 2 September 1872, in A. Goslinga, ed., *Briefwisseling van Mr. G. Groen van Prinsterer met Dr. A. Kuyper, 1864-1876* (Kampen: Kok, 1937), 194-95. Jan W. Sap, *Paving the Way for Revolution: Calvinism and the Struggle for a Democratic Constitutional State* (Amsterdam: VU Uitgeverij, 2001) critically notes Groen's aversion to Huguenot resistance theory, 294-95.

[11] Huguenot resistance theory is well laid out in Julian H. Franklin, ed., *Constitutionalism and Resistance in the Sixteenth Century: Three Treatises* (New York: Pegasus, 1969). Quentin Skinner traces its development and significance in *The Foundations of Modern Political Thought*, vol. II (New York: Cambridge University Press, 1978), 239–348, as does John Witte in *The Reformation of Rights: Law, Religion, and Human Rights in Early Modern Calvinism* (Cambridge: Cambridge University Press, 2007).

[12] Kuyper, "Calvinism and Constitutional Liberties," 296–97.

[13] Jasper Vree, "De dominie van wijk 27, wijk 8, en nog veel meer: Amsterdam 1870-1874," in *Kuyper in de kiem: De precalvinistische period van Abraham Kuyper 1848-1874* (Hilversum: Verloren, 2006), 325–61.

that so frustrated him in the Netherlands back to the Huguenots' adoption of it as a political necessity in the face of military emergency. He hurried on to laud the English Independents for boldly and properly adapting "the Calvinist principle" to their own time and place over against their Presbyterian opponents, who had tried to import the alien French system on the assumption that "Calvinism was a petrifaction, bound to the form it had assumed, take it or leave it." In this battle, Kuyper concluded, the Independents not only had the greater success but the clearer claim on Calvin, "who had unambiguously rejected the idea that one should be tied to an established form." By this argument Kuyper's ideal of a "circle of free, autonomous congregations" bound on a "voluntary, not coerced, relationship with the synod" received the imprimatur of Calvin himself. Likewise the "separation of church and state," which—accordingly to Kuyper—Puritans in old England and New had the virtue to realize, followed "necessarily" from "Calvinistic principle."[14]

The New England case allowed Kuyper to return to civil politics proper, and with the happiest prospects for his thesis. No one could deny that "modern liberties flourish in America without restriction" or that "the people of the Union bear a clear-cut Christian stamp more than any other nation on earth." This was not a coincidental but a causal relationship, Kuyper argued, rooted in the nation's Puritan origins. Kuyper had plenty of sources for this casual conflation of "New England" and "America," since the standard histories of the time (and for several more generations) exercised the same assumption. At the same time, his characteristic organic sociology was at work. Whatever the cultural complexity and the numbers on the ground that made it an exceptional minority by 1776, New England to him still represented "the core of the nation;" and whatever might have developed over the subsequent century via westward movement, civil war, and industrialization, the original Puritan stamp still held on America's core convictions and collective character. To make this claim credible, Kuyper's "Calvinism" now had to leave behind any confessional particulars (he includes Wesleyans in the mix!) and take on enough elasticity to become a broadly cultural pattern of moral earnestness, healthy enterprise, middle-

---

[14] Kuyper, "Calvinism and Constitutional Liberties," 293–97, 299–301; quotations, 293, 294, 306, 300.

class discipline, and public respect for religion.[15]

So arranged, he could hammer home his point: the best of modern liberties were the fruit not of the French Revolution but of Calvinism. To quote him: "With much evil the [French] revolution also brought Europe much good, but this was stolen fruit, ripened on the stem of Calvinism under the nurturing warmth of our martyrs' faith, first in our own land, then in England, and subsequently in America." Kuyper had to acknowledge ruefully that in Europe "what had been refused from the hand of Calvinism was eagerly accepted from the hands of the French heroes of freedom." Yet it would not do to accept that surrogate for, along with "Calvinistic liberties . . . [the Revolution] introduced a system, a catechism, a doctrine; and this system, running counter to God and his righteousness, destroys the bonds of law and order, undermines the foundations of society, gives free play to passion, and gives the lower realm rule over the spirit." Put positively, only Calvinism supplies "the moral element," "the heroic faith," and those intermediate institutions which over the years had become the proper extension of the "lesser magistrates;" all of these, and only these, together give order to liberty and so assure its perpetuation.[16] In sum, Kuyper sees political constitutionalism as the fruit of Calvinist revolution.

II. Sphere Sovereignty

Seven years later, in the autumn of 1880, Kuyper returned to some of these themes in "Sphere Sovereignty." Now he was not speaking at other universities but founding his own. He was speaking from the chancel of the cathedral of Dutch Protestantism, Amsterdam's Nieuwe Kerk, but speaking on behalf of the humble believers in the land who had seemingly been bypassed by time and power. Yet for this group Kuyper was now staking a claim to prospective social and cultural power. His speech needed to be insurrectionary, then, to announce possible reversals in the status hierarchy; at the same time it had to build for the long run, mapping out an order that was both dynamic and stable. The leaders who would be minted at the new

---

[15] Ibid., 286–92; quotations 286, 289. The method and mistakes of Kuyper's appropriation of American history are detailed in James D. Bratt, "Abraham Kuyper, American History, and the Tensions of Neo-Calvinism," in George Harinck and Hans Krabbendam, eds., *Sharing the Reformed Tradition: The Dutch-North American Exchange, 1846-1996* (Amsterdam: VU Uitgeverij, 1996).

[16] Kuyper, "Calvinism and Constitutional Liberties," 298–99, 313, 314, 312.

university would be asserting religiously distinctive claims, yet would play responsibly on the public stage, working for the common good.

Kuyper showed his purpose for "Sphere Sovereignty" by evoking at the earliest opportunity the controlling trope of early-modern political philosophy: absolute and undivided sovereignty. Since French Calvinist resistance had been both the occasion and the victim of that assertion, Kuyper elevating such sovereignty out of human reach to God's hands alone, from whence it was refracted into any number of localized human sovereignties. These were not to be re-gathered into one, Kuyper insisted, until Christ returned in majesty at the final judgment. Any human pretension to claim unitary sovereignty was thus blasphemous on the face of it and bound to wreak woe in practice; this in fact, Kuyper recounted, was the grim thread of world history, from the tyranny of the Caesars to the persecutions of the Hapsburgs, Bourbons, and Stuarts, to the contemporary scene where universalistic claims of revolutionary popular sovereignty on one side matched Hegelian elevations of "the State as 'the immanent God'" on the other.[17] Historically, the antidote to these assaults had been constitutional restrictions on the centralization or exercise of power, particularly the separation and balance of powers as theorized by Montesquieu and ensconced in the United States Constitution. But Kuyper entirely bypassed constitutional measures on this occasion. Rather, he postulated discrete and autonomous spheres of human life to replicate on the ontological level the separation and balance of powers in politics. Not on paper or in formal offices, then, but in the divinely given creation and the evolution of organic societies lay the most promising grounds of resistance to the unitary beast.

For all its theocentric claims about the nature of being and for all its occasion of founding an integrally, distinctively Christian university, "Sphere Sovereignty" proceeds with very modest biblical evidence or theological elaboration. Once again Kuyper appeals to history, but now to a different set of examples and by a different method than was true of his earlier address. Put colloquially, in "Sphere Sovereignty" the villains command the historical highlights; the plot-line is the parade of the unitary beast, contested by valiant yet faltering heroes of liberty. The Netherlands now casts up more of the resistance than in "Calvinism and Constitutional Liberties," but offers a thin case for the theoretical plausibility or future chances of the

---

[17] Kuyper, "Sphere Sovereignty," 469–71; quotation, 466.

harmonious constellation of spheres that Kuyper lauded. The strongest precedent his account can muster on this front is an evocation of "that glorious life, crowned with nobility," that marked the late-medieval Low Countries, "exhibiting in the ever richer organism of guilds and orders and free communities all the energy and glory that sphere sovereignty implies."[18]

Why had no theoretician arisen to explain and warrant the virtues of this order? One had, and on a Calvinistic basis at that! This was Johannes Althusius, author of the definitive compendium of Calvinist, antiroyalist thought *(Politica Methodice Digesta*, 1603) and syndic of Emden in the first quarter of the seventeenth century when that city was "the Geneva of the North" with a strong influence on the emerging Dutch republic and its Reformed church.[19] Indeed, by his writing, civic, and ecclesiastical roles, Althusius qualifies in some historians' estimation as the John Calvin of Emden. His consociational political theory intentionally answered Jean Bodin's theory of unitary sovereignty. It also chartered something very like Kuyper's society of sovereign spheres.

In Althusisus's thought, human nature is indelibly associational, precluding individualism from the start and making communities the building blocks of societies. So also Kuyper begins: "Our human life . . . is so structured that the individual exists only in groups, and only in such groups can the whole become manifest."[20] Each human association, Althusius continues, was empowered by its original purpose to flourish but was also bound by the inherent limits of that purpose so as not to intrude on others—be it another cluster in the same or in an adjoining domain of human activity. Certain powers were delegated upward to the next tier of human interaction by decision of the smaller units, which units (not the individuals in them) remained the constituent members of these broader bodies. Thus, individuals were members of households, the heads of which delegated some of their political power to town councilors who in turn appointed mayors and syndics. For economic purposes, citizens joined guilds; for religious purposes, churches; for recreation, clubs. Successive intermediate levels of as-

---

[18] Ibid., 470.

[19] On Althusius, I have relied on the Introduction by Frederick S. Carney and Preface by Carl J. Friedrich to Carney's translation of Althusius's *Politics* (Boston: Beacon Press, 1964); and on James W. Skillen, "The Political Theory of Johannes Althusius," *Philosophia Reformata* 39 (1974): 170–90.

[20] Kuyper, "Sphere Sovereignty," 467.

sociation then conveyed authority up the scale of more general gatherings: towns constituted a province, provinces a nation, nations an empire.

Human society was thus a pyramid of association where power remained as close to the base as possible, in which no one at any level ruled without the consent of the governed, in which different functions of human life developed freely according to the purposes of that function and not to the call of another, and in which responsible decisions remained closest to those most competent to make and implement them. Moreover, authorities in every domain and at every level were constrained by the laws divine and natural that set norms for that association; thus, individuals within a consociation—the father in the home, guild A in the town economy, province X in the nation—could be disciplined by their fellows or, if need be, by their superiors, for violating their trust.

A more friendly and auspicious antecedent for sphere sovereignty could hardly be imagined. Why did Kuyper not invoke it? Jonathan Chaplin suggests that Althusius had been rendered suspicious for Kuyper by the work of Otto von Gierke, a close contemporary (born 1841) who, in a book published in the same year as "Sphere Sovereignty," completed a harnessing of Althusius to the evolution of the German constitutional state which von Gierke deemed the final synthesis in the inherent dialectic between community and sovereignty, "fellowship" and "lordship," that drove German history.[21] As von Gierke celebrated the newly fashioned (1871) German Empire as the ultimate synthesis between French libertarianism and Russian autocracy, Althusius thus became associated with what Kuyper deemed a grim danger. Methodologically, moreover, von Gierke had secularized Althusius to make his process of human association entirely immanent in its drive and final court of appeal.

But back to Kuyper's speech. What is political theory, named as social ontology and told as historical narrative, doing in a speech that charters a university? The answer lies in "Sphere Sovereignty's" strong evocation of a basic tenet of republican political philosophy, that virtue is the bulwark of

---

[21] On von Gierke, see Antony Black's "Editor's Introduction" to Otto von Gierke, *Community in Historical Perspective: a translation of selections from* Das Deutsche Genossenschaftsrecht [1881], tr. Mary Fischer, ed. Antony Black (Cambridge and New York: Cambridge University Press, 1990), xiv–xxx. Von Gierke published *Johannes Althusius und die Entwicklung der naturrechtlichen Staatstheorien* in 1878. Jonathan Chaplin explained Kuyper's aversion to Althusius via von Gierke in a personal communication to the author, 4 November 2003.

liberty. The antidote to centralizing unitary power is not just spheres orbiting in theoretical sovereignty but in a resolute citizenry whose moral strength animates the spheres with vitality enough to resist the encroaching power. And before that, Kuyper emphasizes, to resist the deterioration *within* a sphere—particularly the oppression and abuse of power that its leaders visit upon the weaker—which invites the state into that sphere's domain: more accurately, which *requires* the state to undertake its divinely given calling to redress abuse of power and reestablish justice. It is self-discipline and self-sacrifice by the people in their respective roles that precludes and withstands statist intervention. But such moral rigor depends much upon morale; if we would fight the sloth and corruption that ultimately lead to oppression, Kuyper repeats, we need hope to live a better way. We need a vision contrary to that vended by the hegemonic threat. In other words, the core of political resistance and the road to social flourishing lie in culture. There the university can and must serve the crucial role.[22] The Free University was to flesh out a robust worldview over against that of the materialist hegemon that was stalking Europe, a worldview that would make of a faithful Reformed remnant a collective player equal in strength—perhaps one day, superior in allure—to the forces animated by secularist naturalism. At the same time the scholars at the university would be conducting the advanced research on pressing problems of modem life needed to articulate alternative policies from a Christian point of view. "Sphere Sovereignty" charters a mandate and arena for Christian public intellectuals.

III. Program

The rhetorical peak that was "Sphere Sovereignty" followed closely upon Kuyper's definitive statement of practical politics, a voluminous commentary on the platform of the Antirevolutionary Party that ran in his newspaper *De Standaard* and that he gathered in book form under the title of *Ons Program*.[23] In this program five spheres in particular come into play. Better, we might say that here "sphere sovereignty" adapted under divine

---

[22] Kuyper, "Sphere Sovereignty," 468, 473–77.

[23] *Ons Program*'s first edition (Amsterdam: J. H. Kruyt, 1879) included the official 21 Articles of the ARP Program, the series of commentary thereon that appeared in *De Standaard* April 1878-February 1879, and additional newspaper essays on the topic, most notably the series "Ordinantiën Gods" which appeared ibid. in 1873, just before Kuyper's first term in Parliament.

warrant a theory of organic social development resembling that of the German Historical School. This thinking had come to Kuyper along his two strongest paths of influence, having been a source of Groen's own thinking, and having become entwined with various currents of Romantic social philosophy across the Continent. Kuyper's particular contribution was to demarcate within this ideal of a free and vibrant society the "fixed radius" and divinely endowed "principle" valorized in his opening paragraphs of "Sphere Sovereignty," along with policy prescriptions for his party to advocate in Dutch politics.

Church. Because his was intentionally a religiously based political program, Kuyper strongly reaffirmed the separation of church and state that had been instituted in the Netherlands in 1848. As we have seen, he grounded the principle in Calvinism itself, wherein the church is stated to proceed from the order of redemption, and the state from the development of creation. Neither has the right or the competence to dictate anything to the other. Even so, Kuyper insisted, religion may, will, and ought to pass over into politics via the "conscience of the legislator" and of the electorate behind him. That is, Kuyper legitimated his party by appealing to the primordial motto—freedom of conscience—of the Dutch war for independence and by expanding its application. "Liberty" included the right to have your religiously grounded ethical prescriptions heard in the councils of state. Yet, they were not to be imposed there simply by invocation of the authority of church or scripture. Rather, any faith-based policy proposal had to be duly passed by 50% + 1 of the parliament via appeal to shared interests and principles. For its part, the church as an institution should raise the entirety of its revenue by voluntary means, but then also have complete control of its properties, appointments, and supervision of clergy and lay members so far as their ecclesiastical behavior was concerned. [24]

School. Public education was the galvanizing issue of Kuyper's party and political career, and understandably so. In the wake of the 1860s' wars of national unification in Germany, Italy, and the United States, schools proved to be the key locus for building and cementing national identity and for improving human capital in an internationally competitive industrial economy. Kuyper affirmed the legitimacy of the latter demand but again appealed to liberty of conscience and developed the principle into his posi-

---

[24] Article 20/Chapter 21 of *Ons Program* treats this topic. "Conscience of the legislator," 103.

tion of *principled pluralism*. By his thinking education necessarily presupposes a common frame of values that directs the school's curriculum and ethos. To impose upon all families a frame from a particular religion, as the Reformed Church had done in the Dutch *ancien regime*, was to violate the conscience of people who did not share that conviction. But so also now in modern times with respect to any secular, putatively but not really "neutral," worldview. The conclusion followed: the state might mandate education for all children per the national interest and the flourishing of its citizens. It also might stipulate quality standards for all. But the content, angle of vision, or interpretive frame within and around the curriculum must be congruent with parental conviction, as children belonged to parents first of all, and not to state or society—or the church. Accordingly, all schools that are responsible to quality standards are "public" in serving the public interest, and all should be supported equitably out of the common till. Kuyper's slogan further prescribed the "confessional school to be the norm," the secular state-run school "a supplement."[25]

The *family*, though the third sphere considered here, was for Kuyper first in every sense of the term. It was the first institution to appear in history and seeded all the rest. Its health was the foundation and surest barometer of a society's wellbeing. It grew from nature, prospered by nurture, and properly taught its members how to balance personal autonomy, mutual dependence, and due responsibility—i.e., it was society in miniature. Likewise its authority was the source of, model for, and limit upon the state. Properly functioning, it exhibited church-like qualities in being crowned with love and becoming a school for morals. It set the first limit on individualism and initiated the upward delegation of powers central to consociational theory. If school and church each had a discrete Article in the Antirevolutionary Program, the family bore upon many. That complicated policy formulation at three points in particular. The state might mandate education, but the family—the "father," Kuyper clarified—defined its terms. The state must promote public health by ensuring pure food and water, among other measures, but—to take the hot controversy of the day—it might not make vaccination compulsory against parental conscience. To prevent anomic individualism the franchise should be extended to all heads of households, not to all adult persons. Normally, that meant voting by hus-

---

[25] *Ons Program*, Article 12/Chapter 13.

bands/fathers; otherwise, by widows/mothers.[26]

Kuyper showed his greatest ambivalence toward the fourth sphere, the *state*. Divinely ordained and the guarantor against chaos and depredation, it deserved obedience and gratitude. Bearing the power of the sword and sharp tendencies toward expansion, it should provoke fear. He refused to see the state as (tracking left to right across the spectrum of contemporary opinion) the unitary expression of the will of "the people," the modern instrument of providence into which the church itself should be absorbed, or the power that would hold together all other domains in unity and order. *Ons Program* stipulated that the state was *among* and not *above* the other spheres. Yet "Sphere Sovereignty" acknowledged that it "rises high *above* them" with the mandate to regulate the other spheres' mutual relations and to intrude within each and any of them whenever individual rights were abused or the weak were exploited by the powerful. In terms of the divine ordinances implanted to guide sphere development, the state arose in response to sin and bore the principle of justice, and so Kuyper most commonly declaimed whenever rival political groups promoted the expansion of state powers. But he also declared at the start of his career that it was simply wrong to see "the state . . . as a purely external means of compulsion." The sharp distinction that the German Historical School taught between a good healthy society, organically developing on its own power, and a negative disciplinary state Kuyper correlated theologically with a divinely endowed creation vis á vis necessary constraints of sin. But within this understanding there was nothing to say that even without sin, a vibrant society would not have arranged for a central agency to coordinate its emerging complexity—just the function that theorists of the modern expansive state prescribed.[27]

Nor was Kuyper a simple state-minimalist in domestic affairs. *Ons Program* called for stricter regulation of prostitution and alcohol abuse so as

---

[26] An apt summary of Kuyper's concept of the family is in Dengerink, *Critisch-Historisch Onderzoek*, 124–27. For the nuances in *Ons Program*, see 295–97, 477–78, 806–07, 848–57.

[27] *Ons Program*, 138–46; "rises high," "Sphere Sovereignty," 468; "purely external means," "Ordinantiën Gods," E. T. "The Ordinances of God," in Skillen and McCarthey," *Political Order and the Plural Structure*, 249.

to promote "public virtue."[28] The budget pressures entailed by such policing would elicit droll comment later on during his prime ministership; the cost of achieving educational equity was much higher still, and more immediately controversial. These proposals also bring us back to the high plains of theory at two points. First, Kuyper varied on how *society* was to be understood. Sometimes he treated it as a separate, fifth sphere, reflecting a tradition that so labeled the domain of voluntary action that lay between household, church, and state. At other times Kuyper treated "society" as a collection of all spheres except the state. In either case his fulsome trust in the powers and dynamics he regarded as inherent in the social sphere from creation is remarkable. Nowhere did he so minimize the effects of sin as in his assumptions about the macro level of social development. Sometimes he could spy a fearful momentum that was greater than any particular part, and on many occasions he noted individual persons, policies, agencies, or communities perverting their social potential. But in formal theory Kuyper more often celebrated than worried about the direction of the whole.

IV. Policy

As a long-time member of the Dutch parliament and prime minister of the Netherlands (1901–05), Kuyper offers an unusual opportunity to observe how a theologian-theoretician translated prescriptions into actual policy on the issues of the day. Education being his galvanizing issue, it also was the site of his most celebrated achievement, yet by no means his only one. He addressed the three most urgent areas of demand in the late nineteenth century with detailed concrete proposals.

1. *Education*: The Antirevolutionary Party insisted start to finish on equitable funding of elementary and secondary education along the lines of principled pluralism. They won the point in steps, from their first triumphs in 1889 to the achievement of full equity in 1917. A notable achievement under Kuyper's prime ministership came with the awarding of full accreditation to Free University degrees in 1905. Notably, Kuyper argued all along that educational equity was connected not just to religious but also to economic justice. To require "double payment" (taxation plus religious school tuition) effectively punished poor parents for, or prohibited them from,

---

[28] *Ons Program*, Article 14/Chapter 15 treats the concept and details of "public virtue."

exercising their freedom of conscience. At the same time Prime Minister Kuyper pushed through legislation chartering vocational schools, night schools, and a technical university to broaden the educational options available to the full range of citizens under the conditions of industrialization.[29]

2. *Franchise*: The democratization of Dutch politics proceeded in tandem with educational pluralization, although usually as its obverse—that is, those who promoted the one opposed the other. The two were finally promulgated together in a "pacification" settlement under wartime exigencies in 1917. Kuyper was something of an exception in promoting both causes all along, with the caveat (finally rejected in 1919) that universal adult manhood suffrage should remain just that—for men only. He argued this on the grounds of maintaining an "organic" as opposed to "individualistic" society; the household franchise (normally exercised by the man as head) would honor the former and forestall the latter. Democratization itself Kuyper advocated as a matter of prudence as well as of justice. The "little people" tended to be more religiously observant than the higher bourgeoisie so that his party would (and did) prosper from franchise extension. Another of his re-structuring proposals also came to pass when representation in the Lower House of the Dutch parliament became calibrated to each party's percentage of the national popular vote. A third proposal, to redesign the Upper House as a chamber of interests, not of the provinces, was not approved.[30]

3. *Labor-capital relations, or "the social question,"* became a burning issue in the Netherlands relatively late owing to the delayed onset of industrialization there. By the 1880s, however, the combination of a prolonged recession in the countryside and a slump in the nascent factory sector posed serious questions of human well-being and social stability. Even before that Kuyper had recognized how much industrialism cost and who was paying the bills. He remained, per sphere sovereignty principles, suspicious of state interventions but equally of "free market" measures out of his observation that both were prone to usurpation by the rich and self-seeking. Counter-

---

[29] Kuyper made a pithy case for educational reform, including its economic dimension, already in a stirring address at Utrecht, "Het Beroep op het Volksgetweten" (Amsterdam: Blankenberg, 1869). For Kuyper's educational reforms as prime minister, see James D. Bratt, *Abraham Kuyper: Modern Calvinist, Christian Democrat*, 312–14.

[30] *Ons Program*, 295–97, 415–25.

parts to our present-day phenomena of regulatory capture and crony capitalism were well known to him and drew his scorn as much as did socialism. Through this maze he attempted to carve out a "middle way" consisting of three elements.[31]

First, just as the state had devised commercial, civil, and criminal codes of law, he espoused a *"law-code for labor"* so that its interests, rights, and obligations would be incorporated in the judicial system; more broadly, labor as a sector would be integrated into the formal structures and procedures of society. Second, he proposed the creation of labor councils in all industries as a balance to management power. These would entail mandatory membership and would negotiate grievances and the terms and conditions of employment subject to binding state arbitration in cases of deadlock. The arrangement reflected Kuyper's ideal of creating checks and balances of power in economic as in political arrangements, and to have the parties at interest handle matters locally according to their greater expertise rather than suffer the dictates of distant and unqualified authorities. Third, Kuyper endorsed the knitting of an effective *social safety net* to mitigate the inevitable harms and limits of the industrial system. These measures included enforcing national standards for safe housing, unemployment and disability insurance, and mandatory health insurance. The latter should be vended precisely on the order of his prescription for education—by private parties with a public option.

From these considerations of Kuyper's theory and its chief practical application we can draw the following common motifs.

1. In his social thinking and political theory, as in his theology, Kuyper was concerned first of all with due *authority*: to garner and stipulate respect for it, but also clearly to delimit its powers and scope. Human depravity made regulatory and punitive power necessary, but its very strength made this power dangerous as well. Accordingly, he was convinced that this combination of limits and potency could be best promoted by a strong ethos of public virtue, a culture of self-discipline and self-restraint written

---

[31] The details of and sources for this paragraph and the next are given in Bratt, *AKMCCD*, 221–32. The key statements by Kuyper are *Het Sociale Vraagstuk en de Christelijke Religie* (Amsterdam: J. A. Wormser, 1891); E. T., *The Problem of Poverty*, ed. James Skillen (Grand Rapids: Baker, 1991); and *Handenarbied* (Amsterdam: J. A. Wormser, 1889); E.T., "Manual Labor," in Bratt, ed., *Kuyper Centennial Reader*, 231–54.

on the individual and collective heart.

2. The key to social flourishing, accordingly, lay for Kuyper more in *culture* than in politics. The ethos of virtue is to be cultivated by education and communication. Notably, Kuyper spent most of his career as a journalist, professor, and preacher, and came secondarily to politics out of the needs and momentum gathered there. In all those roles he recognized (earlier than many others) the power of the public opinion and of mythos, or what we call the hegemonic narrative in a society. He was a master at weaving just such a narrative for his followers and turning them thereby into a persistent movement that achieved far more than its numbers would suggest.

3. Kuyper was much more a *communitarian* than libertarian or individualist. He was fearful of atomism and anomie particularly under the emerging conditions of industrial modernity. The overriding motif in his theology, social theory, and political thinking alike was relationality. We come into the world in, and so must everywhere begin our theorizing with, community. Individual rights are absolutely to be protected, he agreed, but that can and must happen first of all by our embeddedness in community.

4. Kuyper showed a keen eye for *power* in both theoretical stipulations and actual situations. The test of a theory, of a person, and of an institution lay in is its actions toward the poor and weak, just as their chief vulnerability lay in being coopted by the rich and the strong. In this respect his approach may be labeled Christian democratic populism.

5. That said, the best available formula for justice and peace on earth is a *balance of power*, alike in politics, economy, and society. The church is called to aspire to the perfection of the Kingdom of God, and does its best service by calling the norms and ethos thereof to remembrance in the midst of the world; but saints being prone to sin, limiting power by the erection of countervailing powers is a wise and necessary accommodation to our fallenness on earth.

6. At the same time, the brackets of Kuyper's theorizing in all things—political just as much as theological—was the *glory of God*. This was the normative motive through every skein of his thinking, the rhetorical trope at its beginning and end.

7. More than either his disciples or opponents sometimes recognize, Kuyper held a dual, *ambivalent vision* regarding what can be expected of Christians on earth. As he put it in one epochal address, the faithful live on

earth as "a colony of the heavenly fatherland," seeking the good of their earthly fatherland by expending, at the same time as they vigilantly preserve their quality as, leaven.[32] More concretely, believers are to promote God's glory in their national life by refracting the wisdom and distilling the ethics of revelation into policies promoting the common good beyond the secular citizenry's ability to perceive that good.

V. The Spirit of a Movement

Detailed and concrete policy. Sober theology. Institutions that would sustain a movement and stabilize society. Given the accumulation of Kuyper's work reviewed thus far, the last statement of his that we will analyze here sounds a very different chord. The occasion for it came in 1908—well after Kuyper's vision had birthed a complex of institutions that were beginning to realize significant success. The Free University, where Kuyper had taught for twenty years, was now expanding its faculty and student body across a broader range of disciplines. Its graduates were moving up the ranks of the professions, and its clientele was fruitfully engaged in the discussion and application of the writings on the arts, economics, theology, and politics that the faculty were duly putting forth. The Antirevolutionary Party had increased its numbers, seen some of its policy proposals enacted into law, and was currently in charge of the government for the third time. Kuyper was still in command of the party as chair of its Central Committee and as editor of its newspaper, *De Standaard*. But in this third AR Cabinet he was not prime minister, and party members had other newspapers to read as well, some of them voicing pointed critiques of his leadership. Those critiques were also being sounded in party councils by the rising generation of leaders. In fact, that cohort conducted something of a coup in maneuvering through an unexpected set of circumstances to take over the government in 1908, pointedly keeping Kuyper out of the cabinet. In this context Kuyper published a series of articles entitled "Our Instinctive Life" which explored yet another aspect of politics and its ontological footing.[33] It championed

---

[32] Quotation from Kuyper, *Tweeerlei Vaderland* (Amsterdam: J. A. Wormser, 1887), 32.

[33] *Ons Instinctieve Leven* appeared in book form (Amsterdam: W. Kirchner, 1908) after its original newspaper run earlier that year, and is available in English translation as "Our Instinctive Life" in Bratt, ed., *Kuyper Centennial Reader*, 255–77. For the context of its

charismatic leadership and its organic bond with the popular will.

Kuyper begins this account by extolling the instinctive powers of the animal world. This was his "fable of the bees"—more accurately, of the spiders, for whom he shows a fascination comparable to Jonathan Edwards' two hundred years before. The wisdom of the insects partakes of the wisdom of God, Kuyper continues; even more so does the practical intelligence, the knack and knowledge, of ordinary people. In marked contrast to the raptures about front-line scholarship that he proclaimed in "Sphere Sovereignty," Kuyper now characterizes knowledge gained by "reflection," by book study, to be "artificial" and passing. The "perfect" knowledge we shall have in the next world as promised by I Corinthians 13 will be "spontaneous, immediate, and completed at once"—quite more like the practical intuition of everyday life than like the abstract schematizing of academics.[34]

We can recognize here an old theme in Kuyper, one sounded already in his first major cultural address some forty years before, "Uniformity, the Curse of Modern Life." But it was also newly current, part of whole stream of vitalist complaints being sounded left, right, and center, on both sides of the Atlantic, in the early 20th century.[35] Bourgeois civilization with its iron laws of science and industry, its fixed routines of business management and city life, was crushing the unique and the spirited, blighting the individual and the race, draining the life-force and imagination, corroding both the animal virtues and the higher callings that made human life worth living. Kuyper repeated these complaints. Amidst the urban and urbane withered the rich color and variety of traditional rural life, he mourned; under advancing civilization, the collective wisdom that had passed down the generations was giving way to the "calculated," to the "pedestrian and prosaic, the measured and formal." Such routinization was even creeping into the ARP, and inevitably so, Kuyper allowed. But that tendency had to be vigi-

---

controversy, see Dirk Th. Kuiper, *De Voormannen: een social-wetenschappelijke studie* (Meppel: Boom, 1972), 245–51 and 345–47.

[34] Kuyper, "Our Instinctive Life," 257–59; quotations, 258.

[35] "Uniformity" is available in English translation in Bratt, *Kuyper Centennial Reader*, 19–44. It originally appeared as *Eenvormigheid: De Vloek van het Modern Leven* (Amsterdam: H. de Hoogh, 1869). Of many studies of the discontents of modernity, see J. W. Burrow, *The Crisis of Reason: European Thought, 1848-1914* (New Haven: Yale University Press, 2000), and T. J. Jackson Lears, *No Place of Grace: Antimodernism and the Transformation of American Culture, 1880-1920* (New York: Pantheon, 1981).

lantly guarded against lest the holy cause succumb to "spiritual decline and emotional impoverishment."[36]

As we shall see, Kuyper had a very practical objective in view in publishing this polemic, but he was also addressing a problem of modern political organization for which Max Weber and Georges Sorel were drawing up their respective prescriptions at much the same time. In Weberian terms, Kuyper intended to fight the passage from charismatic to bureaucratic authority as much and as long as he could. To that end he defended some procedures he had built into the party from the start over against the proposals that the new cohort wanted to institute. They wished, first, to make policy formation more collaborative, to open study and discussion clubs for all party members, led by men in the junior ranks, so that the ARP would be democratic in means as well as ends. They also proposed to bring trained competence to the head of the table—that is, to replace the abstract and simplistic pronouncements of the clergy sector of party leadership with the trained expertise of lawyers and social scientists.[37] The rising leaders advocating these changes were, let us remember, men trained at Kuyper's university and practicing the mandate he had given them: to conduct the research into modern problems needed to give general AR principles real purchase on the ground.

This Kuyper now scotched. There are three kinds of people in the world, he declared: the large mass of folk who live by practical wisdom, the few genuine scholars whose all-absorbing studies take them to the depths of things, and then the jabbering class of the superficially learned, textbook-trained in second-hand knowledge, who put themselves above but lacked the virtues of the other two groups. The professionals who were most likely to escape this hazard, to have "brought the instinctive and the reflective life into a higher synthesis," Kuyper continued, were in fact the clergy, whose duties in the pulpit sent them back every week to the fonts of deep knowledge and whose parish duties exposed them intimately to the life of ordinary folk. The derivative "amphibians" now contesting for leadership knew not the real life of those they invited to the policy table, Kuyper snapped, otherwise they would know how mistaken their suggestions must

---

[36] Kuyper, "Our Instinctive Life," 268.

[37] Kuiper, Voormannen, 246–47. Kuyper alludes to the proposals satirically in "Our Instinctive Life," 270–71.

be. For Kuyper, lauding the commoners, also reminded them of the "boundaries" that demarcated their "sphere." Having intuitional knowledge, they neither could nor would really wish to take part in policy formation. If confronted with rival proposals, the role of "the non-learned public" was "to use its own instinctive life as touchstone and for the rest to rely on its leaders."[38]

That connection needed to be vibrant and heartfelt, however. This, for all his appeals to custom and tradition, Kuyper sensed to be the modern in politics and the key to his own success. Writing entirely in the third person and in innocently vague language, he lays out in these articles the two roads to his reign. In the series' preliminary discussion of instinctive gifts, where he locates the artist—indeed "all true *talent*, and especially all *genius*"—Kuyper describes how a charismatic speaker operates, and in so doing leaves a self-portrait that was confirmed by any number of observers: the speaker

> takes up his position before the gathering, feels the contact between his spirit and that of his audience, and opens the tap. Almost automatically the words begin to flow, the thoughts leap out, the images frolic—psychological art in action. This is even more true of the *genius*. He does not plod and pick away at things; he does not split hairs or prime the pump. . . . By spiritual X-ray vision he sees through doors and walls and virtually without effort grasps the pearl for which others grope in vain.[39]

Thus there is in Kuyper's typology a fourth category of person besides the earlier three of commoner, scholar, and derivative intellectual—there is the genius, and it is he who lifts up and weaves together policy proposals, social studies, political theory, and tactical considerations into an eloquent statement that accords precisely with "what they themselves [the common voters] instinctively felt in essence."[40] That leadership common people value far more than a spot on a study committee, Kuyper averred.

Charisma cannot remain just occasional in the contests of modern politics, however. It has to be ensconced in ordinary party work without

---

[38] Kuyper, "Our Instinctive Life," 263, 267–68; quotations, 267–68.

[39] Ibid., 260; italics in original.

[40] Ibid., 267.

getting routinized. Kuyper explained how to meet this challenge by having recourse to another French source—not to Calvin or the resistance theorists this time but to Gustav Le Bon and his work on the psychology of the crowd.[41] Written out of long, skeptical retrospect upon the French revolutionary tradition, Le Bon's description of how the crowd becomes a being in itself, with its own will and mind sweeping up those of its individual members, becomes for Kuyper a theoretical warrant for the Antirevolutionary party conventions that he had instituted and that were held every biennial election season. At these meetings the lonely village delegate comes to know that he is part of a vibrant, national movement, Kuyper explains. A written statement of principles becomes a living conviction. A campaign platform becomes the staircase to a better tomorrow. The oratory of genius had its part in the drama, but drama it had to be. A party "must have the means—as the *psychology of the crowd* demands—to convert sober realism into enthusiasm, cool calculation into holy passion. . . . It is by virtue of the power and animation that radiates from these meetings that we have become who we are." Technical expertise—and on this note Kuyper concluded his series—is the armor of Saul in God's good fight, but the intuitive bond connecting the leader genius with the faithful is the stone of David that fells the giant.[42]

VI. Conclusion

Kuyper was a practical politician with a full menu of policy prescriptions. At the same time he was a bard who laid out his political theory in historical narratives. The first of these warranted revolution led by lesser magistrates on constitutional grounds. The second called forth intellectual visionaries to invigorate mediating institutions. The third celebrated the organic bond between the charismatic leader and popular consciousness. The second part of this triad, that laid out as sphere sovereignty, can become—and did become in Dutch Neo-Calvinist history—routinized into place-holding conservatism. The other two notes must be heard as well to grasp Kuyper's full vision and the magic of his inspiration. Revolution and

---

[41] Kuyper cites and develops the theme of Le Bon's *La psychologie de foule* (Paris: F. Alcan, 1895) in ibid., 264–66.

[42] Kuyper, "Our Instinctive Life," 275–77; quotation, 276–77.

charisma are dangerous quantities, of course, and it is sphere sovereignty's job to discipline them. But it is also necessary for sphere sovereignty to be enlivened by their fervor and hope.

Bibliography

Kuyper, Abraham. *Eenvormigheid: De Vloek van het Modern Leven*. Amsterdam: H. de Hoogh, 1869. Translated as "Uniformity, the Curse of Modern Life," in Bratt, ed. *Kuyper Centennial Reader*, 19–44.

———. "Het Beroep op het Volksgetweten." Amsterdam: Blankenberg, 1869.

———. *Het Calvinisme, oorsprong en waarborg onzer constitutioneele vrijheden* [Calvinism, the Source and Stronghold of Our Constitutional Liberties]. Amsterdam: B. van der Land, 1874.

———. *Ons Program*. 1st ed. Amsterdam: J. H. Kruyt, 1879.

———. *Souvereiniteit in Eigen Kring*. Amsterdam: J. H. Kruyt, 1880. Translated as "Sphere Sovereignty," in Bratt, ed., *Abraham Kuyper: A Centennial Reader*, 461–90.

———. *Tweeerlei Vaderland*. Amsterdam: J. A. Wormser, 1887.

———. *Handenarbied*. Amsterdam: J. A. Wormser, 1889. Translated as "Manual Labor," in Bratt, ed., *Kuyper Centennial Reader*, 231–54.

———. *Het Sociale Vraagstuk en de Christelijke Religie*. Amsterdam: J. A. Wormser, 1891. Translated as *The Problem of Poverty*, ed. James Skillen. Grand Rapids: Baker, 1991.

———. *Ons Instinctieve Leven*. Amsterdam: W. Kirchner, 1908. Translated as "Our Instinctive Life," in Bratt, ed., *Kuyper Centennial Reader*, 255–77.

———

Althusius, Johannes. *Politics*. Edited by Frederick S. Carney. Boston: Beacon Press, 1964.

Black, Antony. "Editor's Introduction." In Otto von Gierke, *Community in Historical Perspective: a translation of selections from <u>Das Deutsche Genossen-</u>*

schaftsrecht [1881]. Translated by Mary Fischer, edited by Antony Black. Cambridge: Cambridge University Press, 1990.

Bratt, James D. "Abraham Kuyper, American History, and the Tensions of Neo-Calvinism." In George Harinck and Hans Krabbendam, eds., *Sharing the Reformed Tradition: The Dutch-North American Exchange, 1846-1996* (Amsterdam: VU Uitgeverij, 1996).

———. *Abraham Kuyper: Modern Calvinist, Christian Democrat*. Grand Rapids: Eerdmans, 2013.

———, ed. *Abraham Kuyper: A Centennial Reader*. Grand Rapids: Eerdmans, 1998.

Burrow, J. W. *The Crisis of Reason: European Thought, 1848-1914*. New Haven: Yale University Press, 2000.

Dengerink, J. D. *Critisch-historisch onderzoek naar de sociologische ontwikkeling van het beginsel der "souvereiniteit in eigen kring" in de 19e en 20e eeuw*. Kampen: Kok, 1948.

Dooyeweerd, Herman. *De Wijsbegeerte der Wetsidee*, 3 vols. Amsterdam: H. J. Paris, 1935. Translated by David H. Freeman and William S. Young as *A New Critique of Theoretical Thought*, 4 vols. Philadelphia: Presbyterian and Reformed Publishers, 1953–58.

Franklin, Julian H., ed. *Constitutionalism and Resistance in the Sixteenth Century: Three Treatises*. New York: Pegasus, 1969.

Goudzwaard, Bob. "Christian Social Thought in the Dutch Neo-Calvinist Tradition." In Walter Block and Irving Hexham, eds., *Religion, Economics, and Social Thought*. Vancouver: Fraser Institute, 1986.

Lears, T. J. Jackson. *No Place of Grace: Antimodernism and the Transformation of American Culture, 1880-1920*. New York: Pantheon, 1981.

Le Bon, Gustav. *La psychologie de foule*. Paris: F. Alcan, 1895.

Kuiper, Dirk Th. *De Voormannen: een social-wetenschappelijke studie*. Meppel: Boom, 1972.

Skillen, James W. "The Political Theory of Johannes Althusius." *Philosophia Reformata* 39 (1974): 170–90.

Skillen, James W., and Rockne M. McCarthy, eds. *Political Order and the Plural Structure of Society*. Atlanta: Scholars Press, 1991.

Skinner, Quentin. *The Foundations of Modern Political Thought, vol. 2: The Age of Reformation*. New York: Cambridge University Press, 1978.

Vree, Jasper. "De dominie van wijk 27, wijk 8, en nog veel meer: Amsterdam 1870-1874." In *Kuyper in de kiem: De precalvinistische period van Abraham Kuyper 1848-1874*, 325–61. Hilversum: Verloren, 2006.

Witte, John. *The Reformation of Rights: Law, Religion, and Human Rights in Early Modern Calvinism*. Cambridge: Cambridge University Press, 2007.

And Zeus Shall Have No Dominion, or, How, When, Where, and Why to "Plunder the Egyptians": The Case of Jerome

Dr. E.J. Hutchinson
Assistant Professor of Classics, Hillsdale College

I. Introduction

In *On the Prescription of Heretics* 7, Tertullian famously asked, "What, therefore, does Athens have to do with Jerusalem? What does the Academy have to do with the Church?" [1] Approximately two centuries later, Jerome, in his infamous *Ep.* 22, asks,[2] asks as part of a string of rhetorical questions about Scripture and classical writings, "What does Horace have to do with the Psalter, Vergil with the Gospels, Cicero with the Apostle?" It would be easy to assume from his remark a sharp disjunction for at least some Christian writers between biblical literature and the 'classics'. But this is the same Jerome who, somewhat later, praised the Christian poet Juvencus with the following words:

> *Iuvencus presbyter sub Constantino historiam Domini salvatoris versibus explicavit,* nec pertimuit evangelii maiestatem sub metri leges mittere. (*Ep.* 70.5)[3]

> Juvencus, a presbyter at the time of Constantine, unfolded the history of the Lord our Savior in verses, *nor was he afraid to cast the majesty of the gospel under the laws of meter.*

---

[1] All translations are my own.

[2] Dated by G. Grützmacher, *Hieronymus* (Leipzig: Dieterich, 1901-8), vol. 1, 99, to 384. N. Adkin, in *Jerome on Virginity* (Cambridge: Francis Cairns, 2003), 1, citing Cavallera and Vogüé, places it specifically in the spring of 384. J. Labourt, *S. Jérôme: Lettres, I* (Paris: Les Belles Lettres, 1949), 112, also places the probable date in spring 384.

[3] Grützmacher, *Hieronymous*, vol. 1, 100, dates *Ep.* 70 to 399-403, J. Labourt, *S. Jérôme: Lettres,* (Paris: Les Belles Lettres, 1949-63), III, to 397or 398. The Latin text of Jerome's letters is cited from the edition of I. Hilberg, *CSEL* 54-56 (Vienna: F. Tempsky, 1910-18).

The 'laws of meter' to which Juvencus subjected the Gospel story were, of course, those of the dactylic hexameter—the meter of classical epic whose most famous Roman exponent was Vergil, a poet who heavily influenced Juvencus,[4] as Jerome would have known. It would not be surprising, to be sure, if Jerome's views developed over time, and his statement on Juvencus comes approximately 15 years after *Ep.* 22. As we shall see, however, there are indications even in letters from the mid-380s that his view and use of classical literature were much more complex already in this period than a quick reading of the statement above suggests. In some texts from the mid- to late-390s, his careful balancing act will become more evident.

But why use Jerome as the beginning point for our investigation and not, say, Augustine?[5] Jerome might be remembered chiefly as an exegete and polemicist and not as a cultural or literary theorist of some sort;[6] but one should remember that various areas of interest are often combined in an individual Hieronymian text. Thus, for instance, one of the better places to examine Jerome's ideas about the *classical* past is in *Ep.* 53, where he also shows his *scriptural* skills in a whirlwind tour through both testaments of the Bible. In the same way, some of his "mentoring" texts, such as *Ep.* 22, also contain passages that shed light on literary concerns—in this letter, Jerome casts himself not only as a mentor, but also as a purveyor of literary texts to women.

A more important reason for Jerome as exemplar is Jerome's status as an immensely erudite figure straddling the two worlds (or, perhaps better, the two pasts and presents) that were combining in Late Antiquity in spite of surface conflicts: the world of the Church with its appropriation of the Bible—Old *and* New Testaments—and the "secular" world with its constant re-appropriation of the Greco-Roman past. The end-point of this process is described elegantly by R.A. Markus: "The culture which men of

---

[4] See R.P.H. Green, *Latin Epics of the New Testament* (New York: Oxford University Press, 2006), 50-71. Note especially the following remark: "[I]n the poem as a whole the influence of Vergil is overarching, and its extent and intricacy show the influence of a poet who was thoroughly studied as a school author, as well as being the unchallenged master of Latin epic" (54).

[5] It is of course from Augustine that I borrow the metaphor of "plundering the Egyptians" in my title. See *De doctrina christiana* 2.40.60-42.63.

[6] If one will forgive the anachronism of the application of this terminology to Late Antiquity.

Symmachus' circle and generation regarded as the distinctive property of a pagan élite in an increasingly christianised world became the treasured possession of a Christian élite in an increasingly barbarian world."[7] In the midst of this development we find Jerome, "no doubt the most learned of all the Latin Fathers,"[8] in terms both of Scripture and of the classics. Regarding the latter, the school-authors affected not only the literary style of men such as Jerome, but also their "habit of thought";[9] and no one captivated Jerome's attention more than the Roman poet.[10] As a presbyter/monk and, perhaps, a grammarian,[11] Jerome provides a valuable witness to the crucible of cultures at the end of the fourth century and how Vergil and other classical authors might (and might not) be appropriated to speak to Christian concerns.

His value will be especially evident in the writings to be examined below.[12] After setting the stage with a selection of early examples, we shall move to two letters he wrote to the Christian poet Paulinus of Nola, who also was working for a synthesis of the various influences on his literary art.[13] While Paulinus of Nola, in addition to being a poet, cultivated friendships with several of the most important Christian thinkers of his day,[14] we

---

[7] R.A. Markus, "Paganism, Christianity and the Latin Classics in the Fourth Century," in *Latin Literature of the Fourth Century*, ed. J.W. Binns (London: Routledge & Kegan Paul, 1974), 15.

[8] H. Hagendahl, *Latin Fathers and the Classics* (Göteborg: Elanders boktr. Aktiebolag, 1958), 318.

[9] Hagendahl, *Latin Fathers*, 311.

[10] Hagendahl, *Latin Fathers*, 276.

[11] Hagendahl notes that, according to Rufinus, Jerome performed the duties of a *grammaticus* a few years before 400 in his convent in Bethlehem, and that Jerome never denied this charge (*Latin Fathers*, 325–26).

[12] I shall discuss parts of four letters: *Ep.* 21, to Damasus; *Ep.* 22, to Eustochium; *Ep.* 53, to Paulinus of Nola; *Ep.* 58, to Paulinus of Nola. In his "new taxonomy" of Jerome's letters, A. Cain classifies the first as "exegetical" and the other three as "exhorting." See *The Letters of Jerome: Asceticism, Biblical Exegesis, and the Construction of Christian Authority in Late Antiquity* (New York: Oxford University Press, 2009), 214–15, 218.

[13] Cain notes in his introduction that he does not discuss Jerome's correspondence with Paulinus of Nola (*Letters of Jerome*, 7).

shall focus on his conversation with Jerome, of which Jerome's half alone survives. What sort of advice did Jerome give to him? What sort of model does Jerome himself provide by his own technique in his letters to this budding poet?

It must be stressed that the examples that I have chosen in Jerome are not exhaustive of the surviving evidence of Christian literary theorizing from the late fourth and early fifth centuries (or even of the evidence of Jerome himself), nor are they meant to be. One could examine with profit, for example, the letter and poem Paulinus of Nola himself wrote to his kinsman Jovius on similar subjects,[15] Augustine's own views in relation to Vergil,[16] or the joint effort of Augustine and Paulinus to sway Licentius from a life devoted to secular honors to one devoted to honoring Christ.[17] Rather, I hope that my examples are representative of the problems, tensions, and possibilities caused by the meeting of the classical and Christian worlds, even while detailing the particular responses of one individual. Furthermore, for the purpose of engaging the problem on a theoretical level from a specifically literary perspective, one can find few better examples than Jerome.[18]

---

[14] For a discussion of *amicitia* in some of his epistolary relations, see C. Conybeare, *Paulinus Noster* (New York: Oxford University Press, 2000), 60–90. For Paulinus and his friends vis-à-vis Latin Christian culture, see D. Trout, *Paulinus of Nola* (Berkeley and Los Angeles: University of California Press, 1999), 198–251.

[15] *Ep.* 16 and *Carm.* 22.

[16] See, for example, S. MacCormack, *The Shadows of Poetry* (Berkeley and Los Angeles: University of California Press, 1998).

[17] For Paulinus, see *Epp.* 7 (to Romanianus) and [8] (to Licentius). The latter contains a poem to Licentius in elegiacs, the opening couplet of which combines Vergil and the Bible and thus sets out the program for the Christian poet:

> *quare age rumpe moras et vincla tenacia saecli*
>
> *nec metuas placidi mite iugum domini.*

For Augustine, see *Epp.* 26(1) (to Licentius), 26(2) (Licentius to Augustine), 26(3) (to Licentius), and 27 (to Paulinus). Augustine's letters are cited from the edition of K.D. Daur, *CCSL* 31-31B (Turnhout: Brepols, 2004-2009).

[18] It is true, however, that the Christian poets of Late Antiquity, including Juvencus, Prudentius, and Sedulius in addition to Paulinus of Nola could also be (and have been) examined with profit.

II. *Si certe fuerimus eius amore decepti*: The 380s
A. Ep. 21.13

We shall come to Jerome's famous dream in *Ep.* 22 in due course. But shortly before that letter, Jerome wrote a letter (*Ep.* 21) to Damasus, Bishop of Rome, in which he answers Damasus' queries regarding the Parable of the Prodigal Son (Luke 15:11-32);[19] and this letter too, in its thirteenth chapter, is relevant to Jerome's view of classical literature, and so will be worthwhile to examine first. As Jerome interprets the swine's husks (*siliquae porcorum*) of the parable, he claims that they are the food of demons (*daemonum cibus*): drunkenness (*ebrietas*), luxury (*luxuria*), fornication (*fornicatio*), and all wrongdoing (*universa vitia*). That is, Jerome claims that they represent a series of moral sins.

Shortly thereafter, however, he notes that an alternative interpretation is possible: the *siliquae porcorum* represent secular literature.[20]

> *possumus autem et aliter siliquas interpretari. daemonum cibus est carmina poetarum, saecularis sapientia, rhetoricorum pompa verborum.* (*Ep.* 21.13.4)
>
> We are able, however, also to interpret the husks in another way. The food of demons is the songs of the poets, worldly wisdom, the pomp of rhetoricians' words.

He goes on to emphasize the problematic nature of the deceptive charm of such literature:

> *haec sua omnes suavitate delectant et, dum aures versibus dulci modulatione currentibus capiunt, animam quoque penetrant et pectoris interna devinciunt. verum ubi cum summo studio fuerint ac labore perlecta, nihil aliud nisi inanem sonum et sermonum strepitum suis lec-*

---

[19] Dated by Grützmacher, *Hieronymous*, vol. 1, 99, to 382–84, by Labourt, *Lettres, I*, 165, to 383.

[20] P. Rousseau notes that Augustine, in *Conf.* 3.6.11, uses the swine's husks in a similar fashion, but for Augustine they stand for the teaching of the Manichees. These are more dangerous than the writings of the poets, for Augustine did not believe that what the poets were saying was true, whereas he *did* believe that the Manichees taught the truth at the time of the episode recalled ("Christian Culture and the Swine's Husks: Jerome, Augustine, and Paulinus', in *The Limits of Ancient Christianity*, ed. W. E. Klingshirn and M. Vessey [Ann Arbor: University of Michigan Press, 1999], 173.)

toribus tribuunt: nulla ibi saturitas veritatis, nulla iustitiae refectio repperitur. (*Ep.* 21.13.4)

> These things of themselves delight everyone with their sweetness and, while they seize the ears with verses running in sweet measure, they also penetrate the soul and bind fast the heart inside. But when they have been read with utmost zeal and toil, they bestow nothing on their readers except empty sound and the din of speech; no abundance of the truth is found there, no refreshment of righteousness.

The poets, philosophers, and rhetors do not only charm the ear—they penetrate the soul, and that is exactly the problem, for they bestow only "empty sound and the din of speech."[21]

Perhaps it is a coincidence, but the phrase *inanem sonum et sermonum strepitum* seems to echo a line of the *Aeneid*: *cons**o**nat omne nemus **strepitu** collesque resultant* (8.305).[22] The line forms the conclusion to a description of the singing of myths of Hercules (*talia carminibus celebrant*, 8.303) that culminates in the story of Hercules and Cacus. It is unclear whether Jerome refers to this line or not, but if he does, it is apt: the singers make the hills to resound with the noise of Herculean myths, which from Jerome's perspective would be a dangerous sound—dangerous because devoid of truth. That is, Jerome appears to be hostile to the *form* of classical literature not as such but because it is used to smuggle in content that is really no content at all.[23] It should be noted that Jerome *says* nothing here of the possibility of maintaining the formal eloquence of classical literature to convey Christian truth. But Jerome *does* it implicitly by employing the same sort of *pompa verborum* for which he blasts the rhetors. To take only one example, notice his hissing

---

[21] There is perhaps an echo here of Paul's sentiment in 1 Cor. 13:1: *si linguis hominum loquar et angelorum, caritatem autem non habeam, factus sum velut aes sonans aut cymbalum tinniens* (Vulg.).

[22] This is the only instance I am aware of in which a word from the *sonus/sonare* group and *strepitus* occur in close proximity in Vergil.

[23] I maintain this against A. Mohr, who argues, in comments on the passage *daemonum cibus est carmina poetarum...et pectoris interna devinciunt*, that "Jerome's problem here is clearly with the attractiveness of classical works" ("Jerome, Virgil, and the Captive Maiden," in *Texts and Culture in Late Antiquity*, ed. J.H.D. Scourfield [Swansea: The Classical Press of Wales, 2007], 307).

alliteration on the letter "s" as he criticizes the empty sound of pagan literature, especially as it alternates with nasal "n" and "m" sounds: *nihil aliud nisi inanem sonum strepitum suis lectoribus tribuunt*. These sounds together give the impression of a noisy, senseless buzzing.

Jerome continues with his (ostensible) position of ridding pagan writings of their charming exterior by referring to the instructions for cleansing a captive woman for Israelite marriage in Deuteronomy 21:10-13.[24] The woman is to have her head shaved and her nails cut (and, in the biblical passage, though not in Jerome, to be rid of the clothes in which she was captured). If understood literally, the passage is ridiculous—so says Jerome.[25] Therefore, the woman should be understood as a *figura*:

> itaque[26] *et nos hoc facere solemus, quando philosophos legimus, quando in manus nostras libri veniunt* sapientiae saecularis: *si quid in eis utile* repperimus, *ad nostrum dogma convertimus, si quid vero superfluum, de idolis, de amore, de cura saecularium rerum, haec radimus, his calvitium indicimus, haec in unguium morem ferro acutissimo desecamus.* (Ep. 21.13.6)

> In such a way we too are accustomed to act, when we read the philosophers, when books of *worldly wisdom* come into our hands: if we discover anything useful in them, we convert it to our own dogma, but if we *find* anything superfluous, concerning idols, concerning sexual love, concerning anxiety over worldly affairs, these things we shave off, we make them bald, we cut them back like fingernails with the sharpest blade.

Immediately we notice two echoes from 21.13.4: *sapientiae saecularis/saecularis sapientia* and *repperimus/repperitur*. The earlier reference to "worldly wisdom"

---

[24] This passage is also applied to secular literature in *Ep*. 70.2. For more on this letter and a discussion of the Jerome's different attitude toward the "captive maiden" there, see Mohr, "Captive Maiden," 305-7, 310-12. Mohr argues for a development of Jerome's views culminating in his "most favourable statement of the value of classical literature" in the last chapter of *Ep*. 70 (312). She sees the other extreme in Jerome's dream-narrative in *Ep*. 22 (p. 299). It is my contention that already in the earlier letters, including *Ep*. 22, there are indications of a compromise position vis-à-vis classical literature.

[25] *haec si secundum litteram intellegimus, nonne ridicula sunt?* (*Ep*. 22.13.5).

[26] Reading *itaque* with the codd. and Labourt rather than Hilberg's emendation *atqui*.

claimed that secular literature was the "food of demons," and Jerome claimed that "no refreshment of righteousness" could be found (*repperitur*) there. He is already reversing himself; it now appears that something good for Christians *can* be found there. Moreover, while he warned in the previous passage about formal qualities that were deceptive and unnecessary, and while the Deuteronomy allegory would at first sight appear to be a logical extension of an argument about externals, he instead uses the allegory to exhort his reader(s) to cut away false content concerning idols, love, and care for "the affairs of the age" in order to find the core that is *utile*. Secular learning is in a certain sense permissible, but it is clear that, for Jerome, it is to be conformed—or, rather, "converted"—to the dogma of the Church (*ad nostrum dogma convertimus*), an authority higher than the self. Jerome, then, suggests that radical conversion is necessary not only for persons, but also for learning.

After the image of the captive woman, the next image he employs to urge against secular literature is that of Paul in 1 Cor. 8:9–11, where he discusses the case of a believer eating in an idol's temple. The point of Paul's illustration is that the believer must be careful not to wound the conscience of a weaker brother. Jerome preserves the teaching of Paul, but again allegorizes it in a fashion similar to his treatment of the captive woman and adds an emphasis that helps us to understand his perspective:

> *nonne tibi videtur sub aliis verbis dicere, ne legas philosophos, oratores, poetas, ne in eorum lectione* requiescas? (*Ep*. 21.13.8)

> Doesn't [Paul] seem to you to say under other words that you ought not to read philosophers, orators, poets, lest you *rest* in the reading of them?

One ought not to "abide" or "rest" (*requiescas*) in the reading of pagan literature: this is his gloss for "recline" (*recumbentem*) in the biblical passage itself. Already we see an indication that the problem, in addition to concern for one's brother, is not the reading of the classics *per se*, but the reading of them in exclusion to or to the detriment of studying the Bible—of placing one's treasure, and thus one's heart, in the wrong place.[27]

---

[27] Mohr, "Captive Maiden," does not comment on the use of *requiescas*. She does, however, make the interesting point that "Jerome's concern here needs to be understood in the light of the fact that in the ancient world reading was often done aloud. This is certainly what Jerome has in mind, as he makes clear by his use of the

The point is made clear in Jerome's criticisms of certain priests that follow shortly. The priests he has in mind read the classics (and even memorize Vergil), but the real emphasis comes before that remark in an ablative absolute:

> *at nunc etiam sacerdotes dei* omissis evangeliis et prophetis videmus comoedias legere, amatoria bucolicorum versuum verba cantare, tenere Vergilium et id, quod in pueris necessitatis est, crimen in se facere voluntatis. (*Ep.* 21.13.9)

> But now we see that priests of God, *leaving aside the Gospels and prophets*, read comedies, sing the amorous words of pastoral poetry, memorize Vergil, and commit the crime among themselves willingly which is committed by necessity among children.

These priests of God do not read the Bible at all— and, as we shall see in a moment, there is perhaps some autobiography in this remark.[28] This neglect is a matter of choice and is thus in accordance with their wishes: they wish to find their "rest" in pagan literature. "To rest" in that from which one is supposed to have been liberated is not an option for the Christian. It is a return to Egypt.

The fact that such an extreme is avoidable makes it possible to establish a two-tier approach to classical literature, one that draws on the images of both the captive woman and the Christian reclining in the temple of an idol. The first "tier" is total avoidance: one should not wish *either* to have a

---

words *vox*, *audire*, and *personare* [in the final sentence of 21.13]' (309). Such a concern may also be seen in another comment in 21.13.8: *absit, de ore Christiano sonnet 'Iuppiter omnipotens' et 'mehercule' et 'mecastor'*....

[28] Mohr, "Captive Maiden," 309-10, while she remarks on the possibility of accommodation in *Ep.* 21, does not seem to notice, or at least does not comment on, the emphasis placed by Jerome on the *omission* of the study of the Scriptures. She concludes: 'What we see…in *Letter* 21, written the year before the account of the dream, is not a fearful, guilt-stricken, absolute rejection of classical literature, but an acknowledgement of the Christian tradition of accommodation and a very qualified acceptance of it, the result of study, careful thinking, and the finding of a relationship between classical literature and the Bible through allegory'. The 'relationship' must be 'conducted in such a way that others are not given the wrong idea' (p. 310). Care for one's brother is an important motivation for Jerome, but his implicit point about the *primacy* of Scripture is crucial as well. It is an emphasis we will see again in *Ep.* 22.

captive wife *or* to recline in an *idolium*. If, however, one does choose to read the classics, the allegory of the captive woman provides a procedure for doing it appropriately. Jerome writes:

> *cavendum igitur, ne captivam habere velimus uxorem, ne in idolio recumbamus; aut, si certe fuerimus eius amore decepti, mundemus eam et omni sordium horrore purgemus, ne scandalum patiatur frater, pro quo Christus est mortuus, cum ex voce Christiani carmina in idolorum laudes conposita audierit personare.* (*Ep.* 21.13.9)

> Therefore one should beware not to wish to have a captive wife, nor to recline in the temple of an idol; or, if *certainly* we shall have been beguiled by love for her, let us cleanse her and purge her of all horror-inducing filth, lest a brother for whom Christ died suffer a stumbling-block, when he hears songs composed for the praise of idols sounding forth from a Christian's voice.

The key word here, it seems to me, is the adverb *certe*, "certainly"—an odd word in a conditional clause—for with it Jerome implies that such "deception" or "beguilement" will be the norm for the educated Christian, and, indeed, he includes himself in that number with the first-person plural verb ("if *we* shall have been beguiled").[29] The Christian should, therefore, act with caution. Moreover, it is clear that the *writing* of Christian-classical literature cannot be in view here, for his concern is expressed in the final clause: Christians reciting poems that were written in praise of idols. In conclusion, in *Ep.* 21.13 Jerome argues against an *exclusive* reading of pagan texts; gives advice on how they should be read by Christians, if at all; and acknowledges that engagement with these texts will, in fact, be the norm. His agenda is of a defensive sort against corrupt priests who are not students of the Word. Jerome has left Christian-classical literature untouched, and thus he has left open a way of using even the charming elements of classical literature for the glory of God.

---

[29] Though Mohr cites this passage ("Captive Maiden," 309–10), she does not comment on the significance of *certe*.

B. Ep. *22.30*

It is my contention that we can find a similar position in the famous "dream-scene" of *Ep.* 22.30, written in 384.[30] The dream itself may have occurred between 375 and 377 while Jerome was in the desert of Chalcis,[31] but it is hard to say.[32] The date and location of the dream are, however, immaterial to my purpose here, which is to sketch Jerome's outlook in its retelling several years later in the midst of his exhortation to viriginity.

Jerome sets the stage for his narration of the dream in *Ep.* 22.29 while warning Eustochium, whom he is encouraging to press on in her vow of chastity, about the hazards of classical literature. (The broader context is an exhortation to Eustochium not to associate with dangerous women.) Jerome is discussing a *lifestyle* and admonishes her not to change her behavior simply to fit in. His warnings culminate in his series of rhetorical questions about the supposed incompatibility of Horace and the Psalter, Vergil and the Gospels, and Cicero and Paul,[33] and he immediately supports his point with a reference to 1 Cor. 10:8 (*nonne scandalizatur frater, si te viderit in idolio recumbentem?*), the same passage that he used in *Ep.* 21.13.7–9. In this instance, however, he concedes that "to the pure all things are pure" and that "nothing which is received with thanksgiving ought to be rejected" (Titus 1:15; 1 Tim. 4:4). Thus, it would be easy to argue that, for the Jerome of *this* letter, there is a place in the Christian life for classical literature. But he balances the point about Christian freedom with another warning: *tamen simul bibere non debemus calicem Christi et calicem daemoniorum* (1 Cor. 10:21). I take this to be another acknowledgement that one cannot put faith in or rely on—one cannot abide in—both Christ and idols, just as in *Ep.* 21.

---

[30] Adkin, *Jerome on Virginity*, 1.

[31] For this location and date, see the arguments of J.J. Thierry, "The Date of the Dream of Jerome," *VChr* 17 (1963): 28–40. S. Rebenich, *Jerome* (New York: Routledge, 2002), 20, sets *Ep.* 22 in the context of Jerome's promoting himself as an ascetic champion because "[a]cceptance of his theological and ascetic competence was vital to his ambitious literary programme," so that he "might make himself the spiritual leader of wealthy Christian intellectuals in the western part of the Empire."

[32] Rebenich, who notes that the case has also been made for Antioch on the Orontes at the beginning of the 370s, argues interestingly for an earlier date at Trier (*Jerome*, 9).

[33] *quid facit cum psalterio cum Horatius? cum evangeliis Maro? cum apostolo Cicero?* (*Ep.* 22.29.7).

Paul's remark in 1 Cor. 10:20–21 comes in the context of his discussion of the Lord's Supper:[34] there we learn that one cannot be a communicant of God and of Satan. Thus, Jerome's comment regarding the mingling of the Psalter with Horace, for example, is not a view of mingling *simpliciter*, but rather is a warning against attempting to give the allegiance of faith (brought out by the reference to the Lord's Supper) to both God and Satan. This is Jerome's set-up for his dream—an antagonism caused by the impossibility of serving two masters.[35] Hence, we may not assume that the dream touches on Christians who have ordered their loves correctly using classical literature for Christian ends.

The dream itself leads to the same conclusions for which I argued in *Ep.* 21. Jerome demonstrates that his preference at the time of the dream was for secular literature *to the exclusion of* the Bible, like those priests he had earlier criticized. For if he ever attempted to read Scripture after having indulged himself guiltily on the classics, he was horrified:

> *si quando in memet reversus prophetam legere coepissem, sermo horrebat incultus et, quia lumen caecis oculis non videbam, non oculorum putabam culpam esse, sed solis.* (*Ep.* 22.30.2)

> If ever, having returned to myself, I had begun to read a prophet, his uncultured manner of speaking was horrifying and, since I did not see the light with my blind eyes, I did not think the fault was my eyes', but the sun's.

On the other hand, Jerome's reading of the classics is described almost as though it is an uncontrollable addiction. Regardless of the ascetic rigors that he applied to himself, he knew that, in the end, he would only return to Cicero and Plautus (from the passage immediately preceding the previous):

> *itaque miser ego lecturus Tullium ieiunabam. post noctium crebras vigilias, post lacrimas, quas mihi praeteritorum recordatio peccatorum ex imis visceribus eruebat, Plautus sumebatur in manibus.* (*Ep.* 22.30.2)

> And thus, wretched, I was fasting, knowing that I would later read Cicero. After numerous wakeful nights, after the tears that

---

[34] *non potestis calicem Domini bibere et calicem daemoniorum. non potestis mensae Domini participes esse et mensae daemoniorum* (1 Cor. 10:20-1 [Vulg.]).

[35] One could compare here Matt. 6:24 and Luke 16:13.

the recollection of past sins was drawing out from my interior depths, I was taking up Plautus [to read].

In the midst of his fasting and praying, what he really desired was to read philosophy (and perhaps rhetoric, too) and comedy,[36] and, given what he says about the Bible in 22.30, he had this desire for primarily stylistic reasons. It is in such a context, in the midst of sickness and sin and his looming death, that Jerome is seized in the spirit to the judge's tribunal in the Underworld.[37] Neither the judge (simply called *iudex* and *dominus*) nor the bystanders are identified.[38]

In his finding, the judge makes the same exclusionary point for which I have been arguing: *Ciceronianus es, non Christianus* ("You are a Ciceronian, not a Christian"; 22.30.4). The identification is determined by where Jerome's heart is (*ubi thesaurus tuus, ibi et cor tuum*, 22.30.4, quoting Matt. 6:21, Luke 12:34), and the implication is that his heart still belongs to the classics. Jerome is whipped until the bystanders intercede on his behalf, pleading for mercy because of his youth on the condition that he never read pagan works again (22.30.5).[39] Notice that this is the bystanders' idea, not Jerome's. But after they have spoken, Jerome, under duress, wishes to one-up

---

[36] Cf. his criticism of corrupt priests in *Ep.* 21.13.9: *at nunc etiam sacerdotes Dei omissis evangeliis et prophetis videmus comoedias legere....* Note, however, that Adkin thinks that the alternative MS reading *Plato* should be preferred to *Plautus* (*Jerome on Virginity*, ad 30.2). On the other hand, *Plautus* fits better with Jerome's criticism of derelict priests in 21.13 (cited above): *at nunc etiam sacerdotes Dei omissis evangeliis et prophetis videmus comoedias legere, amatoria bucolicorum versuum verba cantare, tenere Vergilium, et id quod in pueris necessitatis est crimen in se facere voluntatis.*

[37] Thierry, "Date," 32–33, argues that the scene of the dream is in the Underworld (specifically, the Vergilian Underworld), based on, for example, Jerome's statement after the dream is over: *revertor ad superos* (22.30.5), though it is possible that it is meant more generally as "I returned to the realm of the living." Still, the use of *superos* does call to mind its opposite, *inferos*, among whom Jerome would be located during his dream; he would therefore be in the Underworld. Adkin, *Jerome on Virginity*, does not seem to take a position on the issue ad 22.30.3, but in his comment on *revertor ad superos* he states that "[i]t would...appear that in this passage of the *Libellus* J. is thinking of a divine judgment in the underworld."

[38] Adkin, *Jerome on Virginity*, ad 30.3, notes that Rufinus identified Christ as the judge and angels as the bystanders. The identification of God as judge is supported by Jerome's use of Psalm 57:1 (56:2) to address him (*miserere mei, domine, miserere mei*).

[39] Adkin, *Jerome on Virginity*, ad 22.30.5, also notes that the attendants are responsible for Jerome's pardon.

them (*qui tanto constrictus articulo vellem etiam maiora promittere*, 22.30.5) and states that not only reading such works in the future, but even *possessing* them, constitutes a denial of his *dominus*.

Nevertheless, in spite of the torture-induced promise, the main point of the story has to do not with giving up the classics altogether, but with keeping one's studies in a right relationship of priority. In the conclusion of the tale, when the flashback has concluded, Jerome does not say that he never picked up Cicero, or any other ancient author, again. Rather, he was no longer repulsed by the Bible and found new zeal for studying it (...*tanto dehinc studio divina legisse, quanto mortalia ante legeram*, 22.30.6). Jerome now reads the Bible more earnestly than he had ever read anything before. This is the point of the story: that the study of Scripture must outrank any other intellectual pursuit for the Christian.[40] It is, moreover, consistent with what we will find in his advice to Paulinus. That the classics were still an abiding influence on Jerome, even in the composition of the dream itself, has been demonstrated by Thierry.[41] Just because one's treasure is in heaven does not mean that he cannot make investments in the world to increase it.[42]

---

[40] Adkin noticed this as well (*Jerome on Virginity*, ad 22.30): "...[The real significance of the dream] does not lie, as is commonly supposed, in J.'s 'renunciation' of the classics, but rather in the assiduous study of the Bible which he undertook from that moment onwards. The final words of his account, which unlike the 'vow' lie outside the dream itself and are therefore clearly to be taken seriously as a description of reality, proclaim resonantly that this was its consequence: *tanto dehinc studio divina legisse* (30,6). There is no mention whatever of 'abandoning' the classics. Hence J. will have felt no compunction in reading them subsequently.... J.'s problem was not with the classics, but with the Bible.' See also N. Adkin, "Jerome's Use of Scripture Before and After his Dream," *ICS* 20 (1995): 183–90. Because I am convinced that the interpretation offered above is the correct way in which to read this passage, I find claims, such as that of Rousseau ("Christian Culture," 182), that Jerome "nursed...a need to escape from his literary past" to miss the mark. Rather, he sought to reorganize his priorities.

[41] Thierry, "Date," 33–34.

[42] In the exemplary context of the letter, then, Eustochium too needs to remember to keep her priority of Christian virginity in its proper place. Recall the argument above: one must be wary to engage in behavior that will cause others to stumble or if one is only doing it to fit in. Additionally, one must not put his *faith* in anything or anyone but Christ. When one does (as Jerome did), problems arise—hence the way in which he introduces the dream: *referam tibi meae infelicitatis historiam* (22.29.7). He gives it as an example of an attempt to drink both from the cup of Christ and from the cup of demons. If "drinking" here, in its Eucharistic context, has the same strong force as "reclining," as I have claimed, the point, again, regards the

And so, Jerome in these two letters has made no damning indictment against Christians developing a Scripture-centered classical poetics, or against Christians reading and engaging the classics *per se*. In both *Ep.* 21 and *Ep.* 22, we find a principle of priority for the Scriptures and a caution against disregarding them to focus attention and enjoyment primarily on the classics instead. There is still space, then, in which to work out such a Christian-classical poetics, and we shall see some moves in that direction in two of Jerome's letters to Paulinus of Nola.

III. *Nasceretur nobis aliquid, quod docta Graecia non haberet*: Jerome and Paulinus of Nola

Now that objections based on Jerome's supposed prejudice against the classics have been cleared away, Jerome's letters to Paulinus of Nola[43] can provide interesting and useful test-cases to work out the implications of the classics in a Christian framework. Keeping in mind the stipulations about priorities outlined above, let us see how Jerome, in the decade or so following *Epp.* 21 and 22, puts his two-fold knowledge to use in his advice to an erudite Christian writer and poet.

A. Ep. 53

In *Ep.* 53, written sometime in the mid-390s,[44] Jerome makes his first contact with Paulinus, in response to Paulinus' (lost) letter to him. Right away, Jerome delineates their relationship as a "friendship," both new and old (*in principio amicitiarum*; *probatae iam et veteris amicitiae*, 53.1.1). But the friendship is nuanced in an important way: it is based on a shared fear of

---

ordering of one's life and where one places his faith or treasure. This claim, to repeat, economically explains Jerome's own gloss on the dream: *tanto dehinc studio divina legisse, quanto mortalia ante legeram* (22.30.6).

[43] As noted above, this is the only half of their correspondence that survives.

[44] The date of the letter is debated, and whether *Ep.* 53 or *Ep.* 58 was first chronologically has been disputed. I accept the arguments of P. Nautin, "Études de chronologie hiéronymienne (393–97) III," *RÉAug* 19 (1973): 213–21, for the priority of *Ep.* 53. Nautin dates *Ep.* 53 to the summer of 394 (222–24). The letter became a very important part of Jerome's *oeuvre*: M. Vessey, "*Quid facit cum Horatio Hieronymus?* Christian Latin Poetry and Scriptural Poetics," in *Poetry and Exegesis in Premodern Latin Christianity*, ed. W. Otten and K. Pollmann (Leiden: Brill, 2007), notes that "in medieval and later editions of the 'Vulgate'" *Ep.* 53 "serves as a general prologue to the books of the Bible" (29).

the Lord (*timor domini*, 53.1.1) and the study of the Scriptures (*divinarum scripturarum studia*, 53.1.1). The friendship has a dimension of piety and of intellectual pursuit, the latter significantly based on reading (*legimus*, 53.1.2).

But reading of what? One might assume that it is based on the reading of the Scriptures. There is a sense in which this is—or will be, Jerome hopes—true (as he demonstrates in 53.3-10), but Jerome first turns, not to the Bible or to Christian literature, but to a series of classical *exempla* to illustrate the studious aspect of their friendship (and also Jerome's desire to be Paulinus' teacher, a desire that is evident throughout the letter) by referring to a number of thinkers and writers who traveled far and wide to learn from the knowledge of others whom they knew about from their writings (*quos ex libris noverant*, 53.1.2). Included in his list are Pythagoras, Plato, and Apollonius of Tyana. Both Jerome and Paulinus are themselves familiar with these figures through their shared (classical) literary background: the first-person plural verb *legimus* appears twice in the opening section.[45]

It is not until 53.2.1 that Jerome gives a Christian example of the same phenomenon: Paul's journey to see Peter and the other Apostles. It is true that he introduces his comment on Paul with the words, *quid loquar de saeculi hominibus?* Why, indeed? Jerome's implication is that there are sufficient examples in the Christian tradition to make his point, but he only implies this *after* having given a fulsome exposition of his classical knowledge and *after* having chosen purposely to speak *de saeculi hominibus*. Moreover, the classical *exempla* are introduced without a word of criticism. Jerome and Paulinus share a frame of reference rooted both in the Bible and in the classical tradition, and we are given no reason here to view that tradition as problematic—indeed, Jerome draws on its prestige. As if to prove that point once more, Jerome turns again to a classical source to support his contention that there is something special about the *viva vox* of a teacher, so that he must be visited in person.[46]

---

[45] legimus *in veteris historiis quosdam lustrasse provincias, novos populos adisse, maria transisse, ut eos, quos ex libris noverant, coram quoque viderent* (53.1.1); *ad Titum Livium lacteo eloquentiae fonte manantem visendum de ultimo terrarum orbe venisse Gaditanum quendam* legimus (53.1.2).

[46] An anecdote about Aeschines in exile hearing, along with a crowd, the reading of a speech of Demosthenes (which had been given against him) in Pliny *Ep.* 2.3.10. In response to the crowd's amazement at the speech, Aeschines asks, *quid si ipsam audissetis bestiam sua verba resonantem?* (53.2.2). Interestingly, Jerome has translated the question into Latin from the Greek found in Pliny's letter.

It is, of course, undeniable that Jerome offers forceful criticism of one type of the Christian use of classical literature, the cento, in *Ep.* 53. In 53.7.1, he writes:

quasi non legerimus Homerocentonas et Vergiliocentonas ac non sic etiam Maronem sine Christo possimus dicere Christianum....

As if we have not Homer-centos and Vergil-centos, and [as if] we are not thus able to call even Vergil a Christian without Christ....[47]

No poet is named, but, of the three passages he goes on to cite as examples, two in their entirety and the third partially were all applied to the biblical story by Proba.[48] He then states that such exercises are "childish" (*puerilia*) and "similar to the sport of pretentious frauds" (*circulatorum ludo similia*). But his criticism must be set in its proper context. That is, Jerome's purpose is to emphasize the primacy of the study of Scripture, which he had grounded in Paul's commands to Timothy and Titus (especially for the purpose of building the church and refuting error) in 53.3.[49] Jerome's bone of contention in chapter 7 is that certain people are attempting to write about Scrip-

---

[47] I understand a second *quasi* after *ac*, against S. McGill, "Virgil, Christianity, and the *Cento Probae*," in *Texts and Culture in Late Antiquity*, ed. J.H.D. Scourfield, 177.

[48] McGill, "Virgil," 178: *Aeneid* 1.664 and 2.650 were used by Proba at 403 and 624, and part of *Eclogues* 4.6-7 was used at 34. Vessey groups Juvencus with Proba as a possible target of Jerome's criticism: see "Scriptural Poetics," 38 ("Duval shows that [Paulinus'] practice of versifying on biblical themes before ca. 394 conformed in large measure to the methods of writers like Juvencus and Proba and was thus open to the charge of Virgilian pastiche leveled at certain unnamed parties in Letter 53") with Y.-M. Duval, "Les premiers rapports de Paulin de Nole avec Jérôme: moine et philosophe? Poète ou exegete?," *Studi tardoantichi* 7 (1989): 198. The connection is curious, given that Juvencus was not a centonist and that Jerome praises him in *Ep.* 70.5 (cited above) and *De viris illustribus* 84 (a work in which Juvencus is the only poet recognized), and that Jerome cites Juvencus in his *Comm. in Matt.* 1.2.11 (cf. Duval, "Les premiers rapports," 201 n. 101).

[49] Cf. *sancta quippe rusticitas sibi soli prodest et, quantum aedificat ex vitae merito ecclesiam Christi, tantum nocet, si contradicentibus non resistit* (53.3.4); *vides, quantum distent inter se iusta rusticitas et docta iustitia?* (53.3.6). This point is consistent with Jerome's opening words to Paulinus, cited above: *vera enim illa necessitudo est, quam...timor Domini et divinarum scripturarum studia conciliant* (53.1.1). At the same time, Jerome makes it clear in 53.4 that the Apostles are not actually rustics, but are wise. The crucial distinction is between worldly wisdom and Christian wisdom, which can only be learned in Scripture.

ture before they have properly learned it themselves.[50] Furthermore, some "philosophize" (*philosophantur*, 53.7.1) about Scripture among women, while others learn from women what they teach men.

Jerome then singles out, through *praeteritio*, the group that comes to Scripture from secular literature:

> *taceo* de meis similibus, *qui si forte ad scripturas sanctas* post saeculares litteras *venerint et sermone conposito aurem populi mulserint, quicquid dixerint, hoc legem dei putant nec scire dignantur, quid prophetae, quid apostoli senserint, sed ad sensum suum incongrua aptant testimonia....* (53.7.2)

> I am silent about *those similar to me*, who, if they happen to have come to the Holy Scriptures *after secular literature* and to have stroked the ear of the people with well-arranged speech, whatever they say they think to be the law of God, and they do not deign to know what the prophets, what the apostles perceived, but they adjust the testimonies to their own perception, though they are inconsistent [with it].

He includes himself in this group (*de meis similibus*), and we know that Paulinus, in addition to Augustine and many others, comes from it as well, so we may not conclude that Jerome is issuing a blanket condemnation of Scripture-study for former secular *litteratores*. Rather, he is attacking a certain type of *litterator* and is arguing that secular training is *not enough* to understand the Scriptures properly; one needs a teacher.[51] Those trained in classical literature but untaught in the Bible are exceptionally dangerous because they can conceal their ignorance with eloquence: *et sermone conposito aurem populi mulserint.*[52] This is the argument that he uses as a lead-in for his remarks about

---

[50] *hanc garrula anus, hanc delirus senex, hanc soloecista verbosus, hanc universi praesumunt, lacerant, docent, antequam discant* (53.7.1).

[51] Hence, Jerome's comment in 53.6.1: *haec a me perstricta sunt breviter..., ut intellegeres te in scripturis sanctis sine praevio et monstrante semitam non posse ingredi.* For the *insufficiency* of secular study, cf. his comments earlier on the *Verbum* of John: *hoc Plato nescivit, hoc Demosthenes eloquens ignoravit* (53.4.2).

[52] Cf. his comment about those who learn from women: ...*quadam facilitate verborum, immo audacia disserunt aliis, quod ipsi non intellegunt* (53.7.1).

writers such as Proba (*quasi non legerimus...*).[53] The problem is not that such writers read, or even enjoy, Vergil, but that they unthinkingly apply his words to Christ in such a way that they go so far as to conclude that he was a Christian without Christ (*...ac non sic etiam Maronem sine Christo possimus dicere Christianum*, 53.7.3). They should have been taught better.

The reasons outlined in the foregoing, then, explain a number of other features in 53.7 as well as in other parts of the letter. For example, because he is not opposed to Christian use of the classics *per se*, it is not hypocritical for Jerome to round off his criticism of the centonists with an allusion to one of Socrates' famous maxims:

> *puerilia sunt haec et circulatorum ludo similia, docere quod ignores, immo, ut cum stomacho loquar,* nec hoc quidem scire quod nescias. (53.7.3)[54]

> These things are childish and similar to the sport of pretentious frauds: to teach what you do not know; or rather—to vent my spleen—*not even to know that you do not know.*

In addition, Jerome, if my argument above is right, was not being inconsistent at the beginning of this chapter to use a line from Horace, *Ep.* 2.1.117, that expresses disgust at the tendency of even the unlearned to think themselves poets (*scribimus indocti doctique poemata passim*) to give extra weight to his ridicule of the unlearned teaching Scripture. Horace's point vis-à-vis poets is the same as Jerome's vis-à-vis exegetes, and Jerome had in fact used the previous two lines of Horace's poem to show the necessity of teachers at the end of chapter 6.[55] In that chapter, Jerome takes additional evidence for the need for teachers from the world of secular arts, including

---

[53] That is, his derogatory comments are followed directly by the words, "As if we hadn't read centos of Homer and Vergil..."; he is giving an example of the type of Scriptural know-nothings he has just criticized.

[54] I read *cum stomacho loquar* with the MSS and with Labourt and reject Hilberg's emendation *cum Clitomacho loquar*. Hilberg, having emended, then attributes the saying to a "fragment of Clitomachus," but it is more easily read as a reference to Socrates. That Jerome was thinking of Socrates' famous statement while writing this letter is made virtually certain by his comment in 53.9.1: *ceterum Socraticum illud inpletur in nobis: "hoc tantum scio, quod nescio."* McGill, "Virgil," 188 n. 28, also accepts the MS reading.

[55] *quod medicorum est, / promittunt medici, tractant fabrilia fabri* (*Ep.* 2.1.115-16).

grammar and rhetoric, and thus shows that the ancient method of education can serve as a useful model for his proposals concerning Scripture. His comments are introduced in the same way as Jerome's later comments about *mei similes* (*taceo de...*):

> *taceo de* grammaticis, rhetoribus, *philosophis, geometricis, dialectis, musicis, astrologis, medicis, quorum scientia mortalibus vel utilissima est et in tres partes scinditur.* τὸ δόγμα, τὴν μέθοδον, τὴν ἐμπειρίαν. (53.6.1)

> I am silent about *grammarians, rhetors*, philosophers, geometricians, dialecticians, musicians, astrologers, doctors, whose knowledge is indeed most useful for mortals and is divided into three parts: doctrine, method, practice.

He goes on to mention several other kinds of workers and craftsmen, and concludes by saying, ...*absque doctore non possunt esse quod cupiunt* ("...and apart from a teacher, they are not able to be what they desire [to be]"). His endorsement of the usefulness of teachers of all kinds, including schoolteachers, and his flaunting of his own knowledge of classical learning (displayed throughout the letter) renders even more biting his remark that the *poseur*-exegetes act as though "it is not a most vicious way of speaking" (*non vitiosissimum dicendi genus*, 53.7.2) to pervert the Scriptures.[56]

More significantly, my line of argument makes intelligible what follows immediately after chapter 7 in the letter. For Jerome launches into a highlight-reel overview of the Old and New Testaments, commenting (however briefly) on every book of the Hebrew Bible and Greek New Testament and showing himself to be utterly unlike the ignorant expositors he has just criticized; and in this highlight-reel he very frequently describes the Old Testament books in terms of types of classical literature. Job is said to have put forth the rules (λήμματα) of all dialectic: *propositione, adsumptione, confirmatione, conclusione determinat* (53.8.3). Jeremiah wrote in meter (*diversis metris nectit*, 53.8.16). Daniel is referred to as one with an interest in the history of the whole world (*totius mundi* φιλοίστωρ, 53.8.16). David is praised most emphatically of all with the names of the most famous Greek and Latin lyric poets (*Simonides noster, Pindarus et Alcaeus, Flaccus quoque, Catullus et Serenus*, 53.8.17)—a fact that demonstrates that the question, *quid facit cum*

---

[56] Jerome is playing, of course, with the classical *genera dicendi*: *docere, delectare, movere*, and letting the moral sense of *vitium* bleed over into its rhetorical sense.

psalterio Horatius? (22.29), can have more than one answer. Solomon, in the Song of Solomon, wrote an ἐπιθαλάμιον (53.8.17). Finally, 1 and 2 Chronicles are referred to as an *instrumenti veteris* ἐπιτομή (53.8.18), a word often used to denominate summaries or abridgements of longer works of Greek or Roman literature and history.

Jerome's procedure would make no sense if he thought that engagement with such works was poison to the believer, and in fact it shows that he still cares deeply about the classics. If he did not, why would he think it worthy to mention that the book of Job contains the prototype of dialectic, or that David is *Simonides noster?* It would be pointless to identify the biblical writers by such classical terminology unless Jerome wished to bring the classics into conversation with Scripture (while also displaying his own classical and biblical credentials to Paulinus). "But Jerome only brought the pagans to mind," one might argue, "to dismiss them: 'we have already got everything they do.'" Even if this were true, however, his rhetoric still would subvert itself at its very moment of effect, for classical writings are inevitably brought into a relation with Christian and Hebrew writings simply by being called to mind, and the reader is forced to compare them: "we too have versions of these things the Greeks and Romans had. Even if ours are better, theirs are great enough to merit the comparison." Here in particular classical terminology seems to be used to increase the cultural cachet of both Scripture and Jerome.[57] In any case, if my argument about Jerome's true concern in chapter 7 is correct, it would be illogical to assume that he is now, in chapter 8, only engaging in rhetorical posturing and actually thinks that non-Christian writings are worthless. There is no doubt that Jerome, in the aftermath of his dream, would view the classics as *inferior* to Scripture, but that does not necessitate his thinking them *worthless*, and it should be sufficiently clear now that he does not. In this letter as elsewhere, Jerome uses the classics for illustration and argumentative support, often without qualification.[58]

---

[57] Cf. the discussion of the letter's opening above.

[58] Cf. Hagendahl's remark: "The Bible and the Classics are Jerome's two sources of inspiration, and it is not unusual to find both of them quoted in the same passage" (*Latin Fathers*, 302). The two serve to give "double evidence." Most of the time, he gives no preference to one or the other kind of literature, an unprejudiced attitude peculiar, Hagendahl claims, to Jerome (303).

Interestingly, and perhaps significantly, in his run through the New Testament Jerome mentions very little in the way of content; he spends far less space on it than on the Old Testament. In addition, he does not make a single reference to classical works or genres besides calling Acts a *nudam...historiam* (53.9.4), perhaps in a reminiscence of Cicero's description of Julius Caesar's war commentaries. This difference in his treatment of the two Testaments perhaps indicates that Jerome perceives a greater need to bring the Old Testament into dialogue with classical genres and thereby render it more relevant, as a function of the greater problems for interpretation that the Old Testament posed for Christians as compared to the New. In this scenario, the Old Testament books, given new significance by their relationship to the classics, could serve as *progymnasmata* to the study of the New Testament books, with Jerome playing the role of Paulinus' classical-Christian teacher in this didactic letter.

What matters for our purposes, however, is that Jerome seems to be searching for a way in which to integrate his two traditions, not discounting the usefulness of secular learning but noting that it does not of itself make one competent in the Scriptures. At the same time, his survey of the Old Testament shows that classical genres can provide a useful matrix in which to embed his thinking about the Scriptures. Both of these aspects are important in the formulation of a Christian-classical poetics.

B. Ep. *58*

Further confirmation is found in Jerome's next letter to Paulinus, *Ep.* 58.[59] Again, Jerome's letter is a reply to a now-lost letter of Paulinus. In this case, Paulinus had attached a copy of a panegyric he had recently delivered to the emperor Theodosius, on which we will have more to say below. First, however, we shall look to the end of the letter for a brief statement of general principle for the classicizing Christian, one that restates the two-tiered model sketched above. Jerome does not hesitate to praise Paulinus' talent (*magnum...ingenium*, 58.11.1) and eloquence (*infinitam sermonis supellectilem*, 58.11.1). Not only that, but Paulinus already has a certain wisdom (*facilitasque ipsa et puritas mixta prudentiae est*, 58.11.1). To become a better orator (and, presumably, poet)[60] for Christ, he does not need to rid himself of the-

---

[59] Nautin, "Chronologie," 221–22, dates *Ep.* 58 to 395.

se qualities, but he needs to *add* the understanding of the Scriptures. He needs to go beyond where classics alone will take him, as Jerome had also argued in *Ep.* 53 when telling him of his need of a teacher. Jerome now writes to Paulinus:

> *huic prudentiae et eloquentiae si* accederet vel studium vel intellegentia scripturarum, *viderem te brevi arcem tenere nostrorum....* (58.11.2)

> If either *the study or understanding of the Scriptures were added* to this good sense and eloquence, I would see you occupying the citadel of our writers in a short time....

That adding an understanding of Scripture does not demand the obliteration of classical knowledge is shown in practice by Jerome's very next statement. He continues the sentence cited above as follows:

> ...*et ascendentem cum Ioab tecta Sion* canere in domatibus, quod in cubiculis cognovisse*s. accingere, quaeso te, accingere. nil sine magno vita labore dedit mortalibus.* (58.11.2)

> ...and, ascending the roofs of Zion with Joab, [I would see you] *singing on the housetops what you had learned in the bedchambers.* Equip yourself, I beseech you, equip yourself. *Life has given nothing to mortals without great labor.*

The first italicized portion is a reference to Matthew 10:27,[61] and the second is a verbatim quotation of Horace *Serm.* 1.9.59-60. In neither case does Jerome name his source, nor does he disparage the words of Horace. Such sentiments can, apparently, be transferred to the new Christian context,

---

[60] I say "orator" because it is Paulinus' panegyric that has prompted Jerome's comments. Jerome does not mention poetry specifically, but the biblical illustration Jerome uses deliberately calls poetry to mind. He combines an allusion to Joab (possibly 1 Chron. 11:6) with Matt. 10:27; though neither text has to do with singing, Jerome modifies the Vulgate Matthew's *dicite* and *praedicate* to *canere*, "to sing" as well as "to prophesy" (see below on this passage). Vessey, "Scriptural Poetics," 38, notices the change as well (*op. cit.* p. 38), as does Duval, "Les premiers rapports," 200.

[61] *Quod dico vobis in tenebris, dicite in lumine; et, quod in aure auditis, praedicate super tecta* (Vulg.).

even as Paulinus has been transferred from the Senate to the Church.[62] Thus, the pattern is again repeated right away, as Jerome tells Paulinus to prepare riches for himself (*praepara tibi divitias*, 58.11.2)—which I take as an oblique reference to 1 Tim. 6:19, with shades of Matt. 6:19-21 and Matt. 19:21 as well—[63] while he is young, and then supports his point with a quotation of Vergil, *Georgics* 3.67-68, changing only the mood of the verbs from indicative to subjunctive to make sense syntactically with *antequam*.[64]

Not only does Jerome not advocate the obliteration of one's classical learning, but, paradoxically, he suggests that the combination of classicism and Scriptural study actually makes for a more "classical" product—so much is revealed by Jerome's comments on Paulinus' panegyric. For that speech revealed a Ciceronian purity (*Tulliana...puritate*, 58.8.1) in its arrangement and eloquence, and conformed to Quintilianic canons.[65] As such, the speech does not, of course, tell the whole story for Christian literary art, but only forms one part of an envisioned Christian classicism, combining eloquence and Scriptural understanding (*qui talia habes rudimenta, qualis exercitatus miles erit!*, 58.8.2); still, that does not prevent Paulinus from be-

---

[62] *nobilem te ecclesia habet, ut prius senatus habuit* (58.11.2). His use of the classics here, and particularly Horace, recalls his earlier use of Horace, cited above, to disparage unlearned exegetes: *scribimus indocti doctique poemata passim* (53.7.1).

[63] It is likely that the 'riches' here are also meant to ring with Jerome's opening to the letter, a quotation of Luke 6:45: *bonus homo de bono cordis thesauro profert ea, quae bona sunt....*

[64] Jerome writes, *praepara tibi divitias quas cotidie eroges...antequam 'subeant morbi tristisque senectus et labor et durae rapiat inclementia mortis'*. Vergil's lines are:

> *subeunt morbi tristisque senectus*
>
> *et labor, et durae rapit inclementia mortis.*

[65] After remarking that the "Ciceronian purity" of Paulinus' eloquence is found frequently in his *sententiae*, Jerome refers (without naming Quintilian) to *Inst. Orat.* 8 prooem. 31: *iacet enim, ut ait quidam, oratio, in qua tantum verba laudantur* (58.8.2; Labourt and Hilberg both note the reference). Insofar as Paulinus represents the best of classicism and Christianity (for the latter, a humility before the text that allows one to see its majesty and riches), he overcomes the problem that Augustine had to face when he found that he could not penetrate deep into the heart of Scripture. That is, as Rousseau, "Christian Culture," 178 remarks on *Conf.* 5.9, "[Augustine] was distracted by 'speech' and missed in Scripture the *Tulliana dignitas* of secular texts." The Hieronymian/Paulinian pattern allows one to *build* a Ciceronian edifice on a Scriptural foundation without being distracted by its not having one in the first place.

ing called an "orator of Christ" (...*tali Christi oratore*..., 58.8.2), even at this stage. But Paulinus does need to progress in Scriptural understanding for his literary art to mature fully. Jerome details the procedure by referring to important biblical mountains to which he, as a sort of *mystagogus*, would like to lead Paulinus.[66] These are set in contradistinction to classical mountains of poetic inspiration to demonstrate that Christians have something that Greece, though learned, does not have:

> *o si mihi liceret istius modi ingenium non per Aonios montes et Heliconis vertices, ut poetae canunt, sed per Sion et Itabyrium et Sina et excelsa ducere scripturarum, si contingeret docere, quae didici, et quasi per manus mysteria tradere prophetarum, nasceretur nobis aliquid, quod docta Graecia non haberet.* (58.8.3)

> O, if it were permitted to me to lead a talent of that type not through the Ionian mountains and the peaks of Helicon, as the poets sing, but through Zion and Tabor and Sinai and the lofty places of the Scriptures, if it befell me to teach the things that I have learned, and to pass on the mysteries of the prophets from hand to hand, as it were, something would be born to us which learned Greece does not have.

Jerome's statement, then, could be construed as an endorsement for a new Christian poetics since Boeotia (*per Aonios montes et Heliconis vertices*) was a classical locale for *poetic* inspiration[67] and Jerome has replaced them with mountains important in the inspired Scriptures (and, indeed, with the "mountain" of Scripture itself).[68] The Christian writer still needs inspiration,

---

[66] Duval, "Les premiers rapports," 199, makes the same point: Scripture "réclame l'initiation d'un mystagogue."

[67] The opening of Hesiod's *Theogony* is, of course, the most famous example. Duval, "Les premieres rapports," 200, believes that Vergil, *Eclogues* 6.65–66, in particular is evoked in this passage.

[68] It could also indicate, as Vessey, "Scriptural Poetics," would argue (though he does not discuss this particular passage) that Jerome is moving the Alexandrian-Augustan literary center from poetry to biblical exegesis, which would constitute the principle for a new Christian "poetics." His position is not necessarily in conflict with my argument, as there would still be room for poetry of a particular kind—the kind, in fact, that Sedulius and Arator later will write—whether Jerome intended it or not. Poetry would no longer belong to the highest generic expression of literature, but would be subsumed in a broader category of writing *de scripturis*

but it is of a different kind. All that we have discussed so far leads us to conclude that Jerome's statement cannot be strictly a denigration of the classical heritage, but an admission that the Christian's mountains of inspiration come by the divine revelation of the Christian God, and thus were simply *inaccessible* to Greece, however learned, because the Greeks did not have that revelation.[69]

By combining the two heritages in view here, one strikingly ends with a more classical product, as mentioned above. We may observe this in Jerome's arresting comment to Paulinus. If he will work to understand the Scriptures, "...*nihil pulchrius, nihil doctius* nihilque latinius *tuis haberemus voluminibus*" (58.9.2) ("...we would have nothing more beautiful, nothing more learned, *and nothing more Latin* than your books").[70] In this series of comparatives, first note the echo of "learned Greece" in 58.8.3 (*doctius* and *docta Graecia*). Second, note that Paulinus' literary creations, stemming from the study of the classics *and* the Bible, will surpass the previous pinnacle of Latinity (or Roman classicism) that "we" possess. Exactly to whom the "we"

---

sanctis. Thus Vessey goes too far in claiming that "there is no 'place' for poetry as such in the Christian literary system imagined by the monk of Bethlehem" (39), though perhaps his qualification "as such" is crucial. Even if "[t]he literary biblicist...took the place of the poet in the (late) classical literary system" (40)—that is, the exegete now occupies the chief place in literary production—that does not mean that there is no place for the poet, especially the poet whose *ars poetica* is at the same time an *ars scripturalis*. Vessey seems to come back to this position in his closing sentence, where he writes of Jerome's "displacement of Roman poetry by biblical-exegetical prose" (48) and gives additional clarification in a footnote: "Displacement, not replacement" (48 n. 62). Still and all, if I am wrong, there is good company, for Paulinus seems to have been wrong too in his reading of the letter: he did not become a literary biblicist in prose like Jerome, but continued to write poetry—though the full flowering of exegetical poetry would come later—and subsequently encouraged his protégé Jovius to do the same. It may be true, as Duval argues, "Les premiers rapports," 203–205, that Paulinus was an intended target of the cento-criticisms because of some similarities between his *C.* 6 and Proba's *Cento*, and that this caused him to change his manner of composition, but he did not give up poetry altogether.

[69] Recall Jerome's discussion of the *Verbum* in 53.4, where he writes, *hoc Plato nescivit, hoc Demosthenes eloquens ignoravit*.

[70] It is true that *latine loqui* can mean "to speak plainly," but it can also mean "to speak with eloquence," which fits much better with the context here (*LS* s.v. *Latium* B.II.B.1, where the comparative *latinius* is glossed for late Latin as "in better Latin").

implicit in the first-person plural verb pertains is ambiguous. It could be the learned in general, Christians in general, or, more likely, learned Christians, themselves an embodied synthesis of the various cultural forces at work in their literary productions. Furthermore, the classical background is maintained as essential to such a goal. Jerome begins to say, in 58.9.2, that Scriptural study is the *foundation* (to which *si haberes hoc fundamentum* refers), but then takes it back and reconfigures it as the *crowning completion* of Paulinus' work (*immo quasi extrema manus in tuo opere duceretur*).[71] Literature, then, becomes more Roman by becoming more Christian.

My argument for the abiding value of the classics when complemented by Scriptural understanding also helps to explain an interesting feature at the beginning of *Ep.* 58. After opening with a quotation of Luke 6:45 and a reference to Luke 6:44/Matt. 12:33 and thus giving a biblical atmosphere to the letter,[72] Jerome augments it—in the very next sentence—with a whiff of the classics as well by alluding to Vergil, *Georgics* 4.176. That is, Jerome writes to Paulinus:

> *metiris nos virtutibus tuis et* parvos magnus *extollis ultimamque partem convivii occupas, ut patris familiae iudicio proveharis.* (58.1.1)

> You measure me by your virtues and, *great*, you lift up the *small* and take the last place at the banquet, so that you may be promoted by the judgment of the paterfamilias.

In reading Jerome's remark, the man of culture, recollecting his school days, would think of Vergil's words about the bees (*non aliter, si* parva *licet componere* magnis, *Georgics* 4.176).[73]

---

[71] The usefulness of both types of learning for the Christian is again evident in this section through Jerome's own practice. To demonstrate that, while the "outside" (*in cortice*, 58.9.1) of Scripture gleams, the "inner sense" (*medulla*, 58.9.1) is sweeter, Jerome essentially quotes from Plautus *Curc.* 55 (Jerome has *qui esse vult nuculeum, frangit nucem* while Plautus has *qui e nuce nuculeum esse volt, frangit nucem*; Labourt and Hilberg again both note the reference) and then quotes Psalm 119:8 (118:8) in quick succession without differentiating between the two, aside from naming David.

[72] *bonus homo de bono cordis thesauro profert ea quae bona sunt, et ex fructibus arbor agnoscitur* (58.1.1).

[73] The classical atmosphere is enhanced by the reference to a banquet (*convivii*) and to the head of the household (*patris familiae*). Interestingly, these references have

This first nod at Vergil prepares us for the more emphatic direct quotation later in the chapter. Here our discussion of some of Jerome's comments in *Ep.* 53 becomes crucial, because Jerome uses Vergil in what is, for all intents and purposes, centonic fashion.[74] After discussing the last being made first via the example of Paul (58.1.3), who had been changed from a persecutor of the Church into the hardest-working apostle, Jerome uses Judas to exemplify the converse—one who had been in Jesus' inner circle, but then became a betrayer and wretched suicide. Jerome uses two quotations to describe him. The first is Psalm 55:14–15 (54:14–15): *tu autem, homo, dux meus et notus meus; in domo Dei ambulavimus cum consensu.*[75] The second, used to describe his suicide, is *Aeneid* 12.603: *et nodum informis leti trabe nectit ab alta.* The line from the *Aeneid* has been taken over unaltered and applied to an event and person in the Scriptures; that is, Jerome has used the technique of the cento. If my argument above regarding *Ep.* 53.7.3 is incorrect and Jerome is criticizing such a practice *carte-blanche* in that passage rather than criticizing *the kind of writer* who is making the centos, then in our current passage he shows himself to be inconsistent at best, and hypocritical at worst. If, however, the position sketched in the foregoing pages is right and he is arguing for the lesser claim of the use of the classics informed by Scriptural understanding (which the "childish" centos did not evidence, in Jerome's opinion), then Jerome is not only being consistent, but is provid-

---

been given a Christian twist: Paulinus sits in the last spot so that he might be conveyed to the first. Cf. Luke 14:7–11, and note especially v. 10: *sed cum vocatus fueris, vade, recumbe in novissimo loco, ut cum venerit qui te invitavit dicat tibi, "amice, ascende superius." tunc erit tibi gloria coram simul discumbentibus* (Vulg.). That the scriptural allusion has been classicized can be seen by comparing the Vulgate, in which neither *convivium* nor *paterfamilias* are used. For *parvus* and *magnus* in Vergil, cf. also *Eclogues* 1.23 (*sic parvis componere magna solebam*).

[74] C.P.E. Springer, "Jerome and the *Cento* of Proba," *Studia patristica* 28 (1993): 102 n. 29, remarks that "Jerome himself would have had to plead guilty of using cento-like techniques in his own writing." Springer notes that he is indebted to E. Clark and D. Hatch, *The Golden Bough, the Oaken Cross* (Chico, CA: Scholars Press, 1981)) for the observation. See *Golden Bough* 104 and 200 n. 73, where it is documented that Jerome uses in centonic fashion one of the very lines for which he had criticized centonists in 53.7.3 (*talia perstabat memorans fixusque manebat, A.* 2.650).

[75] The text given by Jerome here is fairly close to that found in his revision of the LXX Psalter, which reads: *tu vero homo unianimis, dux meus et notus meus, qui simul mecum dulces capiebas cibos. in domo Deo ambulavimus cum consensu.*

ing a model of how one should go about balancing the classics and the Bible, all in a letter of instruction to a developing Christian-classical poet.

IV. Conclusion

The analysis in the foregoing pages is far from comprehensive. As I noted in the introduction, several other writers could be studied with profit on this question, as well as the rest of Jerome's *corpus*. For that matter, the letters treated above have much more to say on this topic than I have drawn out. What I hope to have done is to have adumbrated one thoughtful approach to this question from one late antique Christian with much invested in both of his "cultures," who, at the same time, espoused an overriding avowal to privilege his Christian faith when the two conflicted or had to be brought into a hierarchical relationship of some kind. The question with which Jerome wrestled is not one of merely historical interest, for all Christians who live in a culture, with its customary traditions and practices—which is to say, all Christians—must deal with this question or one very much like it. If read closely and sympathetically, Jerome (and other Christians of the past) can relieve the claustrophobia of too exclusive an attention to our own circumstances. Not only so, but such writers can provide us, in addition, with "programs of action"[76] to think with and, as we then turn back to our own historical moment, to modify for our own times.

---

[76] I borrow the phrase from Kenneth Burke.

Bibliography

Adkin, N. *Jerome on Virginity.* Cambridge, UK: Francis Cairns, 2003.

——. "Jerome's Use of Scripture Before and After his Dream." *Illinois Classical Studies* 20 (1995): 183–90.

Cain, A. *The Letters of Jerome: Asceticism, Biblical Exegesis, and the Construction of Christian Authority in Late Antiquity.* New York: Oxford University Press, 2009.

Clark, E., and D. Hatch. *The Golden Bough, the Oaken Cross.* Chico, CA: Scholars Press, 1981.

Conybeare, C. *Paulinus Noster.* New York: Oxford University Press, 2000.

Daur, K.D. *Augustinus: Epistulae.* CCSL 31–31B. Turnhout: Brepols, 2004–2009.

Duval, Y.-M. "Les premiers rapports de Paulin de Nole avec Jérôme: moine et philosophe? Poète ou exegete?" *Studi tardoantichi* 7 (1989): 177–216.

Hagendahl, H. *Latin Fathers and the Classics.* Göteborg: Elanders boktr. Aktiebolag, 1958.

Green, R.P.H. *Latin Epics of the New Testament.* New York: Oxford University Press, 2006.

Grützmacher, G. *Hieronymus.* Leipzig: Dieterich, 1901–08.

Hilberg, I. *Sancti Eusebii Hieronymi Epistulae.* CSEL 54–56. Vienna: F. Tempsky, 1910–18.

Labourt, J. *S. Jérôme: Lettres,* Paris: Les Belles Lettres, 1949-63.

MacCormack, S. *The Shadows of Poetry.* Berkeley and Los Angeles: University of California Press, 1998.

Markus, R.A. "Paganism, Christianity and the Latin Classics in the Fourth Century." In *Latin Literature of the Fourth Century*, edited by J.W. Binns, 1–21. London: Routledge & Kegan Paul, 1974.

McGill, S. "Virgil, Christianity, and the *Cento Probae*." In *Texts and Culture in Late Antiquity*, edited by J.H.D. Scourfield, 173–96. Swansea: Classical Press of Wales, 2007.

Mohr, A. "Jerome, Vergil, and the Captive Maiden." In *Texts and Culture in Late Antiquity*, edited by J.H.D. Scourfield, 299–322. Swansea: Classical Press of Wales, 2007.

Nautin, P. "Études de chronologie hiéronymienne (393–97) III." *Revue d'études augustiniennes et patristiques* 19 (1973): 213–21.

Rebenich, S. *Jerome*. New York: Routledge, 2002.

Rousseau, P. "Christian Culture and the Swine's Husks: Jerome, Augustine, and Paulinus." In *The Limits of Ancient Christianity*, edited by W.E. Klingshirn and M. Vessey, 172–87. Ann Arbor: University of Michigan Press, 1999.

Springer, C.P.E. "Jerome and the *Cento* of Proba." *Studia Patristica* 28 (1993): 96–105.

Thierry, J.J. "The Date of the Dream of Jerome." *Vigiliae Christianae* 17 (1963): 28–40.

Trout, D. *Paulinus of Nola*. Berkeley and Los Angeles: University of California Press, 1999.

Vessey, M. "*Quid facit cum Horatio Hieronymus?* Christian Latin Poetry and Scriptural Poetics." In *Poetry and Exegesis in Premodern Latin Christianity*, edited by W. Otten and K. Pollmann, 29–48. Leiden: Brill, 2007.

"The Kingdom of Christ is Spiritual":
John Calvin's Concept of the Restoration of the World

Dr. Matthew J. Tuininga
Oglethorpe University

One of the great paradoxes of John Calvin's theology can be captured in two of the phrases the reformer invokes over and over throughout his *Institutes,* commentaries, and many other works. On the one hand, Calvin constantly emphasizes, "the kingdom of Christ is spiritual." On the other hand, through the kingdom of Christ God has brought about, is bringing about, and will bring about the "restoration of the world," or the restoration of order in the world. Various scholars highlight different sides of this paradox, often for their own ideological or critical purposes. Certain critics claim that Calvin was captive to neo-platonic dualisms of body and soul, earth and heaven, the outward and the inward, so denigrating the significance of the material creation.[1] More appreciatively, some claim that Calvin envisioned the future of Christ's kingdom, and the purpose of the church, in purely "other-worldly" terms.[2] On the other extreme, numerous scholars present Calvin as calling Christians to bring about the transformation of the world into the kingdom of God, or at least as the inspiration for the elite saints who could bring transformation through their zealous activism.[3]

---

[1] See for example R.W. Battenhouse, "The Doctrine of Man in Calvin and in Renaissance Platonism," *Journal of the History of Ideas* 9 (1948): 447–71. For a more subtle example see Heinrich Quistorp, *Calvin's Doctrine of the Last Things,* trans. Harold Knight (London: Lutterworth Press, 1955).

[2] David VanDrunen, *Natural Law and the Two Kingdoms: A Study in the Development of Reformed Social Thought* (Grand Rapids: William B. Eerdmans Publishing Company, 2010), 67–115.

[3] See H. Richard Niebuhr, *Christ and Culture* (New York: HarperCollins, 2001 [1951]), 217–18; Ernst Troeltsch, *The Social Teaching of the Christian Churches,* two vols, trans. Olive Wyon (Louisville: Westminster/John Knox Press, 1992 [1912]); Michael Walzer, *The Revolution of the Saints: A Study in the Origins of Radical Politics* (Cambridge: Harvard University Press, 1965); W. Fred. Graham, *The Constructive Revolutionary: John Calvin and His Socio-Economic Impact* (Richmond, VA: John Knox Press, 1971).

In this paper I argue that Calvin's actual position is more nuanced than either of these positions. I argue that Calvin's understanding of the kingdom of Christ and its relation to this world is best understood in terms of his two kingdoms eschatological framework. Simply put, Calvin believed the spiritual kingdom of Christ does and will restore the material creation, but he interpreted this claim eschatologically. The full restoration, accompanied by some sort of transformation, will come at the end of the present age. In the meantime, protological restoration takes place in the church as human beings are justified and sanctified through the ministry of Christ's spiritual government. At the same time, God preserves the fallen and sinful temporal world through his providence, natural law, and the institution of civil government.

I. The Kingdom of Christ as the Restoration of the World

Calvin's theology of creation and nature is not static. On the contrary, the French humanist-turned-theologian presents creation in terms of its teleological future as the heavenly kingdom of God. The primary way that he does this is in his anthropology, because for Calvin humanity is the apex of creation. As goes humanity, so goes the cosmos, so to speak. For Calvin, human beings were made in the image of God, endowed with immortal souls that impel them upward and forward, in body and in soul, to seek happiness in communion with God. "[T]he state of man was not perfected in the person of Adam" but was "only earthly, seeing it had no firm and settled constancy." Human beings possessed a "living soul" in the image of Adam but they had not yet received the "quickening spirit" they inherit from Christ.[4] Human life was temporal, but had Adam not sinned, humans would have been elevated, body and soul, into the heavenly kingdom of God. "Truly the first man would have passed to a better life, had he remained upright, but there would have been no separation of the soul from the body, no corruption, no kind of destruction, and, in short, no violent change."[5] This is important to stress, because when Calvin talks about the restoration of the world, or about human beings' restoration to their original state, he is not referring to this original state in a static sense, but in the

---

[4] Commentary on Genesis 2:7 [1554], in *Ioannis Calvini opera quae supersunt omnia, Corpus Reformatorum* (volumes 29–87; ed. Johann Wilhelm Baum, August Eduard Cunitz, and Eduard Reuss; 1863–1900) [henceforward *CO*], 23:36.

[5] Commentary on Genesis 3:19 [1554]; *CO* 23:77.

sense of its eschatological purpose.⁶ Calvin writes,

> we cannot think upon either our first condition or to what purpose we were formed without being prompted to meditate upon immortality, and to yearn for the Kingdom of God… For what is that origin? It is that from which we have fallen. What is that end of our creation? It is that from which we have been completely estranged, so that sick of our miserable lot we groan, and in groaning we sigh for that lost worthiness (*Institutes* 2.1.3).⁷

When Adam and Eve fell into sin, however, not only were they estranged from this purpose, but the order of the entire creation was disrupted and subjected to futility and chaos. Only the providence of God, as Susan Schreiner has shown so well, preserves a modicum of order, working by God's invisible omnipotence to prevent disintegration and collapse, by natural law to maintain a measure of human morality, and by ordained coercive political institutions to preserve society.⁸ Human beings lost all of their supernatural or spiritual gifts, Calvin argues, but God has graciously left to them natural or temporal gifts. These gifts can no longer lead human beings upward and forward to the heavenly kingdom, however. They are purely preservative, and deeply flawed.

> Therefore, withdrawing from the kingdom of God, he is at the same time deprived of spiritual gifts, with which he had been furnished for the hope of eternal salvation. From this it follows that he is so banished from the Kingdom of God that all qualities belonging to the blessed life of the soul have been extinguished in him, until he recovers them through the grace of regeneration. Among these are faith, love of God, charity toward neighbor, zeal for holiness and

---

⁶ This is *pace* Richard Prins, "The Image of God in Adam and the Restoration of Man in Jesus Christ: A Study in John Calvin," *Scottish Journal of Theology* 25 (1972): 32–44.

⁷ In the pages that follow, citations from the *Institutes of the Christian Religion* are parenthetical, and quotations are taken from the 1559 edition, translated by Ford Lewis Battles and edited by John T. McNeill (Louisville: Westminster John Knox Press, 1960), except where otherwise specified.

⁸ Susan E. Schreiner, *The Theater of His Glory: Nature and the Natural Order in the Thought of John Calvin* (Grand Rapids: Baker Academic, 1995).

for righteousness. All these, since Christ restores them in us, are considered adventitious and beyond nature: and for this reason we infer that they were taken away (*Inst.* 2.2.12).

The kingdom of Christ is established wherever this restoration has begun to take place, wherever human beings once again turn to the voluntary service of God. This is why Calvin identifies the kingdom so strongly with the church, very often simply saying that the church is Christ's kingdom. But as Torrance argues, Calvin only thinks the church is Christ's kingdom from the perspective of its manifestation in the present age.[9] The kingdom of Christ in its fullest sense involves the restoration of all things. The "true and perfect state of the kingdom of God" entails "the full restoration of all things and perfect happiness."[10] When Christ returns he will "establish perfect order in heaven and earth."[11] Calvin presents his understanding of the kingdom of Christ as the restoration of the world in clear and decisive terms. The sorts of words he typically uses are *instauro*, *restituo*, and *renovatio*, words often translated interchangeably as 'renewal,' 'restoration,' and 'renovation.' The restoration that will occur is a restoration of 'all things' [*omnia*], or of the 'order' [*ordo*] or 'state' [*status*] of creation.

The *locus classicus* for Calvin's discussion of the restoration of creation is his commentary on Romans 8:19–21. Calvin writes, "I understand the passage to have this meaning – that there is no element and no part of the world which, being touched as it were with a sense of its present misery, does not intensely hope for a resurrection." God has "implanted inwardly the hope of renovation [*renovationis*]" to all things.[12] All creatures shall be renewed, not in the particular sense that individual human beings are, but in the sense that "they, according to their nature, shall be participators of a better condition, for God will restore [*restituet*] to a perfect state [*modo melio-*

---

[9] T. F. Torrance, *Kingdom and Church: A Study in the Theology of the Reformation* (Edinburgh: Oliver and Boyd, 1956), 133–34.

[10] Commentary on John 11:27 [1553]; *CO* 47:263.

[11] Commentary on Matthew 25:31 [1555]; *CO* 45:686.

[12] Commentary on Romans 8:19 [1540]; *CO* 49:152. Cf. Schreiner, *The Theater of His Glory*, 97–98.

ris status] the world, now fallen, together with mankind."[13] Calvin admits that it is not entirely clear just what this sort of restoration will entail and he warns against speculation. But he nevertheless specifies two of its most important features. First, the material creation will be liberated from corruption, decay, and death.[14] Second, what it yearns *for*, and will therefore participate in, is "eternal" or "celestial glory."[15]

Calvin makes similar points in his commentaries on 2 Peter 3 and Isaiah 65. On 2 Peter 3 he writes, "Of the elements of the world I shall only say this one thing, that they are to be consumed only that they may be renovated, their substance still remaining the same, as it may be easily gathered from Romans 8:21 and from other passages."[16] Here Calvin uses the Aristotelian distinction between substance and accidents to distinguish between the substance of creation as it will be restored and continue into the kingdom of Christ, and the various phenomena of this temporal world, such as institutions, property, and the arts, that will pass away. There is therefore no basis for speculation that Calvin believed the stuff of culture will endure into the kingdom of Christ, as some scholars think.[17] Calvin makes his position quite clear in his commentary on 1 Corinthians 13. "So far as I can conjecture and am able even to gather in part from this passage, inasmuch as learning, knowledge of languages, and similar gifts are subservient to the necessity of this life, I do not think that there will be any of them remaining."[18]

Thus Calvin does not speak of any sort of *progressive* transformation of the material creation prior to Christ's return, for, as he writes in the Romans commentary, creatures, "being now subject to corruption, cannot be

---

[13] Commentary on Romans 8:21 [1540]; *CO* 49:153.

[14] Commentary on Romans 8:21 [1540]; *CO* 49:153.

[15] Commentary on Romans 8:19 [1540]; *CO* 49:152. Cf. Commentary on Romans 8:17 [1540]; *CO* 49:150–51.

[16] Commentary on 2 Peter 3:10 [1551]; *CO* 55:476.

[17] See, for instance, Cornel Venema, "The Restoration of All Things to Proper Order: An Assessment of the 'Two Kingdoms/Natural Law' Interpretation of Calvin's Public Theology," in *Kingdoms Apart: Engaging the Two Kingdoms Perspective*, ed. Ryan G. McIlhenny (Phillipsburg, NJ: Presbyterian and Reformed, 2012), 26–31; Paul Helm, *Calvin: A Guide for the Perplexed* (London: T&T Clark, 2008), 134–35.

[18] Commentary on 1 Corinthians 13:8 [1546]; *CO* 49:512–13.

restored [*instaurari*] until the sons of God shall be wholly restored [*restituantur*]. Hence they, longing for their renewal [*instaurationem*], look forward to the manifestation of the celestial kingdom [*regni coelestis*]."[19] The order and flourishing of creation is tied up with the order and flourishing of human beings. Having fallen along with them, the creation longs for the restoration to which it will attain when humans have themselves been restored. Again, Calvin makes the same point at length in his commentary on Isaiah 65, warning "that none may think that this relates to trees, or beasts, or the order of the stars, for it must be referred to the inward renewal of man."[20] Or as he puts it in his commentary on John, "Christ was sent in order to bring the whole world under the authority of God and obedience to him, … [for] without him everything is confused and disordered. . . . Now, we ought to judge of this government from the nature of his kingdom, which is not external but belongs to the inner man. . . ."[21]

But Calvin's insistence that it is the whole creation that is restored is not merely abstract or irrelevant to the reformer's broader political theology and ethics. Because all things have been definitively restored by Christ, all things belong to his kingdom. Nonbelievers have forfeited their rights to the earth, to property, or to power before God (though before *human beings* they still hold basic rights rooted in justice),[22] whereas for believers, who are the heirs of the world in Christ, all these things are sanctified.

> God has appointed to his children alone the whole world and all that is in the world. For this reason they are also called the heirs of the world, for at the beginning Adam was appointed to be lord of all on this condition, that he should continue in obedience to God. Accordingly, his rebellion against God deprived of the right, which had been bestowed on him, not only himself but his posterity. And since all things are subject to Christ, we are fully restored by his mediation, and that through faith, and therefore all that unbelievers enjoy may be regarded as the property of

---

[19] Commentary on Romans 8:19 [1540]; *CO* 49:152.

[20] Commentary on Isaiah 66:22 [1559]; *CO* 37:453.

[21] Commentary on Isaiah 42:1 [1559]; *CO* 37:59-60.

[22] See John Witte, Jr., *The Reformation of Rights: Law, Religion, and Human Rights in Early Modern Calvinism* (Cambridge: Cambridge University Press, 2007), 57–58.

others, which they rob or steal.[23]

For those who serve the Lord of all, on the other hand, "there is nothing in the world that is not sacred [*sanctum*] and pure."[24] When believers "enter on the full possession of their inheritance, ... all creatures shall be made subservient to their glory. For both heaven and earth shall be renewed for this end, that according to their measure they may contribute to render glorious the kingdom of God."[25]

All of that said, it must again be stressed that Calvin does not conceive of this restoration or renewal in static terms, or even in terms resembling an idealized version of present human life. For the restoration of human beings and of the world will culminate in the spiritual transformation for which they were always intended. The clearest place where Calvin makes this point is in his commentary on 1 Corinthians 15. Jesus will not restore the body to its original state as experienced by the first human beings, but will "raise it up to a better condition than ever."[26] Christ "brought us from heaven a life-giving Spirit that he might regenerate us into a better life, and elevated above the earth [*terra*]."[27] Calvin uses the same Aristotelian logic to describe the body's transformation as he does with reference to that of the creation in 2 Peter 3. "Let us, however, always bear in mind what we have seen previously – that the substance [*substantiam*] of the body is the same and that it is the quality [*qualitate*] only that is here treated of."[28] "For we now begin to bear the image of Christ, and are every day more and more transformed into it, but that image still consists in spiritual regeneration. But then it will be fully restored both in body and in soul, and what is now begun will be perfected, and accordingly we will obtain in reality what we as yet only hope for."[29]

In the meantime, Calvin could not be more clear about his opposi-

---

[23] Commentary on 1 Timothy 4:3 [1548]; *CO* 52:296.

[24] "[A]ll things are sanctified through Christ." Commentary on 1 Corinthians 10:26 [1546]; *CO* 49:469.

[25] Commentary on Romans 4:13 [1540]; *CO* 49:77.

[26] Commentary on 1 Corinthians 15:45 [1546]; *CO* 49:558–59.

[27] Commentary on 1 Corinthians 15:47 [1546]; *CO* 49:559.

[28] Commentary on 1 Corinthians 15:44 [1546]; *CO* 49:557–58.

[29] Commentary on 1 Corinthians 15:49 [1546]; *CO* 49:560.

tion to any sort of doctrine seeking an earthly political manifestation of the kingdom. The chiliasts, the Anabaptists, and Rome all made this error in one way or another, but it all went back to the basic Jewish misunderstanding that plagued the disciples. They wanted Christ to establish his kingdom immediately, and they expected that establishment in political terms. "They ask him concerning a kingdom, but they dream of an earthly kingdom which should flow with riches, with dainties, with external peace, and with such like good things, and while they assign the present time to the restoring of the same, they desire to triumph before the battle."[30] Only after Christ returns, Calvin says over and over, will the kingdom be fully established. In the meantime it is expressed in righteousness, peace, and the power of the Holy Spirit.

II. Calvin's Two Kingdoms Eschatology

When Calvin argues that the kingdom of Christ is spiritual, he does not mean that it is immaterial. Rather, he means 1) that the power of the kingdom is that of the Holy Spirit, 2) that it fulfills creation's heavenly or eschatological purpose, and 3) that it will be consummated only at Christ's return. Put simply, the kingdom is 1) from the Spirit of God, 2) it leads human beings upward to God, and 3) it leads them forward to eternity. Of course, Calvin believed that Jesus has been made lord of all things by virtue of his ascension and session at the right hand of God. But he also believed that Christ only makes his eschatological kingdom present in the present age in limited ways, where the devil is decisively defeated, and where human beings are restored to voluntary obedience. Outside of that spiritual kingdom Christ continues to rule over his enemies, constraining them by his general providence, by natural law, and by civil government.

> For there are two distinct powers which belong to the Son of God: the first, which is manifested in the structure of the world and the order of nature, and the second, by which he renews and restores fallen nature. As he is the eternal Speech of God, by him the world was made; by his power all things continue to possess the life which they once received; man especially was endued with an extraordinary gift of understanding; and though by his revolt he lost the light of understanding, yet he still sees and under-

---

[30] Commentary on Acts 1:6 [1552]; *CO* 48:8 (Cf. 1:8; 48:10).

stands, so that what he naturally possesses from the grace of the Son of God is not entirely destroyed. But since by his stupidity and perverseness he darkens the light which still dwells in him, it remains that a new office be undertaken by the Son of God, the office of mediator, to renew, by the Spirit of regeneration, man who had been ruined.[31]

Calvin therefore consistently distinguishes between Christ's "spiritual government of the church [*spirituali ecclesiae gubernatione*]" and his "universal government of the world [*universali mundi gubernatione*],"[32] between "that government of God which is general in its nature," and "that special and spiritual jurisdiction which he exercises over the church."[33] Jesus is lord of heaven and earth, but "he is in a peculiar manner the Lord of believers, who yield willingly and cheerfully to his authority, for it is only of 'his body' that he is 'the head' (Ephesians 1:22-23)."[34] In his commentary on Psalm 2 Calvin offers the same distinction: The "beauty and glory of the kingdom ... are more illustriously displayed when a willing people run to Christ in the day of his power, to show themselves his obedient subjects." But this is not the only way that the messiah rules. In his exaltation Jesus is "furnished with power by which to reign even over those who are averse to his authority, and refuse to obey him." These "he shall subdue by force, and compel to submit to him."[35]

The fundamental distinction underlying Calvin's two kingdoms doctrine is the contrast between the present age, marked by corruption and temporality, and the future eternal kingdom of Christ. In his commentary on 1 Timothy Calvin writes, "All that is in the world [*saeculo*] has the taste of its nature, so that it is fading and quickly passes away."[36] Underlying this distinction is the clarification Calvin makes in Book 2 of the *Institutes*.

> I call 'earthly things' those which do not pertain to God or his Kingdom, to true justice, or to the blessedness of the

---

[31] Commentary on John 1:5 [1553]; *CO* 47:6–7.

[32] Commentary on Ephesians 1:23 [1548]; *CO* 51:160.

[33] Commentary on Psalm 67:3 [1557]; *CO* 31:618.

[34] Commentary on Luke 1:43 [1555]; *CO* 45:35.

[35] Commentary on Psalm 2:9 [1557]; *CO* 31:48–49.

[36] Commentary on 1 Timothy 6:17 [1548]; *CO* 52:333.

> future life; but which have their significance and relationship with regard to the present life and are, in a sense, confined within its bounds. I call 'heavenly things' the pure knowledge of God, the nature of true righteousness, and the mysteries of the Heavenly Kingdom. The first class includes government, household management, all mechanical skills, and the liberal arts. In the second are the knowledge of God and of his will, and the rule by which we conform our lives to it. (*Inst.* 2.2.13)

The distinction between earthly and heavenly things corresponds closely to Calvin's classic statement of the two kingdoms doctrine, which contrasts the political kingdom as that which pertains to "food and clothing," "outward behavior," and "life among other men," to the spiritual kingdom which pertains to the "soul," to the "conscience," and to the "inner mind" (*Inst.* 3.19.15). Those thing that pertain to the outward person are earthly things, things that will pass away. Those things that pertain to the inward person are heavenly things, things that will endure as part of the kingdom of Christ. In his commentary on 2 Corinthians 4:17 Calvin articulates this connection explicitly. When the Apostle Paul refers to the "outward man," he argues, the term denotes "everything that relates to the present life. As he here sets before us two men, so you must place before your view two kinds of life—the earthly and the heavenly [*terrenam et coelestem*]. The outward man is the maintenance of the earthly life, which consists not merely in the flower of one's age, and in good health, but also in riches, honors, friendships, and other resources."[37]

Often, of course, Calvin explains the outward/inward distinction in terms of the distinction between the body and the soul. But Calvin emphasizes that the contrast between the body and soul, like that between the flesh and the spirit, is not to be interpreted as a narrow *anthropological* distinction but as an *eschatological* distinction. The terms 'body', 'flesh', and 'outward' denote the whole human being as a participant in the present passing age, corrupted and marred by sin, while the terms 'soul,' 'spirit', and 'inward' denote the human being as a participant in the spiritual kingdom of Christ. "[B]oth terms, flesh as well as spirit, belong to the soul, but the latter to that part which is renewed, and the former to that which still retains its natural character. . . . The inner [*interioris*] man then is not simply the soul,

---

[37] Commentary on 2 Corinthians 4:16 [1548]; *CO* 50:58.

but that spiritual part which has been regenerated by God, and the members signify the other remaining part."[38] Similarly, "the word body means the same as the external man and members," the person insofar as she remains "carnal and earthly."[39] Why use the potentially misleading language of anthropology at all? The primary reason, for Calvin, is that the analogy comes from scripture. But why does the Apostle Paul use it? Because he wanted to "clearly show that the hidden renovation is concealed from and escapes our observation, except it be apprehended by faith."[40]

In other words, the distinction enables believers to make sense of the cruciform character of the Christian life as the means by which they are conformed to the image of Jesus, preparing them to endure suffering in this temporal age, while persevering in hope of the resurrection of the body at the return of Christ. As Paul explains in Romans 8:25–31, in his decree of election God ordained that Christians must be conformed to the image of Jesus, so "connecting, as by a kind of necessary chain, our salvation with the bearing of the cross."[41] Calvin explains that a person's participation in Christ's suffering and death involves them in a process of mortification that is twofold (3.20.42).

> The one is inward—what the Scripture is wont to term the mortification of the flesh, or the crucifixion of the old man, of which Paul treats in the sixth chapter of the Romans. The other is outward—what is termed the mortification of the outward man. It is the endurance of the cross, of which he treats in the eighth chapter of the same epistle.[42]

It is because of the latter that Christians despise, in a sense, the mortal body and the present life. For as the kingdom of Christ "lies beyond this world, . . . we must, by contempt of this present life and mortification of the outward man, set ourselves with the whole bent of our mind to meditation on

---

[38] Commentary on Romans 7:18 [1540]; *CO* 49:132.

[39] Commentary on Romans 7:24 [1540]; *CO* 49:135.

[40] Commentary on Romans 7:22 [1540]; *CO* 49:133–34.

[41] Commentary on Romans 8:28 [1540]; *CO* 49:158–59.

[42] Commentary on Philippians 3:11 [1548]; *CO* 52:50.

a blessed immortality."[43] The point here is not that the body and life are despised *in themselves*. The point, rather, is that Christians despise their *temporal forms* out of longing for their restoration and perfection in the kingdom of God.

It is this dynamic that explains why Calvin uses the two kingdoms doctrine to explain that Christian liberty does not free believers from outward suffering or temporal service in this age. Because of their transience, the political and social circumstances of this age must be distinguished from the spiritual kingdom of Christ, which is eternal. Such "outward things [*rebus externis*]" are to be used only for the "necessity of the present life [*praesentis vitae*], which passes away quickly as a shadow [*instar umbrae subito praeterfluit*]." Thus it is inappropriate "to contend for outward things [*rebus externis*]" which are really "corruptible things [*rebus corruptioni*]."[44] The kingdom of God does not consist in "external things [*rebus externis*]" like meat and drink, according to Romans 14:17, a text Calvin was constantly quoting with this theme in view, but of "spiritual things [*rebus spiritualibus*]" such as "righteousness and peace and joy in the Holy Spirit."[45]

Since the goal of the Christian life is conformity to Christ, Christians approach temporal institutions with a spirit of love, service, and self-sacrifice. In their vocations they embody the same subservience as did Christ, while inwardly they know they are free and will one day be entirely free. "In short," Calvin says, "it is a free servitude and a serving freedom [*In summa, est libera servitus, et serva libertas*]."[46] All political and social relationships are and will be transcended within the kingdom of Christ.

> Hence as the world will have an end, so also will government and magistracy and laws and distinctions of ranks and different orders of dignities and everything of that nature [*politia, et magistratus, et leges, et distinctiones ordinum, et gradus dignitatum, et quidquid tale est*]. There will be no more any distinction between servant and master [*servus a domino*], between king and peasant [*rex a plebeio*], between magistrate

---

[43] Commentary on 2 Corinthians, Argument [1548]; *CO* 50:7. Commentary on James 1:10 [1550]; *CO* 55:388.

[44] Commentary on 1 Corinthians 6:13 [1546]; *CO* 49:397.

[45] Commentary on Romans 14:17 [1540]; *CO* 49:265–66.

[46] Commentary on 1 Peter 2:16 [1551]; *CO* 55:246.

and private citizen [*a privato magistratus*].⁴⁷

From the perspective of the spiritual kingdom of Christ, Calvin argues, the various relations associated with wealth, class, labor, gender, and government are entirely transcended and will one day pass away.

The same dynamic shapes Calvin's view of civil government. In his commentary on Christ's statement, "Render to Caesar what is Caesar's and to God what is God's, Calvin observes,

> Christ's reply ... lays down a clear distinction between spiritual and civil government [*spirituale et politicum regimen*], in order to inform us that outward subjection [*externam subiectionem*] does not prevent us from having within us a conscience free in the sight of God. For Christ intended to refute the error of those who did not think that they would be the people of God, unless they were free from every yoke of human authority [*humani imperii*].⁴⁸

One of the primary differences between spiritual and civil government is that the former creates true righteousness, while the latter can only coerce civil righteousness. As Calvin puts it in one place,

> Hence, the difference between the righteousness of Christ and the righteousness of kings ought to be here noticed. They who rule well can in no other way administer righteousness and judgment than by being careful to render to every one his own, and that by checking the audacity of the wicked, and by defending the good and the innocent. This only is what can be expected from earthly kings. But Christ is far different, for he is not only wise so as to know what is right and best, but he also endues his own people with wisdom and knowledge. He executes judgment and righteousness, not only because he defends the innocent, aids them who are oppressed, gives help to the miserable, and restrains the wicked, but he does righteousness, because he regenerates us by his Spirit, and he also does judgment, because he bridles, as it were, the devil.⁴⁹

---

[47] Commentary on 1 Corinthians 15:24 [1546]; *CO* 49:546–47.

[48] Commentary on Matthew 21:21 [1555]; *CO* 45:601–02.

[49] Commentary on Jeremiah 23:5-6 [1563]; *CO* 38:410.

What Calvin is expressing here corresponds directly to the reformer's fundamental distinction between the second and third uses of the law, which might be called the civil and spiritual uses respectively, and which in turn correspond to spiritual righteousness and civil righteousness. The spiritual and "principal use" of the law constitutes the "proper purpose of the law" because it "finds its place among believers in whose hearts the Spirit of God already lives and reigns" (*Inst.* 2.7.12). The civil use of the law, on the other hand, applies to all human beings, not simply those who are sanctified by the Spirit.[50] Its purpose is neither to sanctify nor to condemn human beings in any ultimate sense, but to give order to temporal society, through coercion if necessary. It is outward in scope, extending to human actions; it cannot touch the inward person nor can it drive her upward and forward to the spiritual kingdom of Christ. As Marc Chenevière puts it, "In obliging men to respect the Decalogue the magistrate does not claim to effect an inward change, but merely to cause them to observe outwardly a relative morality sufficient to secure for them, in spite of themselves, or even contrary to themselves, an existence worthy of the name."[51] In Calvin's words, the "mortal lawgiver's jurisdiction extends only to the outward political order." It cannot touch purposes or intentions; indeed, it can do nothing until "actual crimes are committed" (2.8.6).[52] In a sermon on Deuteronomy 5:17 Calvin declared that when magistrates create laws "their purpose has to do only with the way we govern ourselves with respect to the external civil order to the end that no one might be violated, and that each might have his rights and have peace and concord among men. . . . they cannot reform inner and hidden affections. That belongs to God." Still, Calvin insists, "this constrained and forced righteousness is necessary for the public community of men." Even believers need external enforcement of the law because their sanctification is incomplete (2.7.10).

III. Church and Civil Government

The distinction between the spiritual and civil uses of the law is es-

---

[50] Cf. Commentary on 1 Timothy 1:9 [1548]; *CO* 52:255.

[51] Marc Chenevière, "Did Calvin Advocate Theocracy?," *Evangelical Quarterly* 9 (1937), 166.

[52] Sermon on Deuteronomy 5:17; *CO* 26:328. Cited in Cited in Witte, *The Reformation of Rights*, 64.

sential to understanding Calvin's view of the way in which the church and civil government participate in Christ's restoration of the world. Calvin describes the church as Christ's kingdom in two respects, one with reference to the church's ministry, the other with reference to the society of believers. "When we speak of the kingdom of Christ [*Christi regno*] we must respect two things: the doctrine of the gospel, by which Christ gathers to himself a church, and by which he governs [*gubernat*] it ... and secondly, the society of the godly, who being coupled together by the sincere faith of the gospel, are truly accounted the people of God."[53] The primary reason why the church is Christ's kingdom, as this quote implies, is because *by definition* the church is the place where Christ's spiritual scepter is at work. It is there where the word is proclaimed, and it is by the word that the Spirit regenerates human beings. The proclamation of the word is *the* mark by which both the church and Christ's kingdom are identified. "To sum up, since the church is Christ's Kingdom, and he reigns by his word alone, will it not be clear to any man that those are lying words by which the Kingdom of Christ is imagined to exist apart from his scepter (that is, his most holy word)?" (*Inst.* 4.2.4)

Calvin's locus classicus for this point is Ephesians 4. Significantly, in his commentary on Ephesians Calvin commences his discussion of Christ's spiritual government of the church only after first distinguishing the "universal government [*universali gubernatione*]" of God, by which he "upholds, and maintains, and rules, all things," from that "spiritual one, which belongs to the church [*spirituali tantum, quae ad ecclesiam pertinet*]," by which God graciously draws human beings to himself.[54] Calvin argues that Christ ascended to God's right hand and proceeds to build and grow his kingdom by pouring gifts upon his church, gifts which revolve around the ministry of the word. Christ's "government of the church [*regimen ecclesiae*], by the ministry of the word, is not a contrivance of men, but an appointment made by the Son of God."[55] The ministry, then, is not only the "mode of governing and keeping the church." It is nothing less than "the administration of the Spirit and of righteousness and of eternal life" (*Inst.* 4.3.3). The word has been committed to the church "like a scepter," and it can be said that "by the

---

[53] Commentary on Acts, Dedication to Second Edition [1560]; *CO* 18:157.

[54] Commentary on Ephesians 4:6 [1548]; *CO* 51:192.

[55] Commentary on Ephesians 4:11 [1548]; *CO* 51:196-197.

word the pastors of the church exercise the jurisdiction of the Holy Spirit [*iurisdictionem spiritus*]."[56]

But Calvin doesn't limit the sense in which the church is Christ's kingdom to the simple act of preaching and teaching. He argues that the sacraments and church discipline are "appendages" or extensions of the word, and thus also expressions of Christ's spiritual government. Thus the ministry of the word involves three major tasks: "to instruct the people to true godliness, to administer the sacred mysteries and to keep and exercise upright discipline." Calvin identifies only the preaching of the word and the administration of the sacraments as the marks of a true church, but he views discipline as essential to the church's health and long-term survival (*Inst.* 4.3.6).

Calvin therefore says the same things about church discipline, or the "spiritual jurisdiction [*spirituali iurisdictione*]" (*Inst.* 4.12.1), as he does about preaching. Like preaching, discipline is an "exercise of the office of the keys" by which the kingdom of Christ is opened and closed to human beings. Like preaching "with regard to men it is not so much power [*potestatem*] as ministry" (*Inst.* 4.11.1). Both have the "same power [*potestas*] of binding and loosing (that is, through God's word), the same command, the same promise" (*Inst.* 4.11.2). Of course, the presupposition for such statements, like the presupposition for Calvin's exaltation of preaching, is that the exercise of discipline is within the bounds of the word. Just as a teacher only ministers Christ's spiritual kingdom when he teaches Christ's word, so church discipline is only an expression of Christ's spiritual kingdom when it is an expression of that word. Where it is indeed the word that is at work, however, Calvin does not hesitate to attribute the action to Christ. In that case the voice of the church is ratified in heaven by the one who has "the whole claim to the government of the church, so that he approves and ratifies the decisions of which he is himself the author."[57] "Therefore, that no one may stubbornly despise the judgment of the church, or think it immaterial that he has been condemned by the vote of the believers, the Lord testifies that such judgment by believers is nothing but the proclamation of his own sentence, and that whatever they have done on earth is ratified in heaven" (*Inst.* 4.11.2).

---

[56] Commentary on Psalm 47:3 [1557]; *CO* 31:467-468.

[57] Commentary on Matthew 18:19 [1555]; *CO* 45:516–17.

Of course, Calvin recognizes that the church has an important political dimension. It requires order, decorum, and polity, all of which are political matters that must be ordered by wisdom and prudence consistent with scripture. This can be accomplished either by civil magistrates or, preferably, by the ministers of the church, but the main point is that it is not a spiritual rule. The day and place of worship, the role and attire of women and men, the forms and postures of the liturgy—none of this binds the conscience (*Inst.* 4.10.1–31). In that sense the broader government of the church stands in stark contrast to the ministry of the word, sacraments, and discipline. The former is human, whereas the latter is divine. The former establishes merely outward order, but through the latter means Christ creates true righteousness, so building his kingdom.[58]

Although a number of scholars have claimed that Calvin gives civil government the same essential purpose as the church—the establishment and nurture of the kingdom of Christ through edification and sanctification—it should be clear by this point why this cannot be the case.[59] Calvin is adamant that only by the ministry of the word are human beings regenerated and brought into Christ's kingdom, let alone conformed to Christ's image. In contrast, the civil law can only coerce outward or civil righteousness. To be sure, magistrates can and must submit to Christ's kingship and restoration just like anyone else. But their civil authority never becomes Christ's spiritual kingdom or takes on its ministry.

There are two reasons, I believe, why students of Calvin get confused on this point. First, they observe that Calvin believed magistrates were to enforce the law of God. This is true, of course, but is not true in a simple way. Calvin did not believe a magistrate could enforce the law of God in its ultimate, spiritual sense, but only in its outward, civil sense. What is more, he believed the civil law constantly has to take into account human limits and the hardness of human hearts. Applying Jesus' comments regarding

---

[58] For an excellent study of Calvin's concept of the *adiaphora*, matters indifferent, with reference to the role of women in particular, see John Lee Thompson, *John Calvin and the Daughters of Sarah: Women in Regular and Exceptional Roles in the Exegesis of John Calvin, His Predecessors and His Contemporaries* (Geneva: Droz, 1992).

[59] See especially Harro Hopfl, *The Christian Polity of John Calvin* (Cambridge: Cambridge University Press, 1982), especially 189–212, and to a certain extent William R. Stevenson, Jr., *Sovereign Grace: The Place and Significance of Christian Freedom in John Calvin's Political Thought* (New York: Oxford University Press, 1999), especially 45–61, 174–76.

Moses' law of divorce to numerous other laws of the Torah, for instance, Calvin constantly finds weaknesses even in the Torah's "civil laws [*leges forenses*], the principle of which is not so exact and perfect, since in their enactment God has relaxed his just severity in consideration of the people's hardness of heart [*populi duritiem*]."[60] Calvin thought magistrates should enforce as much of God's law as possible, but he did not think that by declining to punish a crime they were therefore approving it.

Second, scholars observe that Calvin thought magistrates should enforce the first table of the law as well as the second, and that he explicitly called them to establish, defend, and maintain the kingdom of Christ. There is no need for me to multiply quotes here to that effect. But it must be carefully observed what Calvin means when he speaks in this way. For Calvin himself was aware of the charge that giving magistrates the task of caring for religion was a violation of his two kingdoms doctrine. In his commentary on John 18 he addresses the point more clearly than anywhere else. While the Jews slanderously charged Jesus with seeking to overthrow the political order, John's gospel records, Jesus declared that his kingdom is not of this world, because if it was of this world his servants would fight for it with arms. Calvin interprets Jesus' statement as a clear affirmation of the difference between the two kingdoms.[61] But then he asks, "here a question arises, Is it not lawful to defend the kingdom of Christ by arms?" Calvin's answer is that the magisterial defense of the kingdom is made possible precisely *because* of the distinction between the two kingdoms. Then he writes a clear statement describing the sense in which magistrates defend and promote the kingdom of Christ. He speaks in terms of its defense, but he uses the same argument with respect to its establishment and maintenance.

> [T]hough godly kings defend the kingdom of Christ by the sword, still it is done in a different manner from that in which worldly kingdoms are wont to be defended. For the kingdom of Christ, being spiritual, must be founded on the doctrine and power of the Spirit. In the same manner too its edification is promoted, for neither the laws and edicts of men nor the punishments inflicted by them enter into the consciences. Yet this does not hinder princes from *accidentally* defending the kingdom of Christ, partly by ap-

---

[60] Commentary on Exodus 22:1–4 [1563]; *CO* 24:688.

[61] Commentary on John 18:36 [1553]; *CO* 47:403–04.

pointing external discipline and partly by lending their protection to the Church against wicked men.[62]

Calvin's answer carefully distinguishes the direct way in which Christ defends his church and nurtures it through the ministry of the church, and the indirect or accidental way that magistrates do so when they protect the church against attacks and see to it that the ministry is properly established. A consideration of Calvin's letters to foreign magistrates show that he is consistent on this point. Magistrates are called to establish the kingdom of Christ only in the sense that they are to establish and fund the ministry of the church and its discipline. Yet it is the ministry of the church that actually administers Christ's kingdom. Civil government falls under Christ's kingship in the broad sense, but Calvin never identifies it as part of Christ's spiritual kingdom. That is because while civil governments can submit to Christ's kingdom, and in this way submit to Christ's restoration of the world, they cannot bring about that restoration by their own power. They can only do so indirectly, using their preservative and coercive powers to support the work of the church.

Conclusion

Calvin believed that Christ's kingdom is spiritual but he also believed that in the kingdom the whole creation will be restored to its divine purpose. He synthesized these seemingly contradictory claims through his two kingdoms eschatology, which distinguishes the way in which Christ's kingdom breaks into the present age through the spiritual ministry of the church, and its fullfillment at the return of Christ. At the same time, because the kingdom's fulfillment is yet future, Calvin distinguished the temporal and political affairs of this age, ordained by God under Christ's lordship, from Christ's spiritual kingdom. While the church is Christ's kingdom in the present age, because it is in the church that restoration is taking place, civil government can only coerce outward, civil righteousness, and it can only indirectly support Christ's kingom. One day, however, when Christ returns, the political kingdom will pass away, and the restoration of the world will be complete.

Calvin ties these various threads together in his fascinating explanation of the well-known prophecy of Isaiah and Micah that in the kingdom

---

[62] Commentary on John 18:36 [1553]; *CO* 47:403–04. Emphasis added.

of God the nations will beat their swords into ploughshares and their spears into pruning hooks, and that they shall not learn war anymore. Calvin understands the prophecy as a clear indication that the kingdom of Christ will subdue the nations, but not through coercion or the power of the sword. Rather, the nations will unite themselves voluntarily to Israel, having been reformed by the proclamation of the word. The whole prophecy, he argues, is about "God's spiritual kingdom." The means by which Christ rules, his scepter, is the gospel. "We hence see that an earthly empire is not what is here predicted, but what exists through the word and celestial doctrine."[63]

That the kingdom is spiritual, however, does not mean that it holds no relevance for life in the present age. When the prophets declare that the nations will not only be reconciled to God, but also to one another, they mean that those who formerly lived in hatred and lust will devote themselves to kindness. This reconciliation, as a manifestation of God's kingdom, is distinct from his broader government of the world.

> God has indeed ever governed the world by his hidden providence, as he does still govern it. . . . But the Scripture speaks of God's kingdom in two respects [*Sed bifariam loquitur scriptura de regno Dei*]. God does indeed govern the devil and all the wicked, but not by his word, nor by the sanctifying power of his Spirit: it is so done that they obey God, not willingly, but against their will. The peculiar government of God is that of his church only [*peculiare Dei imperium pertinet ad solam ecclesiam*], where, by his word and Spirit, he bends the hearts of men to obedience so that they follow him voluntarily and willingly [*sponte et libenter*], being taught inwardly and outwardly—inwardly by the influence of the Spirit – outwardly by the preaching of the word [*intus, spiritus instinctu: foris, verbi praedicatione*]. . . . This, then, is the beginning of the kingdom of Christ [*exordia regni Christi*].[64]

What is unique here about the *peculiare Dei imperium,* or the *regni Christi,* is that it operates by the outward word and inward Spirit, it establishes obedience that is voluntary and inward, and the place where this happens is solely in the church. The work of the kingdom, Calvin goes on to argue, is to em-

---

[63] Commentary on Micah 4:1-2 [1559]; *CO* 43:341.

[64] Commentary on Micah 4:3 [1559]; *CO* 43:344-345.

power voluntary and genuine righteousness: "that strong men, when thus reproved, shall offer themselves, without any resistance, to be ruled by God. Correction is indeed necessary, but God employs no external force nor any armed power when he makes the church subject to himself, and yet he collects strong nations."[65]

To be sure, this restoration is anything but complete. Only a fraction of the world is Christian, and even Christians continue to struggle with sin. Calvin takes this point as an opportunity to emphasize the continuing importance of civil government, against the Anabaptists, as subservient to the lordship of Christ. He likewise concludes, "We must therefore bear in mind what Micah has previously taught, that this kingdom is spiritual [*regnum hoc spirituale esse*], for he did not ascribe to Christ a golden scepter, but a doctrine."[66]

> [P]eace exists among us only as far as the kingdom of Christ flourishes [*floret Christi regnum*]... Would that Christ reigned [*regnaret Christus*] entirely in us! for then would peace also have its perfect influence. But since we are still widely distant from the perfection of that peaceful kingdom [*perfectione pacifici istius regni*], we must always think of making progress, and it is excessive folly not to consider that the kingdom of Christ [*regnum Christi*] here is only beginning.

The ultimate fulfillment of Isaiah's prophecy could only take place after Jesus' return. "It is enough if we experience the beginning, and if, being reconciled to God through Christ, we cultivate mutual friendship, and abstain from doing harm to any one."[67] David E. Holwerda thus correctly summarizes Calvin's thought when he writes, "The history of salvation which becomes visible in the church contains within it the meaning of the history of the world. And the renewal manifesting itself in the body of Christ is the renewal that embraces the whole creation."[68] With believers

---

[65] Commentary on Micah 4:3 [1559]; *CO* 43:345.

[66] Commentary on Micah 4:8 [1559]; *CO* 43:356–57.

[67] Commentary on Isaiah 2:4 [1559]; *CO* 36:66.

[68] David E. Holwerda, "Eschatology and History: A Look at Calvin's Eschatological Vision," in *Readings in Calvin's Theology* (ed. Donald K. McKim; Grand Rapids: Baker, 1984), 337.

acting according to true righteousness in all the tasks and vocations of life, in response to the ministry of the word, the church thus gives expression to the restoration of the world by the kingdom of Christ.

Bibliography

Battenhouse, R.W. "The Doctrine of Man in Calvin and in Renaissance Platonism." *Journal of the History of Ideas* 9 (1948): 447–71.

Calvin, John. *Institutes of the Christian Religion.* Edited by John T. McNeill. Translated by Ford Lewis Battles. Philadelphia: The Westminster Press, 1960.

———. *Ioannis Calvini opera quae supersunt omnia. Corpus Reformatorum,* volumes 29–87. Edited Johann Wilhelm Baum, August Eduard Cunitz, and Eduard Reuss. Braunschweig: C.A. Schwetschke, 1863–1900.

Chenevière, Marc. "Did Calvin Advocate Theocracy?" *Evangelical Quarterly* 9 (1937): 160–68. Reprinted in *Calvin's Thought on Economic and Social Issues and the Relationship of Church and State,* edited by Richard C. Gamble, 108–17. New York: Garland, 1992.

Graham, W. Fred. *The Constructive Revolutionary: John Calvin and His Socio-Economic Impact.* Richmond, VA: John Knox Press, 1971.

Helm, Paul. *Calvin: A Guide for the Perplexed.* London: T&T Clark, 2008.

Holwerda, David E. "Eschatology and History: A Look at Calvin's Eschatological Vision." In *Readings in Calvin's Theology,* edited by Donald K. McKim, 311–42. Grand Rapids: Baker, 1984.

Hopfl, Harro. *The Christian Polity of John Calvin.* Cambridge: Cambridge University Press, 1982.

Niebuhr, H. Richard. *Christ and Culture.* New York: HarperCollins, 2001 [1951].

Prins, Richard. "The Image of God in Adam and the Restoration of Man in Jesus Christ: A Study in John Calvin." *Scottish Journal of Theology* 25 (1972): 32–44.

Quistorp, Heinrich. *Calvin's Doctrine of the Last Things*. Translated by Harold Knight. London: Lutterworth Press, 1955.

Schreiner, Susan E. *The Theater of His Glory: Nature and the Natural Order in the Thought of John Calvin*. Grand Rapids: Baker Academic, 1995.

Stevenson, William R., Jr. *Sovereign Grace: The Place and Significance of Christian Freedom in John Calvin's Political Thought*. New York: Oxford University Press, 1999.

Thompson, John Lee. *John Calvin and the Daughters of Sarah: Women in Regular and Exceptional Roles in the Exegesis of John Calvin, His Predecessors and His Contemporaries*. Geneva: Droz, 1992.

Torrance, Thomas F. *Kingdom and Church: Study in the Theology of the Reformation*. Edinburgh: Oliver & Boyd, 1956.

Troeltsch, Ernst. *The Social Teaching of the Christian Churches*. Translated by Olive Wyon. Two Volumes. Louisville: Westminster/John Knox Press, 1992 [1912].

VanDrunen, David. *Natural Law and the Two Kingdoms: A Study in the Development of Reformed Social Thought*. Grand Rapids: William B. Eerdmans Publishing Company, 2010.

Venema, Cornel. "The Restoration of All Things to Proper Order: An Assessment of the 'Two Kingdoms/Natural Law' Interpretation of Calvin's Public Theology." In *Kingdoms Apart: Engaging the Two Kingdoms Perspective*, edited by Ryan G. McIlhenny, 3–32. Phillipsburg, NJ: Presbyterian and Reformed Publishing, 2012.

Walzer, Michael. *The Revolution of the Saints: A Study in the Origins of Radical Politics*. Cambridge: Harvard University Press, 1965.

Witte, John, Jr. *The Reformation of Rights: Law, Religion, and Human Rights in Early Modern Calvinism*. Cambridge: Cambridge University Press, 2007.

Participating in Political Providence:
The Theological Foundations of Resistance in Calvin

Andrew Fulford
McGill University

Introduction

Despite ongoing ideological strife, countries in the Anglosphere enjoy relative political stability. But a psychoanalyst or anthropologist studying the artifacts of our popular culture might wonder if our societies are craving something else. Consider the following films and shows, listed in no particular order: *Gladiator*, *V for Vendetta*, Christopher Nolan's *Dark Knight* trilogy, *Captain America: The Winter Soldier*, the Bourne films, *Serenity*, *Tears of the Sun*, *24*, *Person of Interest*, and the list could go on. What all these have in common is a general, at least tacit, support for the idea that justice can sometimes demand using illegal force. In some of these fictional cases, this is taken to the point of armed resistance against the government itself. And outside of the Anglosphere, this idea has a life beyond art. Looking only at very recent history, from the Arab Spring to South Sudan to Ukraine, popular politics often takes the form of revolution and resistance. The appeal of this idea worldwide gives the political theologian pause. Is the apparent widespread support for this kind of act an expression of common grace, a preservation of the light of practical reason in spite of the fall? Or is it simply an expression of the rebellion bound up in the heart of our fallen species?

Dialogue with great minds can be a useful point of access into the larger discussion on these matters, and that's what I plan to engage in here, with John Calvin as my interlocutor. I have chosen the French Reformer for three main reasons: firstly because of his importance to my own ecclesiastical tradition, secondly because of his significance to the West more broadly, and thirdly because there has been lively debate over Calvin's own position on resistance.

Joining that debate, this paper will argue John Calvin's doctrines of nature, sin, and grace can provide theological foundations for armed resistance against unjust rulers, even apart from legal grounds for doing so. The structure of the following argument will proceed as follows. Firstly, it will trace out Calvin's theology on those fundamental *loci*: nature, sin, and grace. Secondly, it will describe Calvin's own position on resistance. Thirdly, it will bring Calvin into comparison with some near contemporaries who took a different perspective on the political question. Fourthly, it will engage in a Calvinian argument against Calvin, attempting to show that the Reformer's theology ought to lead to different conclusions than he took it to. Finally, it will conclude with reflection on the contemporary relevance of Calvin's doctrine. The breadth of Calvin's writings makes comprehensive summary extremely difficult. The following survey will therefore only touch on his teaching insofar as it provides an answer to the question of resistance.

Calvin's Doctrine of Nature and Grace
God and Nature

To truly understand Calvin's teaching on anything, one must begin with his doctrine of God, for from it flows everything else. Calvin teaches that "God's goodness is so connected with his divinity that it is no more necessary for him to be God than for him to be good."[1] In other words, God's goodness is inseparable from his existence. The Reformer teaches, further, that God's will is always just, and that (contrary to the voluntarist view) all his acts flow from this justice.[2]

God's goodness is a law for his actions, and their end is his own glory. In his commentary on Romans 11:36, Calvin writes: "[H]ow unreasonable would it be for creatures… to live for any other purpose than for making his glory known? … [T]he whole order of nature would be strangely subverted, were not God, who is the beginning of all things, the end also."[3]

The Reformer also teaches that all creatures and events in creation are expressions of divine power and providence. He affirms the classic

---

[1] John Calvin, *Institutes of the Christian Religion*, ed. John T. McNeill, trans. Ford Lewis Battles (Philadelphia: The Westminster Press, 1960), II.3.5; hereafter cited only by book, chapter, and section.

[2] *Institutes* I.17.2.

[3] John Calvin on Rom 11:36, in *Calvin's Commentaries*, vol. 19, trans. John Owen (Grand Rapids: Baker, 1996),

http://www.ccel.org/ccel/calvin/calcom38.xv.viii.html (accessed April 8, 2014); hereafter cited according to abbreviated title with biblical reference only.

Christian doctrine of *creatio ex nihilo*,[4] and stresses that God is also "the everlasting Governor and Preserver—... in that ... he sustains, nourishes, and cares for, everything he has made, even to the least sparrow... ."[5] Further, he notes that God providentially governs and upholds every thing he has made in accord with its specific nature: "the several kinds of things are moved by a secret impulse of nature, as if they obeyed God's eternal command, and what God has once determined flows on by itself."[6]

Human Nature

God's providence over human beings thus takes a form suitable to their nature. But what is this nature? In the course of giving his reply, the Reformer raises a false conception in order to refute it. That is, he addresses the possibility that his doctrine entails a kind of fatalism.[7] Calvin replies that God endowed man with "a mind, by which to distinguish good from evil" and that choice, or the will, "was added, to direct the appetites and control all the organic motions, and thus make the will completely amenable to the guidance of reason."[8] By means of these faculties mankind participates in divine providence. As the Reformer writes,

> But the Lord enjoins you to beware, because he would not have [any peril] fatal for you. These fools do not consider what is under their very eyes, that the Lord has inspired in men the arts of taking counsel and caution, by which to comply with his providence in the preservation of life itself. Just as, on the contrary, by neglect and slothfulness they bring upon themselves the ills that he has laid upon them. ... God pleased to hide all future events from us, in order that we should resist them as doubtful, and not cease to oppose them with ready remedies, until they are either overcome or pass beyond all care. I have therefore already remarked that God's providence does not always meet us

---

[4] *Institutes* I.14.20.

[5] *Institutes*. I.16.1.

[6] *Institutes*. I.16.4.

[7] *Institutes* I.17.4.

[8] *Institutes* I.15.8.

in its naked form, but God in a sense clothes it with the means employed.[9]

The significance of this point cannot be overstated for the purposes of this essay. Calvin has harmonized divine providence and human nature in a way that blocks any inference to fatalism and a concomitant practical passivity. Instead, God has cast a shadow of ignorance over the future, and has provided humanity with the powers to prepare for various eventualities, even to "resist" foreseen perils before they come to pass. As Eric Fuchs summarizes the Reformer, "This faith in God's justice and providence, far from leading to an idle fatalism, is to Calvin a powerful call to ethical responsibility... ."[10]

As part of God's providence, human activity properly has the same end as God, which we have seen is his own glory. As André Biéler puts it in his *Calvin's Economic and Social Thought*, for the Reformer "To be human is first and foremost to live for God, through God and with God... ."[11] Rational human beings would perceive this. Indeed, Calvin states the obligation of the law, which republishes the natural law, as: "...God, as he is our Creator, has toward us by right the place of Father and Lord; for this very reason we owe to him glory...."[12] And this obligation includes within itself the doing of righteousness.[13]

This duty to God further includes a debt to human beings, which "we owe to man for the sake of God," and which are summarized in the Second Table of the Law.[14] Calvin thus encapsulates the entire law this way: "First, indeed, our soul should be entirely filled with love of God. From this

---

[9] *Institutes* I.17.4.

[10] Eric Fuchs, "Calvin's Ethics," in *John Calvin's Impact on Church and Society 1509-2009*, ed. Martin Ernst Hirzel and Martin Sallmann (Grand Rapids: William B. Eerdmans Publishing Company, 2009), 146.

[11] André Biéler, *Calvin's Economic and Social Thought*, ed. Edward Dommen, trans. James Greig (Geneva: World Alliance of Reformed Churches, 2005), 163.

[12] *Institutes* II.8.2.

[13] *Institutes* II.8.2.

[14] *Institutes* II.8.50.

will flow directly the love of neighbour."[15] And this love of neighbour expresses itself in doing good to the neighbour.[16]

This law subdivides into further obligations, corresponding to the multifaceted form of the human good. For the purposes of the present investigation, those that pertain to the social and political good of man are most important. The Reformer argues that by nature human beings are instinctively social, and that all people thus have a sense of what good civil order is.[17] He fittingly expounds the meaning of the sixth commandment (you shall not murder) in the following way:

> ...the Lord has bound mankind together by a certain unity; hence each man ought to concern himself with the safety of all. To sum up, then, all violence, injury, and any harmful thing at all that may injure our neighbor's body are forbidden to us. We are accordingly commanded, if we find anything of use to us in saving our neighbors' lives, faithfully to employ it; if there is anything that makes for their peace, to see to it; if anything harmful, to ward it off; if they are in any danger, to lend a helping hand.[18]

And the fifth commandment he explains in this manner: "since the maintenance of his economy pleases the Lord God, the degrees of preeminence established by him ought to be inviolable for us."[19] Magistrates in turn behave in a manner consistent with their calling and "represent in themselves to men some image of divine providence ... and justice."[20] They are ordained so that "their sole endeavor should be to provide for the common safety and peace of all."[21] He stresses, too, that magistrates are

---

[15] *Institutes* II.8.51.

[16] *Institutes* II.8.54.

[17] *Institutes* II.2.13.

[18] *Institutes* II.8.39.

[19] *Institutes* II.8.35.

[20] *Institutes* IV.20.6.

[21] *Institutes* IV.20.9.

more than just necessary evils.[22] Rather, they hold the most honourable of all offices in God's sight.[23]

Calvin thus paints an image of the cosmos as proceeding from the Creator and aimed at his own glorification; this procession takes up human nature within it, including its deliberative faculties, which God has designed to aim at his own glory. Seeking this good entails seeking lesser goods, which in turn includes the social and political good of humanity.

Sin and its Consequences

Unfortunately, sin has affected both humanity's natural gifts and its supernatural gifts. As Biéler notes, Calvin approves of Augustine's view that the fall corrupted man's natural gifts and entirely withdrew his supernatural ones.[24] The natural gifts are the faculties of reason and will. These are corrupted such that the light of reason is immersed in darkness, and the will is in bondage to evil desires.[25] The supernatural gifts that Calvin mentions are "the light of faith as well as righteousness," and "love of God, charity toward neighbor, zeal for holiness and for righteousness."[26] Calvin describes these as above nature and extrinsic to it; he also states that these are the qualities that would have sufficed to attain eternal life.[27] These gifts are entirely removed with the fall, and human beings are banished from the kingdom of God until these are given again in regeneration.[28]

Two points must be made about Calvin's teaching regarding these supernatural endowments. Firstly, they are all apparently actualizations of the natural faculties which still remain. That is, simply going by his list, the supernatural gifts are not extra faculties, but perfections of the natural powers. Secondly, Calvin includes love toward our neighbour as among the supernatural gifts entirely removed, but this must be understood in a qualified

---

[22] *Institutes* IV.20.22.

[23] *Institutes* IV.20.4.

[24] Biéler, 165.

[25] *Institutes* II.2.12.

[26] *Institutes* II.2.12.

[27] *Institutes* II.2.12.

[28] *Institutes* II.2.12.

sense, which will be explained below in the discussion of grace.[29] Nevertheless, abstracted from grace, Calvin leaves human beings with the faculties of intelligence and will, but intrinsically lacking any good use of them.

This corruption of human nature has consequences for society. A world characterized by a full expression of fallen human nature would, to Calvin, clearly be something resembling a Hobbesian war of all against all, the destruction of human society itself. He states this succinctly: "For if he had not spared us, our fall would have entailed the destruction of our whole nature."[30]

It is important to recognize there is no change because of the fall in the moral or natural law that binds human beings. The nature of human beings as such is still directed toward the formation of society, and all people still know the basic principles of civil order are reasonable, and that their sinful actions are against what their minds approve.[31] More will be said about the subjective aspect of this point below, but for the moment it is sufficient to emphasize that the shift in condition that sin eventuates does not change the natural law of human action itself.

Grace

The darkness of this portrait of sin is matched only by the corresponding brightness of Calvin's doctrine of grace. This grace expresses itself in many ways. For the sake of brevity, these can be summarized into two.

Firstly, God extends the gift of reason to all people even after the fall. And as Biéler succinctly comments, "Thanks to these gifts a certain social life remains possible on earth."[32] Calvin is concerned to emphasize that this natural gift is still a gift, but he affirms its common possession: "Therefore this evidence clearly testifies to a universal apprehension of reason and understanding by nature implanted in men."[33] Further, in some sense these gifts are not a replacement of the powers of man's prelapsarian nature, but

---

[29] *Institutes* II.2.12.

[30] *Institutes* II.2.17.

[31] *Institutes* II.2.13.

[32] Biéler, 166.

[33] *Institutes* II.2.14.

a preservation of them. As Calvin writes of "natural" men, "Let us, accordingly, learn by their example how many gifts the Lord left to human nature even after it was despoiled of its true good."[34] Thus, as noted in the section on sin above, this grace leads people in general to perceive the basic principles of civil order.

This perception comes about in some specific ways. Steven Grabill, in his useful *Rediscovering the Natural Law in Reformed Theological Ethics*, argues that Calvin's teaching on conscience is carefully structured to resolve the problem of the noetic effects of sin. Contrary to Marc-Édouard Chenevière, Grabill notes that Calvin holds both conscience and reason together in the unregenerate acquisition of knowledge of right and wrong.[35] He points to Calvin's comments on Romans 2,[36] which note how this process functions: "But observe how intelligently he defines conscience: he says, that reasons come to our minds, by which we defend what is rightly done, and that there are those which accuse and reprove us for our vices...."[37] The discovery of these reasons in connection with civil matters comes through a process directly related to the nature of human beings:

> since man is by nature a social animal, he tends through natural instinct to foster and preserve society. Consequently, we observe that there exist in all men's minds universal impressions of a certain civic fair dealing and order. Hence no man is found who does not understand that every sort of human organization must be regulated by laws, and who does not comprehend the principles of those laws.[38]

It is important to stress at this point that Calvin is directly speaking about unregenerate people in this text, not merely pre-fallen humanity. In teaching this doctrine, he affirms that unregenerate man has and knows his own nature, and moral obligations that follow from it, contrary to the later

---

[34] *Institutes* II.2.15.

[35] Stephen J. Grabill, *Rediscovering the Natural Law in Reformed Theological Ethics* (Grand Rapids: Eerdmans, 2006) 93.

[36] Ibid., 94.

[37] Calvin, *Comm. Rom.* 2:15.

[38] *Institutes* II.2.13.

Reformed theologian Karl Barth.[39] And so we can see the general outlines of Calvin's approach: the social instinct in human nature leads to a perception of the kinds of behavior, especially political behaviors, that are consistent with that good. This entire natural process of the conscience is what God's grace preserves in its function.

Along with preserving this knowledge in all people, God also graciously internally restrains the behavioural effects of corrupted nature.[40] More specifically, while the fallen condition of men would, unrestrained, bring disaster, God "restrains by throwing a bridle over them only that they may not break loose, inasmuch as he foresees their control to be expedient to preserve all that is."[41]

One external means by which God accomplishes this restraint is the law, which Calvin calls the second office of the law.[42] He describes the relation of the law to the unregenerate this way: "All who are still unregenerate feel—some more obscurely, some more openly—that they are not drawn to obey the law voluntarily, but impelled by a violent fear do so against their will and despite their opposition to it."[43] Further, as noted above, magistrates have also been installed in their office by God for the purpose of maintaining "public innocence, modesty, decency, and tranquility...."[44] This divine intention, of course, applies to humanity in general, including the unregenerate.

---

[39] Barth rejects this idea in many places. Grabill, 31, points to an example in, *Church Dogmatics*, IV.1, *The Doctrine of Reconciliation*, ed. G. W. Bromiley and T. F. Torrance, trans. G. W. Bromiley (Edinburgh: T. & T. Clark, 1992), 373. On this note, Calvin also clearly rejects any conception of "Incarnation Anyway", and stresses that the likeness of God in Adam was not based on the model of the future Messiah, but "ought to be sought only in those marks of excellence with which God has distinguished Adam above over all other living creatures." *Institutes* II.12.6. This undermines any theological method that would entail true justice could only be known through an analysis of Jesus' character, since Jesus himself is modeled after the prelapsarian Adam, not the other way around.

[40] *Institutes* II.3.3.

[41] *Institutes* II.3.3.

[42] *Institutes* II.7.10.

[43] *Institutes* II.7.10.

[44] *Institutes* IV.20.9.

In the case of the regenerate, God's grace operates in different ways. Calvin neatly summarizes the mode of divine activity:

> God works in his elect in two ways: within, through his Spirit; without, through his Word. By his Spirit, illuminating their minds and forming their hearts to the love of and cultivation of righteousness, he makes them a new creation. By his Word, he arouses them to desire, to seek after, and to attain that same renewal.[45]

This succinct description addresses two simultaneous concerns. That is, it explains how God ameliorates the effects of sin on both the intellect and the will, and describes how God works both directly upon the soul and indirectly through means, in this case the word of God.

Calvin elaborates on how this instrument functions in his description of the third use of the Law, explaining that it both informs them of God's will and stirs them to do it.[46] Thus, the Spirit uses the Law to resolve both the problem of the intellect (lack of knowledge of God's will), and the problem of the will (implicitly, sloth). The consequence of this saving work is the restoration of the supernatural gifts humanity lost at the fall,[47] which as we noted above are the perfections of the natural faculties of humanity.

The implication of all the above for our present study amounts to this: humanity was created to be a political animal, and despite the effects of the fall, God still intends this purpose to be achieved to some degree, and by various kinds of grace presently accomplishes this end in an imperfect yet real way. The difficulties in knowing the right way to act, and in choosing to do it, are real, but by divine grace are not insurmountable. Further, the obligation God laid upon all human beings to do justice remains as binding as ever. Thus, as we move on to discuss the particular obligations of justice in relation to the state below, we must keep in mind that nothing in Calvin's doctrine makes the achievement of civil justice impossible. His doctrine of God and nature undermine any kind of quietist fatalism, and his doctrine of grace removes the potential barrier that might have been provided in his doctrine of sin.

---

[45] *Institutes* II.5.5.

[46] *Institutes* II.7.12.

[47] *Institutes* II.2.12.

The Case of Tyranny

With this foundation in place, we can now move to the more specific question of Calvin's teaching about resistance, and when it can and cannot be justified. In the course of his final chapter in the 1559 *Institutes*, Calvin comes upon the subject of what submission is owed to magistrates, and especially those of an unjust character. He writes:

> Yet, we need not labor to prove that a wicked king is the Lord's wrath upon the earth…, for a I believe no man will contradict me; and thus nothing more would be said of a king than of a robber who seizes your possessions, of an adulterer who pollutes your marriage bed, or of a murderer who seeks to kill you. For Scripture reckons all such calamities among God's curses.
>
> But let us, rather, pause here to prove this, which does not so easily settle in men's minds. In a very wicked man utterly unworthy of all honor, provided he has the public power in his hands, that noble and divine power resides which the Lord has by his Word given to the ministers of his justice and judgment. Accordingly, he should be held in the same reverence and esteem by his subjects, in so far as public obedience is concerned, in which they would hold the best of kings if he were given to them.[48]

He argues further that just as wives and children have a duty of obedience to their husbands and parents even if the latter are unjust, so it is the case of subjects: "all ought to try not to … inquire about another's duties, but every man should keep in mind that one duty which is his own."[49] Those who are persecuted by magistrates ought rather to reflect upon their faults, consider how they provide the Lord reason for the oppression, and pray to God for aid.[50]

The Reformer does add three exceptions to this rule, however. The first is that God sometimes anoints what we might call charismatic revolutionaries from among his own people to overthrow tyrants.[51] Calvin's basically cessationist approach to revelation puts this exception on weak foot-

---

[48] *Institutes* IV.20.25.

[49] *Institutes* IV.20.29.

[50] *Institutes* IV.20.29.

[51] *Institutes* IV.20.30.

ing, however. As John L. Thompson notes, Calvin falls on the other extreme of the spectrum from Müntzer on the continuation of prophecy.[52] His general mentality is obvious in passages like the one Thompson cites from Calvin's commentary on Genesis:

> Moreover, I perceive that God then commonly made known his will by oracles. Once more, if we consider the magnitude of the affair, it was more fitting that the secret should be revealed by the mouth of God, than manifested by the testimony of man. In our times a different method prevails. For God does not, at this day, reveal things future by such miracles; and the teaching of the Law, the Prophets, and the Gospel, which comprises the perfection of wisdom, is abundantly sufficient for the regulation of our course of life.[53]

Yet in other places Calvin admits a degree of uncertainty about the place of such gifts in his day (and by extension, therefore, ours). Paul Elbert mentions one such text,[54] found in *Institutes* IV.3.4: "Paul applies the name 'prophets' not to all who were interpreters of God's will, but to those who excelled in a particular revelation.... This class either does not exist today or is less commonly seen."[55] Further, as Elbert mentions,[56] Calvin confessed the matter was hard for him:

> If any one is of a different opinion [on the meaning of the term "prophet" in 1 Corinthians 12], I have no objection to his being so, and will not raise any quarrel on that account. For it is difficult to form a judgment as to gifts and offices of which the Church has been so long deprived,

---

[52] John L. Thompson, "Patriarchs, Polygamy, and Private Resistance: John Calvin and Others on Breaking God's Rules," *The Sixteenth Century Journal* 25, no. 1 (1994): 27.

[53] John Calvin on Genesis 25:22, in *Commentaries on the First Book of Moses Called Genesis*, vol. 2, trans. John King (Edinburgh: The Calvin Translation Society, 1850), 43.

[54] Paul Elbert, "Calvin and the Spiritual Gifts," *Journal of the Evangelical Theological Society* 22, no. 3 (1979): 245.

[55] *Institutes* IV.3.4.

[56] Elbert, 243 n.44.

excepting only that there are some traces, or shadows of them still to be seen.[57]

Calvin's general disposition would probably lead him to reject this kind of justification for resistance in practice, but at least in theory his tentative openness to charismatic phenomena would not demand such a rejection.

The second exception is that even private citizens have a duty to passively resist obeying commands of the magistrate that require disobedience to God—that is, in his words, private citizens should let such commands "go unesteemed...."[58] The third appears in his famous teaching that lesser magistrates have a duty to resist tyrannical higher magistrates:

> For if there are now any magistrates of the people, appointed to restrain the willfulness of kings (as in ancient times the ephors were set against the Spartan kings, or the tribunes of the people against the Roman consuls, or the demarchs against the senate of the Athenians; and perhaps, as things now are, such power as the three estates exercise in every realm when they hold their chief assemblies), I am so far from forbidding them to withstand, in accordance with their duty, the fierce licentiousness of kings, that, if they wink at kings who violently fall upon and assault the lowly common folk, I declare that their dissimulation involves nefarious perfidy, because they dishonestly betray the freedom of the people, of which they know that they have been appointed protectors by God's ordinance.[59]

At this point I must acknowledge the difficulty in determining with certainty exactly what kind of resistance Calvin envisages even in this well-known text. In Ralph Keen's provocative article, "The Limits of Power and Obedience in the Later Calvin," he notes some lexical ambiguities in the Reformer's choice of words. More particularly, "moderates" is used by Calvin for the way in which the Spirit acts upon the will of an individual; "intercession" is used by him also to describe the intercession of the saints;

---

[57] John Calvin on 1 Corinthians 12:28, in *Commentary on the Epistles of Paul the Apostle to the Corinthians*, vol. 2., trans. John Pringle (Ediburgh: The Calvin Translation Society, 1848), 416.

[58] *Institutes* IV.20.32.

[59] *Institutes* IV.20.31.

and the French version's *"s'oppose et resister"* had the meanings of "disagree" and "refuse" at the time of his writing.[60] These points might make possible Keen's assertion that "Calvin has passive obedience (for private persons) and moral exhortation (for magistrates) in mind."[61]

Nevertheless, the more likely reading of Calvin's position puts him in continuity with a line of thinking originated by Philip of Hesse. As Quentin Skinner notes, Hesse justified armed resistance on the part of lesser magistrates based on the Imperial constitution of the time.[62] That is, his arguments took as their foundation positive law principles rather than natural law ones. As we will see below, this was the position of Peter Martyr Vermigli, and Skinner notes that it was that of Martin Bucer as well.[63] The evidence that Calvin held this view comes in texts like the one cited above, and in comments he made elsewhere. For example in his letter to Admiral de Coligny regarding the conspiracy of Amboise, he writes: "…that if the princes of the blood demanded to be maintained in their rights for the common good, and if the Parliament joined them in their quarrel, that it would be lawful for all good subjects to lend them armed resistance."[64]

Regardless of the lexical ambiguity Keen notes in the *Institutes* passage, Calvin clearly supports *armed* resistance against superior magistrates in some cases. There have been various attempts in the history of Calvin research, however, to argue that held views more radical than the Hessian line. For the sake of fairness, two recent example of this kind of deserves some engagement.

Two Alternative Readings of Calvin
Skinner on the Institutes

Skinner made lexical arguments in the opposite direction of Keen's, suggesting the Reformer's choice of terms indicates a democratic mind.

---

[60] Ralph Keen, "The Limits of Power and Obedience in the Later Calvin," *Calvin Theological Journal* 27 (1992): 272 n.60.

[61] Ibid.

[62] Quentin Skinner, *Foundations of Modern Political Thought, vol. 2: The Age of Reformation* (Cambridge: CUP, 1978), 195.

[63] Ibid., 205–206.

[64] John Calvin, *Letters of John Calvin*, ed. Jules Bonnet, trans. Marcus Robert Gilchrist (Philadelphia: Presbyterian Board of Publication, 1858), 175.

That is, in using the terms *populares magistratus* not "inferior", by saying they are "appointed" and not "ordained", and by warning that a betrayal on this matter would be a betrayal of the people's liberty, the Reformer suggests the magistrates with authority to resist derive their authority from the people. Skinner contends that Calvin's examples of the ephors, tribunes, and demarchs all confirm this reading.[65] But H. A. Lloyd has convincingly shown that the words Calvin chose derive from Roman law about legal guardianship, and does not imply that the "ward" in question appointed its own guardian.[66]

Nijenhuis on Rebellion in the July 31, 1562 Sermon on 2 Samuel 8

A similar argument appears in a recent essay by Willem Nijenhuis. He contends that Calvin expanded his justification of rebellion in his 1562 sermon on 2 Samuel 8:

> Again taking Abraham as an example of a private person offering armed resistance, he comes this time to the formulation of a second 'reigle commune': not only the lower magistrates, but all citizens are called upon to resist an evil ruler so as to protect the poor. '... And this has been enjoined on all people in general; I tell you, this was said not only to princes, magistrates, and public prosecutors, but also to all private persons ... Consequently, we see that this is a common rule referring to all: ... oppose evil and offer resistance, when support for the troubled poor and the relief they need is called in question.'[67]

In a section from this passage that Nijenhuis omits, Calvin elaborates on his point that the command to do justice and judgment applies even to private individuals:

> For instance, the eighteenth chapter of Genesis states that although Abraham was responsible only to govern his own family, still he said that he would carry out justice to those whom God had given into his charge and placed under his

---

[65] Skinner, 232–33.

[66] H. A. Lloyd, "Calvin and the Duty of Guardians to Resist," *The Journal of Ecclesiastical History* 32.1 (1981): 66–67.

[67] Willem Nijenhuis, *Ecclesia Reformata: Studies on the Reformation*, 2 vols. (Leiden: E. J. Brill, 1994), 2:92.

> protection, and that would teach them what was appropriate and essential so that they could exercise justice and judgment.... .[68]

In light of this evidence Nijenhuis concludes: "It seems that life had become stronger than doctrine, even for the greatest systematist among the Reformers."[69] Unfortunately, it seems that Nijenhuis has perhaps misread Calvin at this point. Nijenhuis alludes in his introduction to the text to the events of Genesis 14, i.e., Abraham's war, but Calvin in the sermon is not appealing to those events; rather, he refers to Genesis 18, where God determines to reveal his plans regarding Sodom to Abraham. There is no armed action of any kind in Calvin's text.

This conclusion forces a question upon those who would agree with Calvin's broader magisterial Reformed theology. The Reformer has permitted some armed resistance in certain situations, but only the basis of positive law. What about situations where there are no such laws on the books? Must those who agree with Calvin's fundamental theology agree with restrictive constitutional justification for resistance, or can they go further? There are at least two major reasons to think they can. Firstly, others who affirm the same broader Reformed theology come to different practical conclusions. Secondly, there are significant tensions within Calvin's own position. The first reason opens up the possibility for reasonable disagreement with Calvin; the second seems to require us to disagree with him. Before discussing Calvin's change of opinion, we will therefore note two other positions on resistance promulgated by Reformed writers roughly around his time. The first is that of Peter Martyr Vermigli, and the second of *Vindiciae, Contra Tyrannos*.

Two Approximate Contemporaries of Calvin on Resistance
Vermigli on Resistance

Vermigli is similar to Calvin in opposing the revolutionary logic of Anabaptists, requiring submission on the part of private citizens, and upholding the authority of the magistrate. This is true even in the case of tyrants. However, he does provide a few notable exceptions to his general

---

[68] John Calvin, *Sermons on 2 Samuel: Chapters 1-13*, trans. Douglas Kelly (Edinburgh: Banner of Truth Trust, 1992), 419.

[69] Nijenhuis, 2:92.

norm. These fall into two basic kinds: exceptions based on perennial facts about reality, and exceptions based on the particular constitutions of various states. There are two cases of the first kind, one of which we have already seen in Calvin. The first one is perhaps the least controversial, i.e., that a people may resist a tyrant if he is attacking the city but has not yet established sovereignty over it.[70] The second one is perhaps, at least for present day readers, the most controversial: Vermigli allows for the possibility that God might anoint a private liberator directly, though he notes that no individual should follow this pattern "unlesse he be such a one as feeleth, and hath a sure trial in himself of the same vocation."[71] This is ultimately permissible because God's authority supersedes that of his deputies, even if they are magistrates.[72]

The third exception is the most interesting, based as it is on constitutional reasoning. In this case it is best to quote Vermigli directly:

> But there be others in the Common weale, which in place and dignitie are inferior unto Princes, and yet in verie deed doe elect the superior power, and by certaine laws doe governe the Commonweale: as at this day we see done by the Electors of the Empire: And perhaps the same is done in other kingdoms. To these undoubtedly if the Prince perfourme not his covenants and promises, it is lawfull to constraine and bring him into order, and by force to compel him to perfourme the conditions and covenaunts which he had promised, and that by warre when it cannot otherwise be doone.[73]

Robert M. Kingdon notes: "Vermigli clearly felt that this election constituted a contract, and if the emperor did not keep his part of it, the electors could force him to obedience."[74] He adds, however, that the Reformer's attempts to suggest this is true of constitutions in general is not

---

[70] Robert M. Kingdon, *The Political Thought of Peter Martyr Vermigli: Selected Texts and Commentary* (Geneva: Librairie Droz, 1980), 101.

[71] Ibid., 68.

[72] Ibid., 68.

[73] Ibid., 99-100.

[74] Ibid., xvii; cf. also p. xix.

convincing on a historical level.[75] And he notes a contradiction appears in Vermigli's corpus on this matter: the Reformer says resistance to the ancient Israelite kings was never permissible because God had ordained a government by succession (not election), yet he also approved of some practices in Denmark and England that contradicted this principle.[76]

Thus, Vermigli allows resistance on the grounds of a normal natural justice (resistance to a foreign invader who has not yet won sovereignty), of supernatural divine intervention in accord with natural justice (God, the ultimate source of authority, directly anointing a liberator), and of positive law principles (the alleged constitutional provision for lesser magistrates to resist higher ones). These exceptions all follow with ease from his general principles: God as the source of law wills order by means of law, and none of these contradict this general rule.

Vermigli's position thus appears identical to Calvin's. Vermigli allows for armed resistance against a magistrate, and not simply moral exhortation. Further, Vermigli's position is based fundamentally on constitutional, positive law grounds, and as it did with Calvin, this conclusion leaves one wondering what the persecuted Reformed might do in a context where no such constitutional provisions are present. This leads us to our third text, the pseudonymously authored *Vindiciae, Contra Tyrannos*.

Vindiciae Contra Tyrannos

Though as with Calvin and Vermigli a complete survey of *VCT* is impossible, we can note areas of agreement with ease. Firstly, once again, the possibility of a charismatically endowed individual liberator is explicitly accepted,[77] though with a qualification similar to Vermigli's: "For if anyone lays claim to that authority for himself, as though he were inspired by the divine spirit, he should certainly make sure that he is not puffed up with pride, that he is not God to himself...."[78] And secondly, *VCT* asserts the right of lesser magistrates, which are present in "every well-constituted

---

[75] Ibid., xvii.

[76] Ibid., xix.

[77] Stephanius Junius Brutus, *Vindiciae, Contra Tyrannos: or, concerning the legitimate power of a prince over the people, and of the people over a prince*, ed. and trans. George Garnett (Cambridge: Cambridge University Press, 1994), 63.

[78] Ibid., 62.

kingdom",[79] to resist as representatives of the people,[80] on the grounds of the king's breach of the law against the people.[81] Going beyond even Vermigli, however, *VCT* defends this conclusion on the basis of natural law reasoning, and not just positive constitutional law. For example, it argues directly regarding the conditionality of the people's agreement to submit: "Yet even if these ceremonies, these rites and these oaths did not occur, yet surely nature itself teaches well enough that kings are constituted by the people on the condition that they command well...."[82] It considers it unthinkable that a people would ever consent to a ruler being free to slaughter them upon a whim.[83] And it responds to the objection that some kingdoms are formed by force rather than consent in this way:

> What, I answer, if a robber, a pirate, or a tyrant... shall have extorted a promissory note at the point of a sword? For is it not well known that faith elicited by force does not bind—and especially in a case where something is promised contrary to good practice... and the law of nature...? For what could be more in conflict with nature than for a people to put itself in fetters and shackles; for it to promise a prince that it would put its own jugular against the point of a knife, and for it to turn its own hand violently against itself—for that is what this clearly amounts to? So there is a mutual obligation between king and people which—whether civil or merely natural; whether tacit or expressed in words—cannot be abrogated in any way, or violated by any right, or rescinded by force.[84]

So *VCT* goes beyond Vermigli and Calvin. But even this is not the full measure of the implications of the text. While *VCT* explicitly rules out private rebellion on the grounds that God has not given such people the

---

[79] Ibid., 47.

[80] Ibid., 46.

[81] Ibid., 45.

[82] Ibid., 139.

[83] Ibid., 104.

[84] Ibid., 139-140.

right of the sword,[85] the logic of the document's answer to its final question seems to undermine this principle. That fourth and final question is: "Whether neighbouring princes may by right, or ought, to tender assistance to subjects of other princes who are being persecuted on account of pure religion, or oppressed by manifest tyranny?"[86] This question directly anticipates contemporary discussions about the principle of international law now known as the Responsibility to Protect (R2P), often invoked in favour of military humanitarian interventions. On this matter, *VCT* argues that neighbouring princes have an obligation to intervene in the case of a tyranny even when the oppression was only in secular matters, and that they have an obligation to do so based in some way on the principles of justice and charity.[87] George Garnett elaborates on this matter: "If the basis for a neighbouring prince's duty to intervene in a case of secular tyranny is the natural obligation of every man to his fellow man, then it is difficult to see why any individual may not act for the same reasons."[88] He shrewdly continues: "If the circumscriptions on the licence of individuals are stripped away – and with them most of the Roman law framework – what remains is a far more anarchic argument, largely based on natural law."[89] In connection with this point, George also highlights the reliance of *VCT* on the arguments of Cicero in this final question,[90] a figure whom Vermigli[91] condemned by name as a *violator* of natural law on this matter, and whom Calvin would probably have condemned implicitly for similar reasons.[92]

Thus in comparison with *Vindiciae, Contra Tyrannos*, we can see that those holding to Reformed theological premises can come to different political conclusions than Calvin did. As suggested above, this can at least show us that reasonable disagreement with the Genevan is possible. But can

---

[85] Ibid., 60.

[86] Ibid., 173.

[87] Ibid., 185.

[88] Ibid., lii-liii.

[89] Ibid., liii.

[90] Ibid., liii.

[91] Kingdon, 24.

[92] *Institutes* II.2.24.

we go further? Can we argue that disagreement with Calvin is necessary? It seems so.

The Problem in Calvin

Returning to the figure in focus in this paper, the question that can immediately arise for contemporary readers is whether Calvin's whole position escapes the charge of inconsistency. And it arguably does not. The Reformer's justification for passivity on the part of private citizens in *Institutes* IV.20 can be divided into several kinds of arguments. The first he briefly passes by is convenience for the common good.[93] The implication here is that anarchy would present significant difficulties for achieving that common end, and that resistance would lead to anarchy. The second argument is more principled, based on the idea that the power of magistrates derives from God, and so deserves a correlative veneration.[94] The third kind of approach is directly Biblical: Calvin cites many texts that enjoin submission to magistrates upon subjects.[95] The fourth is roughly a natural law argument: just as the inferiors in relationships like marriage and family (wives and children) owe obedience regardless of how well their superiors treat them, so do subjects owe unconditional obedience to magistrates.[96]

The problem of consistency arises in relation to all of these arguments, because none of these reasons for subordination would seem to allow the possibility of a justified resistance of any kind, even that of lesser magistrates. But Calvin does exactly this, as we noted above. The Reformer might contend that qualifications on these reasons for obedience are implicit; they require submission to the law firstly, and to superior magistrates as a means to that end. But this liberates others to argue for further implicit qualifications, as *VCT* shows. And the same moral tension that arose in the arguments of *VCT* would seem to arise out of Calvin's own logic: if we have a positive obligation to defend and uphold the good of our neighbour, this might lead to conflict with an oppressive state. Moreover, Calvin's appeal to the authority of God in providentially establishing authorities cuts across his insistence that providence is not fate, but rather that we are called

---

[93] Ibid. IV.20.22

[94] Ibid. IV.20.22.

[95] Ibid. IV.20.22; cf. the various texts he cites to this effect in *Institutes* IV.20.25-28.

[96] Ibid. IV.20.29.

to consciously participate in providence by resisting foreseen perils. He recognizes that providence brings even thieves into our houses, but his attempt to make providence do more for tyrants morally than it does for thieves does not sit easily with a natural sense of justice. Further, in relation to the appropriate submission of natural inferiors to superiors, we should note that Calvin in fact permitted wives to divorce their husbands for adultery or sexual perversion or desertion,[97] as these are grave violations of the covenant of marriage.[98]

In supporting our natural sense of justice while at the same time demanding absolute submission to tyrants when constitutional provisions for resistance are not present, Calvin's positive doctrine leaves us ensnared in a quandary. Theologians today cannot rest content with this situation, however, especially in politically turbulent days such as we are currently experiencing. For this reason, the rest of this essay will attempt to establish that Calvin's more fundamental theology can actually be used to justify resistance, even if the Reformer himself thought otherwise.

The Theological Foundations of Resistance

It is perhaps helpful to return to Calvin's sentiments on the relation of divine providence to human deliberation. As he writes in the *Institutes*:

> considering that whatever creatures are capable of furnishing anything to him are offered by the Lord into his hand, he will put them to use as lawful instruments of divine providence. And since it is uncertain what will be the outcome of the business he is undertaking ... he will aspire with zeal to that which he deems expedient for himself, as far as it can be attained by intelligence and understanding.[99]

Calvin's doctrine of providence inspires the opposite of passive fatalism; it encourages the individual to aim at the best possible outcome using all the means available to him. This has clear relevance to our issue, in that it might allow that a potentially successful revolt could be undertaken if the

---

[97] John Witte, Jr. explains Calvin's views in great detail in his *From Sacrament to Contract: Marriage, Religion, and Law in the Western Tradition*, 2nd ed. (Louisville: Westminster John Knox Press, 2012), 196–98.

[98] Ibid., 189.

[99] *Institutes* I.17.9.

means were available to do so. Providence does sometimes put tyrants in place; but providence also sometimes provides subjects with the capacity to act towards a better future.

The Reformer's logic takes us even further than this. Above, in relation to his exposition of the command "thou shalt not kill", we saw that Calvin argued that the command actually implies our positive obligation to do everything we can to defend our neighbour from evil. Calvin wrote: 'We are accordingly commanded, if we find anything of use to us in saving our neighbors' lives, faithfully to employ it; if there is anything that makes for their peace, to see to it; if anything harmful, to ward it off; if they are in any danger, to lend a helping hand."[100]

The absolute nature of this "everything" would most naturally include armed resistance to tyranny. If the command carries positive obligations to not only refrain from harm, but also to help others, and if the right of the magistrate to compliance is already tacitly limited by the constitutional duties of lesser magistrates, there seems no principled reason why the logic could not ever extend to a popular revolution. Certainly, the moral question seems very much open. As Oliver O'Donovan puts it with regards to the parallel issue of R2P:

> There may well be dangers attached to the kind of humanitarian intervention which has been argued for; but they need to be overwhelmingly conspicuous if they are to provide support for a universal prohibition running counter to the humanitarian instincts of civilised peoples. To turn one's back while a neighbouring community is being slaughtered is not an easy thing to recommend; and international law should not demand it without reasons so strong as to seem, when pointed out, morally irresistible. Certainly, the maintenance of a 'rather tidy legal regime' based on the sovereignty of the nation-state will not suffice.[101]

Calvin's defense of the principles of just war theory could further support this conclusion. In his comments on war in the *Institutes*, he derives the justifiability of war from the general purpose of the state:

---

[100] Ibid. II.8.39.

[101] O'Donovan, *The Just War Revisited* (Cambridge: Cambridge University Press, 2003), 29.

> But kings and people must sometimes take up arms to execute such public vengeance. On this basis we may judge wars lawful which are so undertaken. For if power has been given them to preserve the tranquility of their dominion, to restrain the seditious stirrings of restless men, to help those forcibly oppressed, to punish evil deeds—can they use it more opportunely than to check the fury of one who disturbs both the repose of private individuals and the common tranquility of all, who raises seditious tumults, and by whom violent oppressions and vile misdeeds are perpetuated? If they ought to be the guardians and defenders of the laws, they should also overthrow the efforts of all whose offenses corrupt the discipline of the laws.[102]

Calvin's logic shows why magistrates can exercise judgment on those who are not their proper subjects. His answer implies that fundamental principles of justice demand that those who disturb "the common tranquility of all" be restrained, regardless of normal positive law rules regarding citizenship. The application to the case of tyranny forces itself upon the theorist here. Despite armed resistance being a violation in the strict sense of the criterion of "legitimate authority", one can still intelligibly evaluate a potential act of war against a tyrant on the basis of the rest of the just war criteria. Even apart from the presence of a legally established authority to wage war, those with ethical sense are capable of determining whether a just cause is present that demands armed action. The separability of the criteria opens up a logical space to evaluate the justice of wars against tyrants, and perhaps authorize such action on natural law grounds.

Thus a natural law defense of resistance can be motivated based on principles native to Calvin's thought. But, then, what about the concerns Calvin had about such lines of reasoning? Space cannot permit a point-by-point reply to every relevant argument Calvin made, but a few representative ones can be addressed. They can be categorized into two types: those based on natural law, and those based on scripture.

---

[102] *Institutes* IV.20.11.

Calvin's Difficulties with Resistance
Natural Law Concerns
Hierarchy

While it is true that the Reformer provided a kind of teleological natural law explanation for the existence of magistracy, he also explicitly notes a qualification on the obedience this requires at the end of the *Institutes*:

> ... how absurd would it be that in satisfying men you should incur the displeasure of him for whose sake you obey men themselves! The Lord, therefore, is the King of Kings, who, when he has opened his sacred mouth, must alone be heard, before and above all men; next to him we are subject to those men who are in authority over us, but only in him.[103]

Calvin seems to be appealing to an obvious moral principle at this point. If a means appointed to an end begins to subvert that end, it no longer receives its justification from that end. This logic is indeed commonsensical; it is the same principle used to justify medically necessary amputations. Yet, Calvin taught that the magistrate had a "sole" purpose, "to provide for the common safety and peace of all." Why, then, would the people for whose good the magistrate exists be bound to obey that magistrate when it ceases to act for its proper end? It is not clear that Calvin could avoid falling into the absurdity he recognizes in the parallel case above. That is, unless he took the road his followers later did, and supported a natural law case for resistance.

Peace and Order

Calvin also wanted to preserve a relatively just and peaceful social order, believing that such was natural good of human beings. As an implication of this principle, he upheld the basic principles of just war tradition, as Mark J. Larson has recently shown in his *Calvin's Doctrine of the Christian State*. Included within this tradition are the rules that just wars should be waged for a just cause, and with the right intention, i.e., a just peace. Above I quoted Calvin's justification for war based on the duties of the state, and the examples he gives for justified wars are what would count as just causes. It should be noted that Calvin does not list any minor, frivolous infractions

---

[103] Ibid. IV.20.32.

there. Rather, he speaks of people who disturb "the repose of private individuals and the common tranquility of all, who [raise] seditious tumults, and by whom violent oppressions and vile misdeeds are perpetuated."[104] The Magdeburg Confession around his time, and Calvinist thinkers like Christopher Goodman and "Junius Brutus" after him, would make explicit that resistance is justified not for any failing on the part of the government, but for atrocious and notorious ones, and Calvin's own logic would support this point.

On the matter of right intention, the Reformer upheld the traditional criteria of "last resort" and "prospect of success". With regards to last resort he states plainly:

> For if we are to do far more than that heathen demanded, who wished war to appear as desired peace, assuredly all other means must be tried before having recourse to arms. In fine, in both cases, they must not allow themselves to be carried away by any private feeling, but be guided solely by regard for the public.[105]

And Larson notes[106] an important passage in Calvin's commentaries that supports the principle of prospect of success: "Princes must not allow themselves to sport with human blood, nor must soldiers give themselves up to cruelty, from a desire of gain, as if slaughter were their chief business: but both must be drawn to it by necessity, and by a regard for public advantage."[107]

On the level of natural principles, Oliver O'Donovan notes that the traditional just war criteria of last resort and prospect of success logically flow from the right intention of peace, and this makes sense on an intuitive level.[108] If one is set on a course of violence knowing full well that other

---

[104] Ibid. IV.20.11.

[105] Ibid. IV.20.12.

[106] Mark J. Larson, *Calvin's Doctrine of the State: A Reformed Doctrine and Its American Trajectory, The Revolutionary War, and the Founding of the Republic* (Eugene, Oregon: Wipf & Stock, 2009), 75.

[107] John Calvin, *Commentary on a Harmony of the Evangelists, Matthew, Mark, and Luke*, vol 1., trans. William Pringle (Edinburgh: The Calvin Translation Society, 1845), 195–96.

[108] O'Donovan, 59.

possibilities for peaceful resolution remain untried, or that there is no prospect of armed conflict creating a peaceful social order, including a functioning government, then one cannot be really aiming at peace at all, but rather something more like pure blood lust. And in fact Calvin applied this kind of logic to *jus ad bellum* concerns. He appealed to prospect of success concerns when he counseled against the conspiracy of Amboise: "…I strove to demonstrate to him [Le Renaudie] that he had no warrant for such conduct according to God; and that even according to the world such measures were ill-concerted, presumptuous, and could have no successful issue."[109]

But all this might seem to work contrary to the argument I have been presenting: do they not provide reasons *not* to resist, rather than to do so? This is partly right. The criteria of just cause and right intention do not rule out all possible acts of resistance; if a particular case could meet the criteria, it would be justified. But they would rule out any act that had no reasonable chance of maintaining the kind of relative justice and order that Calvin thought God intended for the present age (as opposed to the perfect justice and peace of the *eschaton*). To put it another way: they would rule out any armed act that would be more likely to produce chaos and rivers of blood than an imperfect but acceptable social order. And so while the line of argument I am pursuing would allow for armed resistance beyond those with official government positions, it would still rule out any course of action with a probability of leading to the anarchy Calvin so dreaded.

One final point should be made here, especially in light of my transgression of the line between constitutionally grounded (lesser magistrate) and naturally grounded (potentially popular) resistance. If we agree that anarchy should be avoided at all costs, and that something as dangerous as popular resistance might be justified only in a specific case where avoiding anarchy seems reasonably likely, an objector could raise a reasonable rejoinder. That is, given how much popular support would be needed for revolutionaries in order for them to establish a new ordered peace after violence, might these individuals not truly be considered as unofficially authorized lesser magistrates? Perhaps it is the case that, in the end, we have simply found a more precisely defined version of the lesser magistrate doctrine. But even if this is so, we have at least more carefully supported the conclu-

---

[109] Calvin, *Letters*, 176.

sion, and brought the logic of the argument more clearly to the surface. Lesser magistrates are not morally significant because they have a title, but because they are more likely to be able to maintain social order through a revolution. It is that ability that matters most, whether an individual or a group has an official status or not.

Biblical Concerns

The Reformer also had exegetical arguments that would seem to undercut the kind of logic being defended here, most notably his rather stark reading of Romans 13's command to submit to governing authorities.[110] There is not space to explore these fully here, but it is worth noting a potential qualification to such arguments. Calvin marshals many passages from scripture against resistance in a general way, and yet seems to regard them all as consistent with his constitutional exception—that duly established lesser magistrates have a duty to resist in certain circumstances. This despite the fact that such an exception is not explicitly present within the texts themselves. No doubt Calvin would say that they are implied in it, since the principle they express is the duty to obey the law, and such exceptions are part of that law. Might we then suggest that the same kind of logic would apply to Calvin's natural law grounds for resistance? That is, if the scriptures presuppose the existence of natural law (as Calvin certainly thought), might we not say that the biblical texts in question also assume the natural law "exceptions" to the general rule of obedience?

Conclusion

While the conclusion of this argument is already a practical one, the analysis of its underlying principles provides grounds for applications on issues beyond revolution. The argument above suggests Calvin's theology can allow that the natural duty to do justice might sometimes supersede their obligation to the magistrate. On his principles, the state exists as means to serve the end of justice, not the other way around, making justice the greater good that demands obedience. At the same time, this justice is one tempered by the gracious divine intent to preserve the common good, a relatively peaceful human society through history. In other words, political judgment itself is properly considered a means to an end of the common

---

[110] *Institutes* IV.20.22; 25-28.

good, and we must seek the former insofar as it upholds the latter. A great number of implications follow from this general teaching; a few can be suggested here.

First, given the ethical parallels between resistance and humanitarian intervention, Calvin's logic sheds light on the latter question as well as the former. Second, even in my "Calvinian argument against Calvin", in fact the Reformer's overall system remains anti-utopian in nature. It recognizes the persistence of sin and so the imperfectability of humanity; it absolutely condemns wars or acts of violence that contravene the general divine will for a relatively just and relatively stable social order. Third, it recognizes a standard of justice rooted in natural law (which is something Calvin does explicitly anyway). This provides common ground for political reasoning with those outside the community of faith. More specifically, Calvin's position has something to say even to oppressed groups in non-Christian societies since it roots its motivation for resistance in principles of justice that bind, are knowable by, and can be obeyed even by unregenerate people.

To put the matter more directly, I have essentially argued that Calvin's doctrine provides a foundation for democratic politics. As Calvin scholar Winthrop S. Hudson once wrote, there are two pillars on which democratic thinking rests: "(1) the idea of limited sovereignty, of a government under law, of limits beyond which government cannot go and to which it must conform; (2) the right of resistance when these limits are exceeded."[111] No serious student of Calvin would deny that Calvin affirmed the first pillar, and clearly he affirmed a version of the second. My argument is that his principles provide for a more robust version than even he realized.

At this point we can step back and see the big picture logic of Calvin's system. God, as goodness and justice himself, created a world that would reflect his goodness and justice. Within that world, he created human beings who are rational, capable of deliberation, and social, meant to live in love toward each other. Human beings are also hierarchical, naturally sorting into levels of subordination. The fall threatened to destroy this design, but by God's common and special grace he intends to preserve, and does preserve, a relative social peace. The state continues to have the mandate to facilitate society's accomplishment of this goal by means of coercion. Yet

---

[111] Hudson, "Democratic Freedom and Religious Faith in the Reformed Tradition," *Church History* 15.3 (1946): 181.

the state may turn from facilitating a relatively just and peaceful social order to actively and egregiously opposing it. In such a situation, Calvin argued that lesser magistrates with the constitutional duty to resist must do so, and that the people were free to provide them with armed support. I have argued that on Calvin's principles, one could contend that the members of the society whose good the magistrate was supposed to serve may act directly to restore that good by means of armed resistance, even apart from constitutional grounds for doing so. The most fundamental principle always remains: every human being has a standing obligation to seek justice and to "seek the peace of the city", for that is what most closely echoes God's ultimate purpose—i.e., his own glory—on a human register. And it would be fair to say that it is this version of Calvin's system that continues to loom over history. As Nijenhuis writes: "The radical accents which were heard every more clearly… have had a lasting influence in areas where Calvinism became the predominant religion. Outside these limits, they continue to reverberate to the present day."[112]

---

[112] Nijenhuis, 2:94.

Bibliography

Barth, Karl. *The Doctrine of Reconciliation*. Vol. IV.1 of *Church Dogmatics*. Edited by G. W. Bromiley and T. F. Torrance. Translated by G. W. Bromiley. Edinburgh: T. & T. Clark, 1992.

Biéler, André. *Calvin's Economic and Social Thought*. Edited by Edward Dommen. Translated by James Greig. Geneva: World Alliance of Reformed Churches, 2005.

Brutus, Stephanus Junius. *Vindiciae, Contra Tyrannos: or, concerning the legitimate power of a prince over the people, and of the people over a prince*. Edited and translated George Garnett. Cambridge: Cambridge University Press, 1994.

Calvin, John. *Calvin's Commentaries*. Vol. 19. Translated by John Owen. Grand Rapids: Baker, 1996. http://www.ccel.org/ccel/calvin/calcom38.xv.viii.html (accessed April 8, 2014).

———. *Commentary on a Harmony of the Evangelists, Matthew, Mark, and Luke*. Vol 1. Translated by William Pringle. Edinburgh: The Calvin Translation Society, 1845.

———. *Commentaries on the First Book of Moses Called Genesis*. Vol. 2. Translated by John King. Edinburgh: The Calvin Translation Society, 1850.

———. *Commentary on the Epistles of Paul the Apostle to the Corinthians*. Vol. 2. Translated by John Pringle. Ediburgh: The Calvin Translation Society, 1848.

———. *Institutes of the Christian Religion*. Edited by John T. McNeill. Translated by Ford Lewis Battles. Philadelphia: The Westminster Press, 1960.

———. *Letters of John Calvin*. Edited by Jules Bonnet. Translated by Marcus Robert Gilchrist. Philadelphia: Presbyterian Board of Publication, 1858.

———. *Sermons on 2 Samuel: Chapters 1–13*. Translated by Douglas Kelly. Edinburgh: Banner of Truth Trust, 1992.

Elbert, Paul. "Calvin and the Spiritual Gifts." *Journal of the Evangelical Theological Society* 22, no. 3 (1979): 235–256.

Fuchs, Eric. "Calvin's Ethics." In *John Calvin's Impact on Church and Society 1509–2009*, edited by Martin Ernst Hirzel and Martin Sallmann, 145–158. Grand Rapids: Eerdmans, 2009.

Grabill, Stephen J. *Rediscovering the Natural Law in Reformed Theological Ethics*. Grand Rapids: Eerdmans, 2006.

Hudson, Winthrop S. "Democratic Freedom and Religious Faith in the Reformed Tradition." *Church History* 15, no. 03 (1946): 177–94.

Kingdon, Robert M. *The Political Thought of Peter Martyr Vermigli: Selected Texts and Commentary*. Geneva: Librairie Droz, 1980.

Larson, Mark J. *Calvin's Doctrine of the State: A Reformed Doctrine and Its American Trajectory, The Revolutionary War, and the Founding of the Republic*. Eugene, OR: Wipf & Stock, 2009.

Lloyd, H. A. "Calvin and the Duty of Guardians to Resist." *The Journal of Ecclesiastical History* 32, no. 01 (1981): 65–67.

Nijenhuis, Willem. *Ecclesia Reformata: Studies on the Reformation*. Vol. 2. Leiden: E. J. Brill, 1994.

O'Donovan, Oliver. *The Just War Revisited*. Cambridge: Cambridge University Press, 2003.

Thompson, John L. "Patriarchs, Polygamy, and Private Resistance: John Calvin and Others on Breaking God's Rules." *The Sixteenth Century Journal* 25, no. 1 (1994): 3–27.

Witte, John, Jr. *The Reformation of Rights: Law, Religion, and Human Rights in Early Modern England.* Cambridge: Cambridge University Press, 2007.

"Bavinck's bug" or "Van Tilian" hypochondria? An analysis of Prof. Oliphint's assertion that cognitive realism and Reformed theology are incompatible

Laurence O'Donnell
Calvin Theological Seminary

I. Introduction

The following is an analysis of two essays by Prof. K. Scott Oliphint wherein he levels criticisms against Herman Bavinck's (1854–1921) formulation of realism as the cognitive foundation for non-theological knowledge (hereafter: philosophy).[1] The form of the reply, a loosely-interpreted scholastic *quaestio*, reflects Bavinck's own presentation of the topic.[2]

A. The question stated

The question Oliphint raises is not regarding the *principium essendi* of theology or philosophy; for he admits that he and Bavinck hold the same view on this point: the triune Lord is the *principium essendi* of all that exists.

The question is not regarding the *principium cognoscendi* of theology; for Oliphint admits that he and Bavinck hold the same view on this point: Holy Scripture is the cognitive *principium unicum* of theology.[3]

Rather, the question regards the *principium cognoscendi* of philosophy. It has two parts: (1) whether Bavinck's affirmation of cognitive realism in phi-

---

[1] Oliphint, "The Prolegomena Principle: Frame and Bavinck," in *Speaking the Truth in Love: The Theology of John M. Frame*, ed. John J. Hughes (Phillipsburg, NJ: P&R, 2009), 201–32; Oliphint, "Bavinck's Realism, The Logos Principle, and *Sola Scriptura*," Westminster Theological Journal 72, no. 2 (2010): 359–90.

[2] David S. Sytsma notes that, formally, Bavinck's assertion of realism vis-à-vis rationalism and empiricism can be read along the lines of a scholastic *quaestio*. "Herman Bavinck's Thomistic Epistemology: The Argument and Sources of his Principia of Science," in *Five Studies in the Thought of Herman Bavinck, A Creator of Modern Dutch Theology*, ed. John Bolt (Lewiston, NY: Edwin Mellen, 2011), 19.

[3] Cf. Oliphint, "Bavinck's Realism," 361; with Oliphint, "The Prolegomena Principle," 207–08.

losophy is compatible with his affirmation that Holy Scripture is the cognitive *principium unicum* of theology, and (2) whether Bavinck's formulation of the Logos as the external and internal cognitive foundation of philosophy is compatible with his affirmation of cognitive realism. Oliphint denies both; we affirm both.

B. *The state of the question*
1. *Past and present scholarship*

Even though it is our intent to analyze this question systematically rather than historically, it is important nevertheless to place the question in its historical context; for Oliphint's formulation of the question—which itself is an instance of the perennial question of the proper relation between theology and philosophy—is rooted in the anti-scholastic intellectual milieu that arose in the early twentieth century at the Free University in Amsterdam and was imported into North America via several streams, one of which being the apologetics of Cornelius Van Til (1895–1987) of whom Oliphint is an ardent disciple.[4] John M. Frame, another disciple of Van Til, has debated the same issue with Richard A. Muller and David F. Wells.[5] More recently J. V. Fesko and Guy M. Richard have argued that Van Til's rejection of natural theology—which position is a correlate of his rejections of scholasticism and realism—is out of accord with the Westminster Standards, with the views of prominent Westminster divines, and with the catholic tradition appropriated by Reformed doctors throughout the early and

---

[4] On Oliphint's esteem of Van Til, see Oliphint, "Desert Bloom in Amarillo," *New Horizons* (July 2010), http://opc.org/nh.html?article_id=666; Oliphint, "Foreword," in Cornelius Van Til, *The Defense of the Faith*, ed. K. Scott Oliphint, 4th ed. (Phillipsburg, NJ: P&R, 2008), xi–xiii; and Oliphint, "The Consistency of Van Til's Methodology," *Westminster Theological Journal* 52, no. 1 (1990): 49.

[5] Whether *sola Scriptura* can rightly serve as the *principium cognoscendi* of non-theological knowledge is the underlying issue in the debate between Frame and Muller. See Frame, "Muller on Theology," *Westminster Theological Journal* 56, no. 1 (Spring 1994): 133–51; Muller, "The Study of Theology Revisited: A Response to John Frame," *Westminster Theological Journal* 56, no. 2 (Fall 1994): 409–17. The same underlying issue was subsequently debated in Frame, "In Defense of Something Close to Biblicism: Reflections on *Sola Scriptura* and History in Theological Method," *Westminster Theological Journal* 59, no. 2 (Fall 1997): 269–91; Muller, "Historiography in the Service of Theology and Worship: Toward Dialogue with John Frame," *Westminster Theological Journal* 59, no. 2 (Fall 1997): 301–10; and Wells, "On Being Framed," *Westminster Theological Journal* 59, no. 2 (Fall 1997): 293–300.

high periods of Protestant doctrinal fluorescence.[6] Additionally, T. David Gordon and John Bolt have argued, albeit implicitly, against Van Til's position,[7] and Donald MacLeod has attempted to forge a middle way of sorts between the opposing views.[8] In this light Oliphint's "Bavinck's bug" critique is simply the most recent restatement of Van Til's position.[9]

There are no extant studies aimed directly at responding to Oliphint's criticisms. However, David Sytsma has recently published a trenchant historical-theological essay on the argument and sources of Bavinck's epistemology. In his summary of scholarship regarding Bavinck's formulation of the *principia* of science, he notes Van Til's criticisms but does not attempt a response other than stating that Van Til's repudiation of Bavinck's affirmation of "common notions" is "a significant departure from both catholic and Reformed tradition."[10] As will become evident below, Sytsma provides a more historically contextualized, more accurate, and more compelling reading of Bavinck's formulations than does Oliphint (or Van Til). Theodore G. Van Raalte's essay in the same volume analyzes Bavinck's philo-

---

[6] "Natural Theology and the Westminster Confession of Faith," in *The Westminster Confession into the 21st Century: Essays in Remembrance of the 350th Anniversary of the Westminster Assembly*, vol. 3, ed. J. Ligon Duncan III (Ross-shire, Scotland: Mentor, 2009), 223–66.

[7] Gordon, "How My Mind Has Changed: The Insufficiency of Scripture," *Modern Reformation* 11, no. 1 (2002): 18–23; Bolt, "*Sola Scriptura* as an Evangelical Theological Method?," in *Reforming or Conforming: Post-Conservative Evangelicals and the Emerging Church*, ed. Gary L. W. Johnson and Ronald N. Gleason (Wheaton, Ill: Crossway Books, 2008), 154–65. Oliphint interprets Bolt's essay as a challenge to the "Van Tilian" position on *sola Scriptura*, especially as that position has been as expounded by Frame, and he polemicizes against Bolt's thesis accordingly: cf. Oliphint, "The Prolegomena Principle," 212–13, 228–30; with Oliphint, "Bavinck's Realism," 364–65, 389–90.

[8] "Bavinck's Prolegomena: Fresh Light on Amsterdam, Old Princeton, and Cornelius Van Til," *Westminster Theological Journal* 68, no. 2 (2006): 261–82. Insofar as Macleod omits Van Til's criticisms of Bavinck's thought, his interpretation of the two positions is unconvincing. Nevertheless, he does highlight the significant continuity that attains between the two positions.

[9] The recent essay by Dan Strange, who appropriates John Frame's formulation of *sola Scriptura* and applies it to politics in the United Kingdom, can be included among recent "Van Tilian" formulations: "Not Ashamed! The Sufficiency of Scripture for Public Theology," *Themelios* 36, no. 2 (2011): 238–60.

[10] "Herman Bavinck's Thomistic Epistemology," 43; cf. ibid., pp. 2–4, 18.

sophical epistemology from another angle: the moral epistemology undergirding Bavinck's use of natural law theory.[11] Both of these studies provide grist for the reply to objections below.

2. The historical context of Oliphint's "Van Tilian" criticism

Oliphint levels his criticism against Bavinck's thought explicitly upon the basis of Van Til's earlier criticism.[12] According to Van Til, Bavinck's epistemological formulations are beholden to "scholasticism," which term Van Til defines as a wrongheaded attempt to synthesize the antipodes of pagan (Greek) philosophy and Christian theology. The crux of Van Til's critique is his assertion that Holy Scripture is the cognitive *principium unicum* of theology *and* philosophy. Upon this premise he concludes that cognitive realism is incompatible with a truly Christian view of philosophy insofar as realism posits reason (i.e., perception of the extra-mental world via sense experience) as its cognitive foundation rather than Holy Scripture. In Van Til's view this formulation entails rationalistic autonomy.

What Oliphint overlooks in his appropriation of Van Til's criticism is that the criticism is in fact an appropriation of Herman Dooyeweerd's (1894–1977) definition of "scholasticism" and corresponding criticisms of Bavinck's "scholastic" epistemology.[13] Noting the true origin and context of

---

[11] "Unleavened Morality? Herman Bavinck on Natural Law," in *Five Studies in the Thought of Herman Bavinck*, 57–100.

[12] Cf. Oliphint, "The Prolegomena Principle," 206; with Oliphint, "Bavinck's Realism," 360. The passage Oliphint cites is Cornelius Van Til, *An Introduction to Systematic Theology: Prolegomena and the Doctrines of Revelation, Scripture, and God*, ed. William Edgar, 2nd ed. (Phillipsburg, NJ: P&R, 2007), 94–95. Van Til levels several more criticisms against Bavinck's thought, all of which relate to the underlying issue of the validity of Reformed scholasticism especially with respect to philosophical epistemology. All of Oliphint's criticism are recapitulations of Van Til's criticisms. For a catalog and analysis of the latter, see Brian G. Mattson, "Van Til on Bavinck: An Assessment," *Westminster Theological Journal* 70, no. 1 (2008): 111–27; Sytsma, "Herman Bavinck's Thomistic Epistemology," 2–4; Laurence O'Donnell, "Kees Van Til als Nederlandse-Amerikaanse, Neo-Calvinistisch-Presbyteriaan apologeticus: An Analysis of Cornelius Van Til's Presupposition of Reformed Dogmatics with special reference to Herman Bavinck's *Gereformeerde Dogmatiek*" (ThM thesis, Grand Rapids, MI: Calvin Theological Seminary, 2011), http://j.mp/ODonnell_ThM_Thesis, chs. 5–7.

[13] See O'Donnell, "Kees Van Til," ch. 6; regarding the influence of the Free University philosophers upon Van Til, cf. John Bolt, "Een gemiste en een nieuwe kans: Herman Bavinck over openbaring en religie," in *Ontmoetingen met Herman Bavinck*,

this criticism illuminates its connection to a larger question that was being debated at the Free University in Amsterdam: the validity of Reformed scholasticism, especially its affirmation of an eclectic, modified Aristotelian-Thomistic cognitive realism.[14] At the risk of overgeneralization one way this debate can be summarized is as a dispute between Bavinck's successor in the chair of dogmatics and fellow advocate of Reformed scholasticism, Valentijn Hepp (1879–1950), and two philosophy professors at the same school—Dooyeweerd and D. H. Th. Vollenhoven (1892–1978)—both of whom were overtly antagonistic toward Reformed scholastic modes of thought. For instance, Dooyeweerd concludes his lengthy analysis of the anti-Christian "scholasticism" he sees in Abraham Kuyper's (1837–1920), Jan Woltjer's (1849–1917), and Bavinck's proclivities for philosophical realism with the following ultimatum: "an urgent and necessary process is laid upon us by virtue of our reformational calling to come to a critical choice between the principles of the Reformation and the traditional philosophical ideas that sprung from an entirely different root."[15] By "traditional philosophical ideas" he means Reformed scholasticism's appropriation of philosophical concepts from the catholic tradition such as body-soul dualism, the Logos theory, the *analogia entis*, the *universalia in re* and *ante rem in mente divina*, and cognitive realism.

The fruits of this project appear in such works as Vollenhoven's *Calvinism and the reformation of philosophy* (1933) and Dooyeweerd's *Philosophy of the cosmonomic idea* (1935–36), which are proposals for a non-scholastic rebirth of Reformed philosophy, and Dooyeweerd's diatribe against scholasticism,

---

ed. George Harinck and Gerrit Neven, Ad Chartas-reeks 9 (Barneveld: De Vuurbaak, 2006), 153; and Bolt, "Editor's Preface," in *Five Studies in the Thought of Herman Bavinck*, vi–vii; with the literature cited in Sytsma, "Herman Bavinck's Thomistic Epistemology," 3n7.

[14] On the nature of the general philosophical orientation of Reformed scholasticism, see Richard A. Muller, "Reformation, Orthodoxy, 'Christian Aristotelianism,' and the Eclecticism of Early Modern Philosophy," *Nederlands Archief voor Kerkgeschiedenis* 81 (January 1, 2001): 306–25; cf. Sytsma, "Herman Bavinck's Thomistic Epistemology," 47.

[15] Herman Dooyeweerd "Kuyper's Philosophy of Science," trans. D. F. M. Strauss, in *On Kuyper: A Collection of Readings on the Life, Work & Legacy of Abraham Kuyper*, eds. Steve Bishop and John H. Kok (Sioux Center, IA: Dordt College Press, 2013), 178; cf. Dooyeweerd, "Kuyper's wetenschapsleer," *Philosophia Reformata* 4 (1939): 232.

Reformation and Scholasticism in Philosophy (1949). Such strong stances against classical Reformed thought brought forth equally strong reactions against such "amateurish tinkering," as Hepp saw it, with sardonic titles such as Hepp's *Threatening deformation*[16] (1936) and Hendrik Steen's *Deformed philosophy* (1937). Bitter division ensued. Tensions remained unresolved through World War II.[17]

Van Til was not only aware of the controversy surrounding this project but also explicitly sided with the Free University philosophers regarding their vision to replace Reformed scholasticism's allegedly pagan philosophical corruptions with a truly Reformed philosophy. His programatic claims regarding the need to purify the "scholastic" elements left over in the philosophical formulations of his theological forefathers, the so-called old Amsterdam and old Princeton theologians, hearken back to this Free University dispute and indicate that he saw his own life's work in Reformed apologetics as participating in an American version of this anti-scholastic rebirth movement.[18] "It is thus that Kuyper's vision," proclaims Van Til in a 1968 address to the American Association of Christian Schools,

---

[16] Given the Free University debate over "Reformed principles" and Dooyeweerd's claim to purify Kuyper's Calvinism it could be that Hepp's title, *Dreigende deformatie*, hearkens backhandedly to "Deformatiën der Theologie," in Kuyper's *Encyclopaedie der heilige godgeleerdheid*, vol. 2., §29.

[17] See "Vollenhoven and Dooyeweerd," in Arie Theodorus van Deursen, *The Distinctive Character of the Free University in Amsterdam, 1880–2005: A Commemorative History*, trans. Herbert Donald Morton (Grand Rapids: Eerdmans, 2008), 169–76; the "amateurish tinkering" characterization is from van Deursen's summary, p. 175; J. Glenn Friesen, "The Investigation of Dooyeweerd and Vollenhoven by the Curators of the Free University" (self-published essay, 2005), http://j.mp/FriesenVU; "The Academic Context" and "Vollenhoven's Program," in Anthony Tol, *Philosophy in the Making: D. H. Th. Vollenhoven and the Emergence of Reformed Philosophy* (Sioux Center, IA: Dordt College Press, 2010), 42–74. On Van Til's relationship with Klaas Schilder (1890–1952), another important figure in the Dutch anti-scholastic renewal movement, see George Harinck, "'How Can an Elephant Understand a Whale and Vice Versa?' The Dutch Origins of Cornelius Van Til's Appraisal of Karl Barth," in *Karl Barth and American Evangelicalism*, ed by. Bruce L. McCormack and Clifford B. Anderson (Grand Rapids, MI: Eerdmans, 2011), 13–41.

[18] See Van Til, *An Introduction to Systematic Theology*, chs. 3–5; Van Til, *The Defense of the Faith*, chs. 2, 11–13. On Dooyeweerd's influence upon Van Til's thought, see O'Donnell, "Kees Van Til," ch. 6. Also note Van Raalte's comment: "Very likely Dooyeweerd's approach to the history of philosophy influenced Van Til." "Unleavened Morality?," 59n6.

expanded and clarified by Vollenhoven and Dooyeweerd may help us in our task in undertaking the cultural mandate for ourselves today. Would that more of those who have seen something of Kuyper's vision as he set it forth in the chapel at Princeton Seminary, might be willing to follow through with Vollenhoven and Dooyeweerd.[19]

Placing Oliphint's "Bavinck's bug" criticism in light of this background yields three salient contextual markers for our analysis. First, the criticism is rooted in a twofold philosophical commitment that arose in twentieth-century Dutch neo-Calvinism: a rejection of the Reformed scholastic philosophical tradition—along with its medieval precursor, especially the scholasticism of Thomas Aquinas[20]—and a corresponding affirmation of some sort of "truly Reformed" or "purely biblical" philosophical alternative.[21] This desire for anti-scholastic philosophical rebirth runs contrary to Bavinck's appropriation of the patristic, medieval, and Reformed scholastic affirmation of philosophical eclecticism.[22] As Sytsma notes:

[D]espite Bavinck's various criticisms of Roman Catholic

---

[19] "The Christian Philosophy of Life," an unpublished address "to the mid-Atlantic chapter of the AACS, Philadelphia, March 29, 1968" (Eric D. Bristley, *A Guide to the Writings of Cornelius Van Til 1895–1987* [Chicago: Olive Tree Communications, 1995], s.v. 1968.I); included as "Appendix 2" in William White Jr., *Van Til, Defender of the Faith: An Authorized Biography* (Nashville: Thomas Nelson, 1979); quote at p. 233.

[20] Van Til's interpretation of Aquinas's "scholasticism" (which largely follows Dooyeweerd's) has been challenged regarding its accuracy. See "Nature and Grace" in Arvin Vos, *Aquinas, Calvin, and Contemporary Protestant Thought: A Critique of Protestant Views on the Thought of Thomas Aquinas* (Grand Rapids, MI: Christian University Press, 1985), ch. 6; Norman L. Geisler, *Thomas Aquinas: An Evangelical Appraisal* (Grand Rapids: Baker, 1991), ch. 1.

[21] On the development of a so-called purely Reformed philosophy, see Bolt, "Editor's Preface." For a contemporary Dooyeweerdian definition of "Christian philosophy"—a definition that provides less of an antithetical interpretation regarding Dooyeweerd's intent to formulate a specifically Christian philosophy than the generalized pure-vs-impure motif we present here—see Gerrit Glas, "What is Christian Philosophy?," trans. John Kok, *Pro Rege* 40, no. 1 (September 2011): 1–17.

[22] See "Dogma and Greek Philosophy," in Herman Bavinck, *Reformed Dogmatics*, vol. 1, *Prolegomena*, ed. John Bolt, trans. John Vriend (Grand Rapids, MI: Baker Academic, 2003), 607–09 (#157).

and Thomistic doctrine on the relation of nature and grace, his largely positive evaluation of the integration of Greek philosophy in the early church and the goal of scientific theology underlying the rise of scholasticism contrasts not only with the negative evaluation of Harnack, but also those in the Dutch Reformed tradition such as Herman Dooyeweerd, Cornelius Van Til, G. C. Berkouwer and others who followed in their path.[23]

Second, the past and present disputes regarding Van Til's rejection of Reformed scholasticism (and his corresponding rejection of realism) are largely intramural in scope and have had limited impact in mainstream philosophical scholarship.[24]

Third, Oliphint's criticism is not novel. It is a recapitulation of Van Til's criticism, which itself is a recapitulation of Dooyeweerd's criticism. This is not to say that one may draw a straight line from Dooyeweerd through Van Til to Oliphint; for significant differences appear in the ways that Dooyeweerd and Oliphint develop their formulations of a purely Christian alternative to Bavinck's impure Reformed scholasticism. For instance, whereas Dooyeweerd rejects neo-Calvinist formulations of the Logos principle as a scholastic devolution from truly Christian principles, Oliphint asserts a so-called *sola Scriptura* form of the Logos principle as an corrective to Bavinck's allegedly derelict Thomistic formulation.[25] But the underlying goal of their criticisms is the same: to purge Bavinck's Reformed scholasticism of its allegedly un-Christian impurities.

We will proceed through the *quaestio* as follows: first, we will state Oliphint's objections; second, contrary views in general (*sed contra*) and in particular (*respondeo*); third, our replies to Oliphint's objections.

---

[23] "Herman Bavinck's Thomistic Epistemology," 8–9.

[24] E.g., Gerrit Glas remarks that Dooyeweerdian Reformational philosophy is "underestimated, qua content and impact, in philosophical circles still today," despite the fact that it has attained relative prominence within several Dutch universities. "What is Christian Philosophy?" 7.

[25] See Dooyeweerd, "Kuyper's wetenschapsleer," 208–19; Oliphint, "Bavinck's Realism," 375–88; cf. Bolt, "Editor's Preface," pp. vi–vii, n. 4.

II. Objections
A. *"Bavinck's bug"*

Oliphint avers, "[T]here is in Herman Bavinck's otherwise most useful analysis of epistemology and theological prolegomena a viral infection—call it Bavinck's bug—that, if it spreads, will serve to undermine the basic foundation of his own Reformed theology."[26] He provides slightly more clarity on the nature of "Bavinck bug" in two parallel statements. First: "Could it be that the clear affirmations of a revelational epistemology are more explicit [in Bavinck's thought] when discussing dogmatics, and less explicit when discussing epistemology more generally? It would appear so."[27] Second:

> With respect to knowledge generally, or knowledge that obtains in other theoretical fields, such as science, Bavinck seems to waver on his revelational commitment. To be clear, it is not the case that he sets up a dichotomy between what he says concerning dogmatics and what he says concerning science. But it is, without question, the case that his analysis of scientific foundations, generally speaking, could easily (and perhaps [more] consistently . . .) be interpreted as an argument for a generic, universally recognized epistemological foundation.[28]

In light of these statements the rationale undergirding Oliphint's criticism can be restated more clearly as follows:

---

[26] "The Prolegomena Principle," 201; cf. ibid., pp. 202, 211, 228. The formal sharpness of Oliphint's criticism is lessened a bit in his second rendition of the article, but the underlying criticism remains the same: either Bavinck must affirm *sola Scriptura* as the cognitive foundation of non-theological knowledge, or he must affirm a Christian-pagan compromise. "What, then, is Bavinck's epistemology? Is it, in fact, consistent with the theology that he himself explicates? Is it the case, we could ask, as both Vos and Van Til seem to indicate, that Bavinck's realism is itself grounded in "common sense" principles (Vos) or in some principle or principles that differ from the one *principium* of the existence of the God of Scripture (Van Til)?" Oliphint, "Bavinck's Realism," 360.

[27] "Bavinck's Realism," 362.

[28] "Bavinck's Realism," 362. "Generic" and "universally recognized" are used here as derogatory terms that mean "autonomous" or "non-Christian" or "anti-theistic." In other words, Oliphint thinks Bavinck's epistemology devolves into a form of Pelagian natural theology that allows pagans the same epistemic soundness as Christians regarding the interpretation of general revelation.

1. God is the sole source (*principium essendi*) for all human knowledge.

2. Holy Scripture is the sole cognitive foundation (*principium cognoscendi*) for all human knowledge, theological or otherwise.

3. Bavinck asserts that sense experience of the external world is the *principium cognoscendi* of philosophical sciences.

4. Ergo, Bavinck's philosophical *principum cognoscendi* is incompatible with his theological *principium cognoscendi*; enter "Bavinck's bug."

The definition of the basic principles of Christian epistemology according to which he levels this allegation are as follows: "(1) that God's revelation provides the foundation for *all* our knowing and living and that (2) because God's revelation is the *principium* for all knowledge, it cannot be the case that some other methodological process can be affirmed as a ground for knowledge."[29] Thus the crux of Oliphint's criticism is that a dialectical relationship attains between Bavinck's purely biblical theological epistemology and his impure, unbiblical philosophical epistemology. All of Oliphint's subsequent criticisms derive from this overarching objection.

1. Scottish Common Sense Realism

Oliphint cites a passing statement in Geerhardus Vos' review of the first edition of Bavinck's *Gereformeerde Dogmatiek* and, through a long series of inferences, concludes that Bavinck's philosophical epistemology is incompatible with his theological epistemology.[30] His rationale may be summarized as follows:

1. Vos identifies Bavinck's philosophical epistemology with that of James McCosh (i.e., Scottish Common Sense Realism).

2. McCosh's epistemology is the same as Thomas Reid's.

3. Thomas Reid asserts that, although the human mind receives its being from God, it nevertheless serves as its own cognitive principle of knowledge; that is, the human mind functions autonomously in its acquisition of knowledge. Hence for Reid God is the essential principle of knowledge but not the cognitive principle of knowledge.

---

[29] "The Prolegomena Principle," 205.

[30] Cf. Oliphint, "The Prolegomena Principle," 205–07, 221–25, 227; with Oliphint, "Bavinck's Realism," 359–60, 372–75, 388. The portion of Vos' review cited by Oliphint is "Gereformeerde Dogmatiek—Vol. One" in *Redemptive History and Biblical Interpretation: The Shorter Writings of Geerhardus Vos*, ed. Richard B. Gaffin Jr. (Phillipsburg, NJ: P&R, 1980), 478.

4. Since Bavinck holds the same view as McCosh, and since McCosh holds the same view as Reid, then Bavinck must hold the same view as Reid: God is merely the essential principle of knowledge, not the cognitive principle.

5. Ergo, Bavinck's philosophical epistemology contradicts his theological epistemology; for in the latter God's revelation provides *both* the essential and cognitive principle of knowledge.

2. Universals

Oliphint asserts that Bavinck's Thomistic, moderate-realist theory of universals—the essence of which is the assertion that universals exist *in re* and *in mente hominis post rem*—is ultimately a non-Christian formulation.[31]

B. *The Logos principle*

Oliphint avers that Bavinck's formulation of Christian realism "is insufficient as an application of the Logos principle in epistemology."[32] His rationale is as follows. First, he defines the "Logos principle":

> The Logos principle is not, as is most often thought, a general capacity of reason, or the ability to receive the basic, common sense, principles of the world, at least not directly. Rather, the Logos principle *just is* the knowledge of God, through the Logos, that all men, by virtue of their being created, necessarily and for eternity, *have*. We do not merely have the capacity by virtue of our reason, to know God; we know him by virtue of his activity through the Logos.[33]

Second, he interprets Bavinck's formulation of the Logos' relation to epistemology to be that of merely imparting to humanity the capacity for

---

[31] Cf. Oliphint, "The Prolegomena Principle," 213–28; with Oliphint, "Bavinck's Realism," 363–89. Dooyeweerd levels a similar criticism against Bavinck's formulation regarding *"universalia ante rem in mente divina* and *universalia in re."* Dooyeweerd, "Kuyper's wetenschapsleer," 213.

[32] Cf. Oliphint, "Bavinck's Realism," 387; with Oliphint, "The Prolegomena Principle," 225–26.

[33] "Bavinck's Realism," 387.

reason, conscience, and the *sensus divinitatus*.³⁴

III. *Sed contra*

Whereas Oliphint asserts that *sola Scriptura* must be the sole cognitive principle of theology and philosophy, Aristotle demonstrates in *Posterior Analytics* (32.88b10) that "[i]t is ridiculous to say that the principles are the same [for all sciences]." Thomas Aquinas, commenting on this passage, asserts that "it is impossible and ridiculous to hold that the principles of one science are the same as those of another science" for "it would follow from this that all things in the sciences were the same and, consequently, that all the sciences were one science." He also recalls Aristotle's corresponding demonstration regarding the impossibility "to demonstrate by passing from one genus to another."³⁵ Moreover, according to Professor Muller the Reformed orthodox theologians maintained that "in the case of true or Christian natural theology, Scripture cannot be the *principium cognoscendi*." Rather, as seen for instance in Johann Heinrich Alsted's (1588–1638) and Samuel Maresius's (1599–1673) treatises on natural theology, "nature" in the sense of "reason, universal experience, and the Book of Nature (*Liber Naturae*)" is the cognitive principle of natural theology and Holy Scripture that of supernatural theology.³⁶

IV. *Respondeo*

The assumption undergirding Oliphint's "Bavinck's bug" criticism is that the Reformed principle of *sola Scriptura* is a necessary and sufficient condition of the cognitive foundation not only for theology but also for philosophy. Hence he infers, "[W]e should not allow a methodological separation such that method in theology, specifically, differs, at root, from method, more generally, in science. Where the foundations of method are

---

³⁴ "Bavinck's Realism," 387n78; cf. ibid., 362–63; Oliphint, "The Prolegomena Principle," 209, 226n65.

³⁵ Thomas Aquinas, *Commentary on Aristotle's Posterior Analytics*, trans. Richard Berquist (Notre Dame, Indiana: Dumb Ox Books, 2007) I.43.c; cf. I.15.

³⁶ Richard A. Muller, *Post-Reformation Reformed Dogmatics*, vol. 1., *Prolegomena to Theology* (Grand Rapids: Baker Academic, 2003), 436 and 436n123; cf. 280. The references are to Johann Heinrich Alsted, *Praecognitorum theologicorum* I.ix, *Theologia Naturalis* I.i, and Maresius, *Collegium Theologicum* I.xxiii. See also Muller's explication of Reformed natural theology in *Prolegomena*, ch. 6.

concerned, what is true for one discipline should be true for them all."[37] This assumption is a category mistake insofar as theology and philosophy are distinct sciences that operate in different genres and proceed upon different *principia*.[38]

If Oliphint's criticism is pressed to its logical conclusion, then not only are Scripture and universal human experience contradicted but also an endless slew of absurdities follow in philosophy and the special sciences such as that a theory of numbers and the entire science of mathematics must be deduced from the Bible, that the laws of logic must be deduced from the Bible, that a medical student must study the Bible instead of *Grey's Anatomy*, that a gentleman's choice between boxer shorts or briefs must be determined by Holy Scripture alone, that whether one's toilet paper should hang over the top or under the bottom of the roll must be determined by Holy Scripture alone. For logically speaking if *sola Scriptura* is truly the *principium unicum* for *all* knowledge theological or otherwise, then humans are obliged to deduce *all* knowledge of themselves and of the external world from that alleged *principium* via the method appropriate to that foundation: exegesis of the Bible. Yet this supposition is absurd.

1. Ambiguous terms

Whereas Oliphint caricatures Bavinck's formulations as "confusing,"[39] Bavinck defines his terms unequivocally and uses them clearly and in accord with their standard use in the Reformed tradition. After surveying the classical meaning and purpose of the technical term *principium*—"that whence something either is or becomes or is known"—as it derives from Aristotle's use of *arche* in *Metaphysics* V.1 and was appropriated by the fathers, the medieval theologians, and the Reformed orthodox, Bavinck then defines the three *principia* of Reformed theology: God is the *principum essendi*; God's self-revelation is the principium *cognoscendi externum*; the Holy Spirit's illumination is the *principium cognoscendi internum*.[40] Next, he defines the three

---

[37] "The Prolegomena Principle," 204.

[38] Cf. Muller, *Prolegomena* 6.2.B (pp. 287–88).

[39] Cf. Oliphint, "The Prolegomena Principle," 207; with Oliphint, "Bavinck's Realism," 360.

[40] Cf. Bavinck, *Reformed Dogmatics*, 1:210–14 (##62–63); with Muller, *Prolegomena* 9.3 (pp. 431–45).

principia of philosophy as parallel with, though distinct from, theology's *principia*: God (specifically, God as Logos) is the *principium essendi*; the created world is the *principium cognoscendi externum*; the light of reason, which shines forth from the Logos and enlightens the mind in order that it can recognizes the Logos in created things—is the *principium cognoscendi internum*.[41] Therefore, Bavinck's formulation is not confusing; rather, what is confusing is that neither Oliphint nor Van Til define *principium*. They appropriate the *principia* terminology from Bavinck but then use it in an idiosyncratic manner such as conflating *principium unicum* with "method."

2. Misguided interpretations

Whereas Oliphint criticizes Bavinck for asserting not only that the human intellect operates "abstractly" (i.e., autonomously) but also that God is merely the *principium essendi* of knowledge and *not* the *principium cognoscendi*,[42] Bavinck asserts the opposite on both accounts. Regarding the former, he explicitly rejects rationalistic (i.e., "abstract" or Socinian) natural theology: "A religion and a natural theology [in general], as rationalism conceives it, does not exist. For the religion and the natural theology we know was not acquired by us apart from special revelation but became our own from and in the light of Holy Scripture."[43]

Furthermore, following the Reformed orthodox tradition Bavinck maintains that "the origin of common notions is Christ," not rationalistic autonomy.[44] He also explicitly repudiates the deistic assumption in Oliphint's criticism, namely, that God gives humanity its intellect and then sits idly by while human exercise their intellects autonomously; for he insists:

> The world itself rests on revelation; revelation is the presupposition, the foundation, the secret of all that exists in all its forms. . . In every moment of time beats the pulse of eternity; every point in space is filled with the omnipresence of God; the finite is supported by the

---

[41] *Reformed Dogmatics*, 1:233.

[42] Cf. Oliphint, "The Prolegomena Principle," 227; with Oliphint, "Bavinck's Realism," 388.

[43] *Reformed Dogmatics*, 1:209; cf. pp. 104–08, "The Impact of Philosophy" (##32–33).

[44] Sytsma, "Herman Bavinck's Thomistic Epistemology," 43–45; quote at p. 43.

infinite, all becoming is rooted in being. . . . The foundations of creation and redemption are the same. The Logos who became flesh is the same by whom all things were made. . . Notwithstanding the separation wrought by sin, there is a progressive approach of God to his creatures. The transcendence does not cease to exist, but becomes an ever deeper immanence. . . General revelation leads to special, special revelation points back to general. The one calls for the other, and without it remains imperfect and unintelligible. Together they proclaim the manifold wisdom which God has displayed in creation and redemption.[45]

Finally, immediately after defining the *principium cognoscendi internum* of philosophy as the light of reason, Bavinck concludes, "So, in the final analysis *it is God alone who* from his divine consciousness and by way of his creatures *conveys the knowledge of truth to our mind—the Father who by the Son and in the Spirit reveals himself to us.*"[46] Hence the conclusion that Oliphint derives from this passage—that Bavinck affirms rationalistic autonomy—is directly contrary to Bavinck's own explicit affirmation that the Holy Trinity is involved at every point in the cognitive process.

3. Conflation of theology and philosophy

Whereas Oliphint everywhere conflates theological and philosophical *principia* based on the assumption (appropriated from Van Til) that Holy Scripture is the cognitive *principium unicum* of theology and philosophy, Bavinck distinguishes the *principia* of theological science and non-theological science.[47] Without such a distinction there remains no grounds for distinguishing the nature and purpose of theology from all other sciences, and all human knowledge in every field of inquiry becomes a sub-discipline of theology.[48]

---

[45] Herman Bavinck, *The Philosophy of Revelation: The Stone Lectures for 1908–1909, Princeton Theological Seminary* (New York: Longmans, Green, and Co., 1908), 27–28; cf. Van Raalte, "Unleavened Morality?," 88–89.

[46] *Reformed Dogmatics*, 1:233 (emphasis added).

[47] See "Scientific Foundations" and "Religious Foundations" in Bavinck, *Reformed Dogmatics*, chs. 7–8.

[48] "Unlike Bavinck's clear distinction between revealed and rational *principia*, Cornelis Van Til emphasized the noetic effects of the fall to such an extent that he

Additionally, whereas Oliphint's position removes all foundational cognitive distinctions between theology and philosophy and hence universalizes the jurisdiction of theology's *principia*, Bavinck limits the jurisdiction of theology to its own domain. Contra Schleiermacher, who in his prolegomena makes theology subservient to philosophy, Bavinck argues that Christian theologians do not "treat topics that actually lie outside the territory of dogmatics, belong to other sciences, and can only come up as 'borrowed propositions' [Lehnsätze] in the introduction of dogmatics."[49] In other words since the scope of theology is bounded by its unique *principia*, theologians are limited to drawing theological conclusions from theology's unique cognitive foundation (Holy Scripture), operating with the unique mode of certainty that theology employs (faith), aiming its operations toward theology's unique end (eternal union with God), and refraining from either imposing its unique foundation, method, mode, and end on other sciences or allowing other sciences (such as philosophy in Schleiermacher's case) to impose their foundations, methods, modes, and ends on theology.

4. Contradiction of Scripture, Reformed confessions, and experience

Oliphint's conflation not only reduces all sciences to theology but also contradicts the affirmations of natural revelation in Holy Scripture, the Reformed confessions, and universal human experience. Regarding Scripture, Paul asserts that all people know God's eternal power and divine nature by means of created things (Rom. 1:18–20) and that during the time of Israel's theocracy the Gentiles knew God apart from the law, that is, apart from Holy Scripture (Rom. 2:14–16). But if Scripture itself avers that all people know God through nature and that Gentiles know God's law without Holy Scripture, it cannot be that *sola Scriptura* is the sole cognitive foundation of these two extra-biblical, natural forms of knowledge.[50]

---

apparently collapsed such a distinction by requiring that the truth of general human knowledge be based on the *testimonium Spiritus Sancti.*" Sytsma, "Herman Bavinck's Thomistic Epistemology," 18.

[49] *Reformed Dogmatics*, 1:208–10; quote at p. 210 (emended); cf. Bavinck, *Gereformeerde Dogmatiek*, 7th ed. (Kampen: Kok, 1998), 1:181–82.

[50] See the standard Reformed arguments for affirming the necessity of natural theology based upon these Romans passages (and other biblical passages) as found, e.g., in Francis Turretin, *Institutes of Elenctic Theology*, ed. James T. Dennison, Jr., trans. George Musgrave Giger (Phillipsburg, NJ: P&R, 1992), 1.3 (pp. 1:6–9); Wilhelmus à Brakel, *The Christian's Reasonable Service in which Divine Truths concerning the*

Regarding the Reformed confessions, the Westminster Confession of Faith (I.1, 6; XX.4; XXI.1) and the Westminster Larger Catechism (qq. 2, 60, 121, 151) distinguish between matters that are known on the basis of Holy Scripture from those that are known by the "light of nature."[51] Likewise, the Belgic Confession (art. 2) affirms a Christian realist position with respect to the "beautiful book" of nature in which all humans perceive God's self-revelation.[52] Additionally, the material content of the doctrine of common notions is found in the Canons of Dort (III/IV, a. 4).[53] Such distinctions regarding the light of nature, especially those of the Westminster Standards, are commonplace in the Reformed confessional tradition.[54]

Covenant of Grace are Expounded, Defended against Opposing Parties, and their Practice Advocated as well as The Administration of this Covenant in the Old and New Testaments, ed. Joel R. Beeke, trans. Bartel Elshout (Grand Rapids, MI: Reformation Heritage Books, 1992), ch. 1; James Ussher, *A Body of Divinity: Or, the Sum and Substance of Christian Religion*, ed. Michael Nevarr (Birmingham, AL: Solid Ground Christian Books, 2007), 1st head (esp. pp. 3–4). Cf. Muller, *Prolegomena*, ch. 6.

[51] Regarding the circumscription of the scope of Scripture in ch. I of the Westminster Confession, see Gordon, "How My Mind Has Changed: The Insufficiency of Scripture." One eminent, classical interpreter of the Larger Catechism defines "light of nature" as follows: "From the light of nature in man, by which we understand that reason which he is endowed with, whereby he is distinguished from, and rendered superior to, all other creatures in this lower world, whereby he is able to observe the connexion of things, and their dependence on one another, and infer those consequences which may be deduced from thence. These reasoning powers, indeed, are very much sullied, depraved, and weakened, by our apostacy from God, but not wholly obliterated; so that there are some remains thereof, which are common to all nations, whereby, without the help of special revelation it may be known that there is a God." Thomas Ridgeley, *A Body of Divinity: wherein the doctrines of the Christian religion are explained and defended. Being the substance of several lectures on the Assembly's Larger Catechism*, ed. John M. Wilson, rev. (New York: Robert Carter & Brothers, 1855), 10. Regarding Van Til's epistemological views vis-à-vis the Westminster Standards's teaching on the "light of nature," see Fesko and Richard, "Natural Theology and the Westminster Confession of Faith."

[52] See Bavinck's notes on the Belgic Confession, art. 2, and the Reformed tradition's affirmation of natural theology in *Reformed Dogmatics*, 1:87–88, 233.

[53] Sytsma, "Herman Bavinck's Thomistic Epistemology," 41–42; see also Van Raalte, "Unleavened Morality?," 73–76.

[54] Cf. *Anglican Catechism* (1553); *The Thirty-Nine Articles* (1562/63) XVIII; *The Stafforts Book* (1599) s.v. *De persona Christi*; *The Cambridge Platform* (1648) XIV.3; *The Geneva Theses* (1649) IV.2; *The Savoy Declaration* (1658) I.i, vi, X.iv, XX.ii., XXII.1, which

Hence the "Van Tilian" supposition that *sola Scriptura* is the sole necessary and sufficient cognitive principle of all knowledge and hence that realism contradicts *sola Scriptura* is out of accord with Reformed confessional orthodoxy insofar as these confessions recognize the light of nature as a necessary and sufficient cognitive foundation for true natural knowledge despite its insufficiency to serve as a cognitive foundation for saving faith.

Regarding universal human experience, no one opens the Bible in order to decide whether to wear blue or brown socks. To do so would be to violate the nature and scope of Holy Scripture: the Bible is not a divine revelation of binding rules of haberdashery but of the power of God in Jesus Christ *unto salvation* (Rom. 1:16). Likewise, no one opens the Bible in order to determine whether a highway should be paved with asphalt or concrete, whether a lumberman should use an axe or a chain saw, whether a red or white wine will pair better with fish, and so forth ad infinitum. Again, Holy Scripture *cannot* answer these questions insofar as they pertain to non-theological sciences—civil engineering, forestry, culinary arts, respectively—each of which proceed upon different principles than theology, have different objects of study than theology, are bounded by different scopes than theology, and employ different methods than those employed by theology. Just as it would be absurd in the science of forestry for a forester to infer that Christ has only one nature based upon the lifespan of conifers, so also it would be absurd in theology for a theologian to infer that conifers are not truly gymnosperms based upon the two natures of Christ. Therefore, to conflate theology's unique cognitive principle with the common cognitive principle of all non-theological sciences is to patently contradict universal human experience regarding the starting point for knowledge in non-theological sciences: human sense perception of the external world.

5. False dichotomy

Oliphint's criticism assumes that merely distinguishing the *principia* of theology and philosophy somehow entails rationalistic autonomy. It then infers the following ultimatum regarding the cognitive principle of philosophy: either supernatural revelation or realism, *sola Scriptura* or scholasticism, theonomy or autonomy. However, the assumption behind this inference

---

places recapitulate the Westminster Standards; *The Formula Consensus Helvetica* (1675) XX; *The London Baptist Confession* (1677) I.1, 6, etc., which also recapitulates Westminster; likewise, *The Baptist Catechism* (1693) q. 3.

finds no warrant in Bavinck's thought or in the Reformed scholastic tradition from which he drew his principles. Bavinck nowhere pits natural revelation over against supernatural revelation in the manner assumed by Oliphint. Both in Bavinck's thought and in the Reformed tradition reason is not a cognitive principle that asserts itself over against supernatural revelation but a human faculty—a tool for understanding both natural and supernatural revelation—that itself is a gift, a *revelation*, of the Logos.[55]

The unsoundness of this ultimatum paradigm and its underlying assumption can be seen more clearly when contrasted with concrete examples from the Reformed tradition of the relation between philosophy and theology. Peter Martyr Vermigli (1499–1562) stands in a long line of Protestant doctors who lectured on Aristotle's moral philosophy in Protestant universities including Calvin's Genevan Academy.[56] If Oliphint's position is valid and sound, then the very act of presenting such lectures is a violation of *sola Scriptura*; for Holy Scripture, not Aristotle, must be the sole cognitive foundation for ethics. What this position overlooks, however, is that when Reformed theologians such as Vermigli delivered these lectures, they did so on the basis of several distinctions, the chief of which being the following: "All our knowledge is either revealed or acquired. In the first instance it is theology, in the other philosophy."[57] For these Reformed thinkers Aristotle's *Nicomachean Ethics*, for example, is not moral theology but moral philosophy, a science that is no more repugnant to theology than is "astrology or the nautical or military arts, or else fishing and hunting, and also knowledge of human law that everyone understands as necessary for public administration."[58] For Vermigli, this distinction does not entail a lessening of Holy Scripture's role as the *norma normans* of philosophy. Rather, he asserts that

---

[55] Cf. Muller, *Prolegomena*, 283, 433.

[56] "The practice of commenting on Aristotle to complement biblical lectures was common in Reformed seminaries in the sixteenth century." Peter Martyr Vermigli, *The Peter Martyr Library, Volume Nine: Commentary on Aristotle's Nicomachean Ethics*, ed. Emidio Campi and Joseph C. McLelland, Sixteenth Century Essays & Studies 73 (Kirksville, MO: Truman State University Press, 2006),x. In addition to Vermigli, John Sturm, Martin Bucer, Girolamo Zanchi, and Konrad Gesner lectured on Aristotle's works (ibid., x–xi). See also Donald Sinnema, "The Discipline of Ethics in Early Reformed Orthodoxy," *Calvin Theological Journal* 28, no. 1 (April 1, 1993): 10–44.

[57] *Commentary*, 7.

[58] *Commentary*, 15.

the Christian religion is inflamed by knowledge of pagan ethics, for we understand through comparison how far those things taught in scripture surpass philosophy. For it is a common saying that when opposites are compared with one another they become clearer. . . Therefore, whoever knows both faculties will more easily avoid the mistake of the one, namely, of human philosophy, especially when properly demonstrated.[59]

Accordingly, all throughout his commentary on Aristotle's *Ethics*, Vermigli concludes each section by both correcting Aristotle's errors according to Holy Scripture and stating where Aristotle's views are in accord with Scripture.[60] Vermigli's commentary, then, presents us with a concrete example that does not fall prey to the horns of Oliphint's false dichotomy. Vermigli distinguishes the cognitive foundations, scopes, and aims of theology and philosophy while simultaneously maintaining the role of Holy Scripture as *norma normans* for philosophy.

The preface to Edward Reynolds's (1599–1676) *Treatise on the Passions and Faculties of the Soul* (1640) provides another example, one from a Westminster Divine writing close to the time of the Westminster Assembly, of how distinguishing the foundations of philosophy and theology does not entail rationalism. So does Francis Turretin's (1623–1687) discussion of philosophy's relation to theology.[61] More examples could be adduced here.[62] Nevertheless, these few are sufficient to show that Bavinck's distinguishing the *principia* of theology and philosophy stands in a long line of Reformed orthodox thought that draws this distinction without the Socinian entailment assumed but nowhere proven in "Bavinck's bug."

6. No universal moral epistemology

If held consistently the consequences of Oliphint's position are dire with respect to moral epistemology. For example, the fact that the Bible is neither universally available nor univocally understood leads to the problem

---

[59] *Commentary*, 16.

[60] E.g., see *Commentary*, 35–36; cf. ibid., xi, xviii, 5.

[61] *Institutes* I.3–4, 8–13.

[62] E.g., see Heinrich Heppe, *Reformed Dogmatics Set Out and Illustrated from the Sources*, ed by. Ernst Bizer, trans by. G. T. Thomson (London: George Allen & Unwin, 1950), ch. 1 (esp. sections 12–16).

of a non-universal morality:

1. Holy Scripture is the sole, universal cognitive foundation for morality.

2. But not all people have read the Bible, and even fewer have understood the Bible's meaning correctly.

3. Ergo only very few actual human beings—Christians who have read the Bible and have understood it correctly—obtain epistemic access to the moral order.

But if this rationale is sound, then it follows that the majority of the world's population (i.e., anyone who is a non-Christian or any Christian who fails to read the Bible correctly) is excluded by definition from having cognitive access to the moral order. Yet such a position is contrary to the same Romans passages mentioned above and to universal human experience of right and wrong. For example, murder, theft, and rape are just as morally impermissible in Muslim, Buddhist, and secular humanist cultures as in Christian ones.

7. *Bipolar Bavinck*

Oliphint asserts that, despite the dialectic in Bavinck's thought between *sola Scriptura* and cognitive realism, "[h]e has the remedy to his problems within his own system."[63] In other words Oliphint claims to know Bavinck's thought better than Bavinck does himself, and in the name of maintaining consistency with *sola Scriptura*, he recommends a restructuring of the fundamental principles in Bavinck's philosophical epistemology: the elimination of cognitive realism. However, neither Bavinck himself nor the Reformed tradition within which he operated saw a contradiction in the distinction between affirming *sola Scriptura* as the cognitive foundation of theology and affirming human sense perception (of the self and the external world) as the cognitive foundation of philosophy.[64] Therefore, to object to this distinction on the ground that it introduces an inconsistency with re-

---

[63] Cf. Oliphint, "The Prolegomena Principle," 228; with Oliphint, "Bavinck's Realism," 389.

[64] Sytsma remarks that "the 'special view of the intellect' on the part of the Reformed is ultimately grounded in the doctrine of the divine ideas in the Logos, which in Bavinck's opinion, when purged of any subordinationism or emanationism, is both a Scriptural *and* Greek doctrine." "Herman Bavinck's Thomistic Epistemology," 45.

spect to *sola Scriptura* is to impose upon Bavinck's thought a norm that is foreign to it and to the Reformed tradition. Furthermore, insofar as this foreign norm is assumed rather than proved, conclusions based upon it are instances of question begging. For these reasons Oliphint's assertion that, although Bavinck's realism contradicts his theology, the former may be fixed by the latter, is both subjective and unsound. Such attempts to interpret Bavinck's thought in terms of a "multiple Bavincks" thesis are fundamentally misguided.[65]

V. Reply to objections
A. *"Bavinck's bug"*

Despite claiming that this "viral infection" threatens the health of Bavinck's entire dogmatic enterprise, Oliphint strains to provide a clear definition of this systemic "bug." In both articles his attempts to state Bavinck's errors are prefaced with so many qualifying caveats (i.e., "it seems," "it could be," "perhaps," etc.) that one is left with the impression that the allegations lack soundness on purely formal grounds. An unqualified assertion is nowhere to be found. In the most odd instance of these caveats Oliphint admits that he cannot prove whether Bavinck's bug exists: "While it cannot perhaps be definitively shown that Bavinck held that issues of prolegomena required a radically different method from that of theology, there is little question that Bavinck affirmed such a thing."[66]

The non sequitur here strongly suggests that the "Bavinck's bug" allegation is an instance of *petitio principii*. Oliphint nowhere proves that Van Til's criticism—which is the foundation of his own criticism—is correct. He assumes the existence of the "bug" before analyzing Bavinck's formulations on their own terms.

Likewise, Oliphint's definition of the basic cognitive principles of Christian epistemology is full of ambiguity. For example, it is not clear whether he uses *principium* in the sense of *principium essendi* or *principium cognoscendi*. Nor is it clear whether he uses "foundation" as a synonym for *princip-*

---

[65] See James Eglinton, "How Many Herman Bavincks? *De Gemeene Genade* and the 'Two Bavincks' Hypothesis," in *The Kuyper Center Review, Volume 2: Revelation and Common Grace* (Grand Rapids, MI: Eerdmans, 2011), 279–301; Eglinton, *Trinity and Organism: Towards a New Reading of Herman Bavinck's Organic Motif*, T&T Clark Studies in Systematic Theology 17 (London: T&T Clark, 2012), ch. 2.

[66] "The Prolegomena Principle," 204.

ium. Additionally, the relationship between *principium* and "methodological process" is undefined and hence invites criticism on the ground that an argument's first principles are not the same thing as an argument's method.[67]

1. Scottish Common Sense Realism

The string of inferences beginning with Geerhardus Vos' statement is unsound for several reasons. First and foremost, the conclusion is assumed in the unstated first premise. Oliphint never demonstrates *why* realism is incompatible with revelation or *how sola Scriptura* is the cognitive principle of non-theological science; rather, he merely presupposes that these are valid and sound assertions. At most Oliphint demonstrates only *that* Bavinck distinguishes theological and philosophical epistemology not *how* such a distinction entails rationalistic autonomy.

In the second place, Oliphint infers too much from Vos' review. In the same paragraph to which Oliphint refers Vos himself neither asserts nor implies that Bavinck's distinction regarding the *principium cognoscendi* of theology (i.e., Holy Scripture) and science (i.e., Christian realism) is self-contradictory; if anything his silence on the matter implies that the two distinct cognitive principles are harmoniously related.[68] Additionally, rather than interpreting Bavinck's view of revelation as too narrow (as does Oliphint), Vos criticizes Bavinck for making his definition of "revelation" *too broad* insofar as his assertion that "revelation" coincides with all of God's acts both in nature and grace conflates the older distinction between God's creative and redemptive acts.[69] Finally, Oliphint oddly turns Vos's passing, neutral comment about McCosh which was meant merely to introduce one aspect of the unknown Dutch author's thought by means of an apples-to-apples comparison with a known Princetonian's thought into a pejorative criticism. In all these ways what Oliphint concludes from Vos's review contradicts Vos's own interpretations of Bavinck's thought.

In the third place, Oliphint cites no evidence from Bavinck's writings to demonstrate either that Bavinck's realism is the same as McCosh's or

---

[67] Oliphint levels this same criticism against Bolt. Yet, his own formulation lacks the clarity that he finds lacking in Bolt's. See Oliphint, "Bavinck's Realism," 364n21.

[68] Vos, *Redemptive History*, 478.

[69] Vos, *Redemptive History*, 479.

that it is the same as Reid's. Rather, he merely raises questions regarding the relationship between Bavinck's thought and the formulations of these philosophers.[70] Nevertheless, he draws the conclusion that Bavinck's epistemology is the same as McCosh's and Reid's as if he has demonstrated the connection. Insofar as this "conclusion" lacks proper grounds, the string of inferences underlying it is not a sound argument but an assumption.

2. Universals

Regarding Oliphint's allegation that Bavinck's Aristotelian-Thomistic theory of universals is non-Christian, here again we are confronted by confusing caveats. Oliphint admits that Bavinck affirms that all "knowledge must be grounded in revelation" and that in his view the *principia* of science "are themselves rooted in the Triune God." Despite this admission, Oliphint insists that "it is not clear that this 'rooting' takes the *principium cognoscendi* as seriously as it should."[71]

What Oliphint means by this last phrase is not entirely clear. He immediately cites passages from Bavinck's *Reformed Dogmatics* wherein Bavinck affirms basic elements of Aristotelian epistemology that have been refracted through Thomistic and Reformed scholasticism such as the pure potency of the intellect, the necessity of the external world as a stimulus for the mind's *tabula rasa*, the existence of *veritates aeternae*, the conceptualist formulation of universals that posits their existence *in re* and *in mente hominis post rem*, and the assertion that sense perception is the starting point for human knowledge. Oliphint finds all of these affirmations to be problematic; for he

---

[70] E.g., Oliphint asserts, "If it is indeed the case that Bavinck's epistemology is a realism, which itself is in the neighborhood of Reid's approach, then there are serious questions that need to be asked." The corresponding footnote claims that this assumption—the very thing that requires grounding in order to form a valid assertion—in fact does *not* need to be treated: "The relationship of Aquinas's views, affirmed by Bavinck, and Reidianism need not detain us here." Oliphint, "The Prolegomena Principle," p. 222 & n. 55, respectively. Likewise, Oliphint raises the question of whether Bavinck's formulation of the Logos principle falls prey to Arthur Holmes' criticism of realism (Oliphint, "Bavinck's Realism," 376n55); yet, he then *asserts* that Bavinck's use of the Logos principle needs to be clarified on this very point without providing any proof that Bavinck's formulation of this point is indeed unclear (ibid., 376).

[71] "Bavinck's Realism," 363.

immediately asks: "is this, indeed, in the end, a revelational epistemology?"[72] In other words, "[I]s it the case that a realistic approach to universals, guided by Aquinas, can move us in the direction of a Christian epistemology?"[73] After pursuing lengthy excurses on Aquinas' theory of universals, Aquinas' theory of participation, Scottish Common Sense Realism, and the biblical Logos principle,[74] Oliphint answers this question in the negative, albeit not without much ambiguity:

> The confusion in Bavinck may be this: it seems in the majority of cases, Bavinck attributes to the Logos, not specifically the *principium cognoscendi*, but the *principium essendi*, in much the same way as Thomas Reid did. That is, if what we say about the Logos is that he is the originator of the intellect, and of reason, or that (as Reid says), our "first principles" of reasoning "are the gift of heaven," all we have said thus far is that God, or the Logos, is the *principium essendi* of knowledge. He is the one who is the cause of the knowledge that we have. . . . What we need for an epistemological principle is not simply a *causal* principle (though that is necessary), but rather a principle *of knowledge*.[75]

Oliphint's conclusion is ambiguous for two reasons. First, by employing probability qualifiers (i.e., "may be this," "it seems"), he presents his conclusion as more of a hypothesis than an actual conclusion. Second, he significantly weakens—if not contradicts—his own characterization of "Bavinck's bug" as an affirmation of "*a radically different method* from that of theology"[76] by admitting that the "bug" is a matter of degree rather than a matter of principle:

---

[72] "Bavinck's Realism," 364.

[73] "Bavinck's Realism," 365. Note the ambiguous terms here: "revelational epistemology" is equated with "Christian epistemology." Also note the *petitio principii* again: whether there is such a thing as "Christian epistemology" for non-theological knowledge and whether Bavinck intended to formulate such a "Christian epistemology" are assumed in the affirmative without any evidence to warrant these assumptions.

[74] "Bavinck's Realism," 365–88.

[75] "Bavinck's Realism," 388–89.

[76] "The Prolegomena Principle," 204 (emphasis added).

> In conclusion, we should reiterate here that Bavinck has said much that moves, without question, in the direction we have moved above. He has the remedy to his problems within his own system. However, to be consistent, an epistemology of realism, we should see, is not able to be sustained if what is hoped for is some kind of universal *principia* in which all must participate.[77]

Moreover, though Oliphint rejects that universals exist *in re* and *in mente hominis post rem*, he provides no alternative explanation as to whether perceptions in the human mind accurately reflect the external world, and, if so, how the mind-world relation is to be formulated. Since Oliphint rejects Bavinck's Thomistic realism, and since it thus would be inconsistent for him to sneak realism in through the back door, then the question arises as to whether he intends to wed his allegedly non-realist Logos principle to rationalism, empiricism, idealism, nominalism, or another form of cognitive anti-realism.

The following reply is sufficient for the portion of this objection regarding whether Bavinck asserts that God is merely the essential but not the cognitive principle of knowing.

B. *The Logos principle*

Whereas Oliphint criticizes Bavinck's formulation of the Logos principle for giving humanity merely the capacity for reason rather than actual knowledge of God, Bavinck does not assert that the Logos provides merely the capacity without the actuality of knowledge. This is obvious in the very passage to which Oliphint refers:

> All life and all knowledge is based on a kind of agreement between subject and object. Human beings are so richly endowed because they are linked with the objective world by a great many extremely diverse connections. They are related to the whole world. Physically, vegetatively, sensorily, intellectually, ethically, and religiously there is correspondence between them and the world; they are microcosms.
>
> [. . .] *God not only forged these connections between human beings and the world; from moment to moment he also consistently maintains them and causes them to function. It is the one*

---

[77] "Bavinck's Realism," 389; cf. Oliphint, "The Prolegomena Principle," 207.

selfsame Logos who made all things in and outside of human beings. He is before all things, and they still continue jointly to exist through him (John 1:3; Col. 1:15–17). In addition, Scripture makes known to us the Spirit of God as the source and agent of all life in humanity and the world (Gen. 1:2; Ps. 33:6; 104:30; 139:7; Job 26:13; 33:4), especially of the intellectual, ethical, and religious life (Job 32:8; Isa. 11:2).[78]

Bavinck's language of divine agency in relation to the human act of knowing is directly in line with the Thomistic tradition on this point. For example, Aquinas asserts "that for the knowledge of any truth whatsoever man needs Divine help, that the intellect may be moved by God to its act." Likewise: "We always need God's help for every thought, inasmuch as He moves the understanding to act." Again: "Every truth by whomsoever spoken is from the Holy Spirit as bestowing the natural light, and moving us to understand and speak the truth."[79]

Furthermore, based upon the same Romans 1 passage to which Oliphint refers, Bavinck explicitly asserts that all humans have actual knowledge of God for which they are culpable rather than a mere capacity for knowledge:

> Pagans fell into idolatry and unrighteousness because they did not acknowledge God (Rom. 1:18ff.). But that knowledge of God penetrates the heart and arouses there an assortment of affections, of fear and hope, sadness and joy, guilt feelings and forgiveness, misery and redemption, as these are pictured to us throughout Scripture but especially in the Psalms.[80]

Finally, in addition to misinterpreting Bavinck's formulation on divine agency with respect to philosophical knowledge, Oliphint's criticism both omits an analysis of the cornerstones of Bavinck's formulation of cognitive realism—the *intellectus agens, veritates aeternae*, and divine

---

[78] *Reformed Dogmatics*, 1:586 (emphasis added).

[79] *Summa theologiae*, trans. Laurence Shapcote, O.P., ed. John Mortensen and Enrique Alarcon (Lander, WY: The Aquinas Institute, 2012) 1–2.109.1c, ad 3, and ad 2 respectively; cf. ad 2 with Aquinas, *Lectura super Johannem*, ch. 1, lect. 3, sect. 103; and with Aquinas, *De veritate* I.8 sed contra.

[80] *Reformed Dogmatics*, 1:268; cf. 1:315, 1:341, 2:30, 2:56, 2:69, 2:76, 2:433, et passim.

illumination[81]—and sidesteps the crux of the matter: whether the knowledge imparted to humans by the Logos is mediate or immediate. If mediate, then what is the medium? If the medium is created things—and if realism is disallowed as a valid epistemological option—then in Oliphint's view what is the nature of the cognitive process by which human minds obtain knowledge from the Logos via created things? If immediate—if the Logos's revelation does not employ the external world as its medium and if there is no adequation between mind and thing—then how would Oliphint's position avoid rationalism, idealism, or pantheism?

VI. Conclusion

"Bavinck's bug" does not exist. It is a mythical creature that lives exclusively in "Van Tilian" folklore. Its sole strength lies in the ability of its small community of supporters to perpetuate a false dilemma based upon a category mistake: the assumption that either one must affirm Holy Scripture as the sole necessary and sufficient cognitive principle of theology *and* philosophy or one must affirm rational autonomy as the sole cognitive foundation of one's philosophy. This idiosyncratic position arose under the influence of twentieth-century theological and philosophical developments at the Free University in Amsterdam. Ironically, this view is incompatible with Holy Scripture itself, despite its intention to defend the necessity of Scripture vis-à-vis philosophy. Furthermore, this position is out of accord with the Reformed confessions, the formulations of classic Reformed orthodox theologians, and universal human experience. The resulting reductionism of this position—when pressed to its logical conclusion—entails endless absurdities regarding the cognitive process in non-theological sciences. Finally, this view omits a positive statement regarding the crux of the entire matter—the nature of the relation between human perception, the external world, and the Logos. The only "viral infection" that needs purging, then, is Oliphint's recapitulation of Van Til's anti-scholastic hypochondria.

---

[81] See Sytsma, "Herman Bavinck's Thomistic Epistemology," 22–45.

Bibliography

Aquinas, Thomas. *Commentary on Aristotle's Posterior Analytics*. Translated by Richard Berquist. Notre Dame, IN: Dumb Ox Books, 2007.

———. *Summa theologiae*. Edited by John Mortensen and Enrique Alarcon. Translated by Laurence Shapcote, O.P. Lander, WY: The Aquinas Institute, 2012.

Bavinck, Herman. *Reformed Dogmatics*. Edited by John Bolt. Translated by John Vriend. 4 vols. Grand Rapids: Baker Academic, 2003–08.

———. *The Philosophy of Revelation: The Stone Lectures for 1908–1909, Princeton Theological Seminary*. New York: Longmans, Green, and Co., 1908.

Bolt, John. "Een Gemiste En Een Nieuwe Kans: Herman Bavinck over Openbaring En Religie." In *Ontmoetingen Met Herman Bavinck*, edited by George Harinck and Gerrit Neven, 143–64. Ad Chartas-Reeks 9. Barneveld: De Vuurbaak, 2006.

———. "Sola Scriptura as an Evangelical Theological Method?" In *Reforming or Conforming: Post-Conservative Evangelicals and the Emerging Church*, edited by Gary L. W. Johnson and Ronald N. Gleason, 154–65. Wheaton, Ill: Crossway Books, 2008.

Brakel, Wilhelmus à. *The Christian's Reasonable Service in Which Divine Truths Concerning the Covenant of Grace Are Expounded, Defended against Opposing Parties, and Their Practice Advocated as Well as The Administration of This Covenant in the Old and New Testaments*. Edited by Joel R. Beeke. Translated by Bartel Elshout. 4 vols. Grand Rapids, MI: Reformation Heritage Books, 1992.

Bristley, Eric D. *A Guide to the Writings of Cornelius Van Til 1895–1987*. Chicago: Olive Tree Communications, 1995.

Deursen, Arie Theodorus van. *The Distinctive Character of the Free University in Amsterdam, 1880–2005: A Commemorative History*. Translated by Herbert Donald Morton. Grand Rapids: Eerdmans, 2008.

Dooyeweerd, Herman. "Kuyper's Philosophy of Science." Translated by D. F. M. Strauss. In *On Kuyper: A Collection of Readings on the Life, Work & Legacy of Abraham Kuyper*, eds. Steve Bishop and John H. Kok, 323–41. Sioux Center, IA: Dordt College Press, 2013.

———. "Kuyper's Wetenschapsleer." *Philosophia Reformata* 4 (1939): 193–232.

Eglinton, James. "How Many Herman Bavincks? De Gemeene Genade and the 'Two Bavincks' Hypothesis." In *The Kuyper Center Review Volume 2: Revelation and Common Grace*, edited by John Bowlin, 279–301. Grand Rapids, MI: Eerdmans, 2011.

———. *Trinity and Organism: Towards a New Reading of Herman Bavinck's Organic Motif*. T&T Clark Studies in Systematic Theology 17. London: T&T Clark, 2012.

Fesko, J. V., and Guy M. Richard. "Natural Theology and the Westminster Confession of Faith." In *The Westminster Confession into the 21st Century: Essays in Remembrance of the 350th Anniversary of the Westminster Assembly*, vol. 3, ed. J. Ligon Duncan III, 223–66. Ross-shire, Scotland: Mentor, 2009.

Frame, John M. "In Defense of Something Close to Biblicism: Reflections on Sola Scriptura and History in Theological Method." *Westminster Theological Journal* 59, no. 2 (1997): 269–91.

———. "Muller on Theology." *Westminster Theological Journal* 56, no. 1 (Spr. 1994): 133–51.

Friesen, J. Glenn. "The Investigation of Dooyeweerd and Vollenhoven by the Curators of the Free University." Unpublished essay, 2005. http://j.mp/FriesenVU.

Geisler, Norman L. *Thomas Aquinas: An Evangelical Appraisal*. Grand Rapids: Baker, 1991.

Gordon, T. David. "How My Mind Has Changed: The Insufficiency of Scripture." *Modern Reformation* 11, no. 1 (2002): 18–23.

Glas, Gerrit. "What Is Christian Philosophy?" Translated by John H. Kok. *Pro Rege* 40, no. 1 (2011): 1–17.

Harinck, George. "'How Can an Elephant Understand a Whale and Vice Versa?' The Dutch Origins of Cornelius Van Til's Appraisal of Karl Barth." In *Karl Barth and American Evangelicalism*, edited by Bruce L. McCormack and Clifford B. Anderson, 13–41. Grand Rapids, MI: Eerdmans, 2011.

Heppe, Heinrich. *Reformed Dogmatics Set Out and Illustrated from the Sources*. Edited by Ernst Bizer. Translated by G. T. Thomson. London: George Allen & Unwin, 1950.

Macleod, Donald. "Bavinck's Prolegomena: Fresh Light on Amsterdam, Old Princeton, and Cornelius Van Til." *Westminster Theological Journal* 68, no. 2 (2006): 261–82.

Mattson, Brian G. "Van Til on Bavinck: An Assessment." *Westminster Theological Journal* 70, no. 1 (2008): 111–27.

Muller, Richard A. "Historiography in the Service of Theology and Worship: Toward Dialogue with John Frame." *Westminster Theological Journal* 59, no. 2 (1997): 301–10.

———. *Post-Reformation Reformed Dogmatics*. Vol. 1, *Prolegomena to Theology*. Grand Rapids: Baker Academic, 2003.

———. "Reformation, Orthodoxy, 'Christian Aristotelianism,' and the Eclecticism of Early Modern Philosophy." *Nederlands Archief Voor Kerkgeschiedenis* 81 (2001): 306–25.

———. "The Study of Theology Revisited: A Response to John Frame." *Westminster Theological Journal* 56, no. 2 (1994): 409–17.

Oliphint, K. Scott. "Bavinck's Realism, The Logos Principle, and Sola Scriptura." *Westminster Theological Journal* 72, no. 2 (2010): 359–90.

———. "Desert Bloom in Amarillo." *New Horizons*, July 2010. Available at http://opc.org/nh.html?article_id=666.

———. "The Consistency of Van Til's Methodology." *Westminster Theological Journal* 52, no. 1 (1990): 27–49.

———. "The Prolegomena Principle: Frame and Bavinck." In *Speaking the Truth in Love: The Theology of John M. Frame*, edited by John J. Hughes, 201–32. Phillipsburg, NJ: P&R, 2009.

Ridgeley, Thomas. *A Body of Divinity: wherein the doctrines of the Christian religion are explained and defended. Being the substance of several lectures on the Assembly's Larger Catechism*. Edited by John M. Wilson. New York: Robert Carter & Brothers, 1855.

Sinnema, Donald. "The Discipline of Ethics in Early Reformed Orthodoxy." *Calvin Theological Journal* 28, no. 1 (1993): 10–44.

Strange, Dan. "Not Ashamed! The Sufficiency of Scripture for Public Theology." *Themelios* 36, no. 2 (2011): 238–60.

Sytsma, David S. "Herman Bavinck's Thomistic Epistemology: The Argument and Sources of His Principia of Science." In *Five Studies in the Thought of Herman Bavinck, A Creator of Modern Dutch Theology*, edited by John Bolt, 1–56. Lewiston, NY: Edwin Mellen, 2011.

Tol, Anthony. *Philosophy in the Making: D. H. Th. Vollenhoven and the Emergence of Reformed Philosophy* Sioux Center, IA: Dordt College Press, 2010.

Turretin, Francis. *Institutes of Elenctic Theology*. Edited by James T. Dennison, Jr. Translated by George Musgrave Giger. 3 vols. Phillipsburg, NJ: P&R, 1992.

Ussher, James. *A Body of Divinity: Or, the Sum and Substance of Christian Religion*. Edited by Michael Nevarr. Birmingham, AL: Solid Ground Christian Books, 2007.

Van Raalte, Theodore G. "Unleavened Morality? Herman Bavinck on Natural Law." In *Five Studies in the Thought of Herman Bavinck, A Creator of Modern Dutch Theology*, edited by John Bolt, 57–100. Lewiston, NY: Edwin Mellen, 2011.

Van Til, Cornelius. *An Introduction to Systematic Theology: Prolegomena and the Doctrines of Revelation, Scripture, and God*. Edited by William Edgar. 2nd ed. Phillipsburg, NJ: P&R, 2007.

———. *The Defense of the Faith*. Edited by K. Scott Oliphint. 4th ed. Phillipsburg, NJ: P&R, 2008.

Vermigli, Peter Martyr. *The Peter Martyr Library*. Vol. 9, *Commentary on Aristotle's Nicomachean Ethics*. Edited by Emidio Campi and Joseph C. McLelland. Sixteenth Century Essays & Studies 73. Kirksville, MO: Truman State University Press, 2006.

Vos, Arvin. *Aquinas, Calvin, and Contemporary Protestant Thought: A Critique of Protestant Views on the Thought of Thomas Aquinas*. Grand Rapids, MI: Christian University Press, 1985.

Vos, Geerhardus. *Redemptive History and Biblical Interpretation: The Shorter Writings of Geerhardus Vos*. Edited by Richard B. Gaffin Jr. Phillipsburg, NJ: P&R, 1980.

Wells, David F. "On Being Framed." *Westminster Theological Journal* 59, no. 2 (Fall 1997): 293–300.

White, Jr., William. *Van Til, Defender of the Faith: An Authorized Biography*. Nashville and New York: Thomas Nelson, 1979.

De-Klining From Chalcedon: Exegetical Roots Of The "R2k" Project

Rev. Benjamin Miller

Since the publication of David VanDrunen's *Natural Law and the Two Kingdoms* (hereinafter *NLTK*) in 2010, and his *Living in God's Two Kingdoms* (hereinafter *LGTK*) the same year,[1] the level of critical engagement with what has been variously termed "the Escondido theology" or the "R2K" position associated with Westminster Seminary California, has risen dramatically.[2] Perhaps foremost in recent exchanges has been the question of the validity of VanDrunen's historical claims, particularly with respect to the teachings of the magisterial Reformers, but also with respect to such important figures as Augustine, the Puritans and Presbyterians of the sixteenth- and seventeenth-century British Isles, Abraham Kuyper, Herman Bavinck, and representatives of the "Neo-Calvinist" tradition. What has not received much attention to date is something that lies deep beneath the surface of the Escondido R2K project—the biblical theology and exegesis of Meredith G. Kline.[3]

The Klinean Roots of the R2K Project

Kline taught Old Testament at Westminster Seminary California from 1981 until 2002, and remained professor emeritus there until his death

---

[1] David VanDrunen, *Natural Law and the Two Kingdoms: A Study in the Development of Reformed Social Thought* (Grand Rapids: Eerdmans, 2009); and *Living in God's Two Kingdoms: A Biblical Vision for Christianity and Culture* (Wheaton: Crossway, 2010).

[2] E.g., John Frame, *The Escondido Theology: A Reformed Response to Two Kingdoms Theology* (Lakeland, FL: Whitefield Media Productions, 2011). Some of the liveliest interactions have been hosted on The Calvinist International site (http://calvinistinternational.com/category/two-kingdoms-2/, accessed 9 June 2014, and sources cited therein). Another notable contribution is the recent collection of essays in Ryan C. McIlhenny, ed., *Kingdoms Apart: Engaging the Two Kingdoms Perspective* (Phillipsburg, NJ: P&R Publishing, 2012).

[3] Only very recently has VanDrunen himself offered a full-scale exegetical work comparable to his earlier historical project in *NLTK*. See his *Divine Covenants and Moral Order: A Biblical Theology of Natural Law* (Grand Rapids: Eerdmans, 2014).

in 2007. Significantly, his influential *Kingdom Prologue: Genesis Foundations for a Covenantal Worldview* was published in two parts in 1981 and 1983, and was a classroom text from which a generation of WSCal students learned biblical theology. Among these was David VanDrunen, who received his MDiv from WSCal during Kline's tenure, and whose thorough familiarity with Kline's system of thought is evident in *NLTK*.[4]

Near the end of his historical study, VanDrunen situates Kline within (his reading of) the Reformed natural law/two kingdoms tradition, but also points out what is unique in Kline's contribution—and here his sympathy with Kline's work in Genesis starts to emerge. He sees Kline as basically consistent with (his reading of) "traditional Reformed two kingdoms ideas about the different origins, natures, purposes, and functions of the church as the redemptive kingdom of Christ on the one hand and the state and other cultural institutions and activities on the other" (the accuracy of this portrayal of the Reformed tradition is, of course, fiercely contested, cf. note 3 above). Similarly, he thinks "Kline's treatment of creation, the image of God, and the covenant of works . . . communicates a classic Reformed doctrine of natural law, albeit without using that terminology."[5] However, Kline's "most important creative contribution to the tradition . . . is probably his explicit articulation of the older ideas in terms of Reformed covenant theology." Specifically, Kline grounds "political and cultural life in God's work of creation and providence rather than in his work of redemption" and insists "on a sharp distinction between holy and common realms of life." VanDrunen believes

> Kline's distinction between the cultural realm as founded in the covenant of common grace and the church as founded in the redemptive covenant of grace in a way paralleling the earlier Reformed distinction between the two kingdoms as expressed in state and church suggests a more explicit connection between the central biblical categories of covenant and kingdom than the earlier tradition provided.

---

[4] VanDrunen, *Natural Law and the Two Kingdoms*, 411–421.

[5] Ibid., 416, 418.

He goes so far as to suggest that Kline's

> (somewhat unwitting) development of the Reformed natural law and two kingdoms traditions was in some respects more theoretically and practically coherent than that of the figures considered [by VanDrunen] in previous chapters and is linked in much more explicit detail to the covenant theology that has so often served as an organizing substructure for the system of Reformed doctrine.[6]

Put succinctly, Kline isn't just faithful to the Reformed NL/2K tradition (as VanDrunen reads it); he's more *biblically* faithful – he has grounded the "traditional" view in biblical covenant theology.

VanDrunen's conceptual reliance on Kline is even more evident in *LGTK*, albeit with fewer explicit references to his former teacher. In this more popular volume, VanDrunen introduces two lines of argument that sound strange to ears accustomed to refrains such as "all of life redeemed" and "all of Christ for all of life." One line of argument (we'll call it his "distinction argument") runs as follows:

> Scripture requires a high view of creation and of cultural activity, but it also requires a distinction between the holy things of Christ's heavenly kingdom and the common things of the present world. It requires a distinction between God's providential sustaining of human culture for the whole of the human race and his glorious redemption of a chosen people that he has gathered into a church now and will gather into the new creation for eternity. Some people indeed fall into unwarranted "dualisms," but dualism-phobia must not override our ability to make clear and necessary *distinctions*. Some people indeed are guilty of promoting a godless and amoral "secular" realm, but the fear of a godless secularism should not eliminate our ability to speak of a *divinely-ordained common* kingdom that is legitimate but not holy.[7]

Later he describes the origins and nature of these two kingdoms more precisely:

---

[6] Ibid., 420–21.

[7] VanDrunen, *Living in God's Two Kingdoms*, 26 (emphasis in original).

Early in Genesis God established two covenants, by which the two kingdoms were formally established. In his covenant with Noah God entered covenantal relationship with the entire human race (and with the entire creation), promising to preserve its cultural activities such as procreating and securing justice. This was the formal establishment of the "common kingdom." In his covenant with Abraham, by contrast, God entered covenantal relationship with a chosen people, upon whom he bestows eternal salvation by faith, thereby distinguishing them from the rest of the human race. This was the formal establishment of the "redemptive kingdom." God's people are thus called to live under both covenants – that is, in two kingdoms. On the one hand, they respect the terms of the Noahic covenant as they pursue a variety of cultural activities in common with unbelievers. On the other hand, they embrace the terms of the Abrahamic covenant of grace as they cling to the promises of salvation and eternal life in a new creation and as they gather in worshiping communities distinguished from the unbelieving world.[8]

Setting aside the question whether this adequately accounts for "redemptive" elements in the Noahic context (see below), how do these two covenants/kingdoms relate to God's purposes in creating the human race in the first place? What, in other words, has either Noah or Abraham to do with Adam? This brings us to VanDrunen's other line of argument (which we'll call his "direction argument"): "Redemption does not consist in restoring people to fulfill Adam's original task, but consists in the Lord Jesus Christ himself fulfilling Adam's original task once and for all, on our behalf. Thus redemption is not 'creation regained' but 're-creation gained.'"[9]

Later he develops what this means for the direction (orientation, or purpose) of human cultural life:

---

[8] Ibid., 29. VanDrunen has published at least two articles that expand considerably his brief reflections on the Noahic covenant in *LGTK*: "Natural Law in Noahic Accent: A Covenantal Conception of Natural Law Drawn from Genesis 9," *Journal of the Society of Christian Ethics* 30:2 (Fall–Winter 2010): 131–49; and "The Two Kingdoms and the Social Order: Political and Legal Theory in Light of God's Covenant with Noah," *Journal of Markets and Morality* 14:2 (Fall 2011): 445–62. See also his recent *Divine Covenants and Moral Order*, 95–132.

[9] Ibid., 26.

> The Lord Jesus, as a human being—as the last Adam—has attained the original goal held out for Adam: a glorified life ruling the world-to-come. Because Jesus has fulfilled the first Adam's commission, those who belong to Christ by faith are no longer given that commission. Christians already possess eternal life and claim an everlasting inheritance. God does not call them to engage in cultural labors so as to earn their place in the world-to-come. We are not little Adams. Instead, God gives us a share in the world-to-come as a gift of free grace in Christ and then calls us to live obediently in this world as a grateful response. Our cultural activities do not in any sense usher in the new creation. The new creation has been earned and attained once and for all by Christ, the last Adam. Cultural activity remains important for Christians, but it will come to an abrupt end, along with this present world as a whole, when Christ returns and cataclysmically ushers in the new heavens and new earth.[10]

There's something odd here. By framing Adam's cultural life as so entirely directed toward attaining "a glorified life ruling the world-to-come," and by making attainment of that glorified life a matter of strict merit, VanDrunen is forced to erect an impenetrable wall between the life of believers under grace and the life for which God made humans in the first place. Life under redeeming grace must be *absolutely* non-Adamic: believers are saved not only from Adam's sin but also from his commission (which was a matter of meritorious righteousness). What are we to do, then, with all of the "merely human" things in which the redeemed find themselves employed in this world?

VanDrunen's solution (cf. his "distinction argument" reviewed above) is to radically partition human life after the Fall: life on the one (redemptive) side consists simply in believing Jesus has fulfilled the creation mandate, and worshipping Him; all other human activities, cut off from God's first purposes in Eden, His final purposes in the *eschaton*, and His redeeming grace in the interval between the two, are legitimate but "profane." They are allowed to continue because God hasn't yet destroyed the earth (this is the grace of the Noahic covenant)—but He surely will destroy it, and with it all cultural activities and institutions of believers and unbe-

---

[10] Ibid., 28.

lievers alike. To argue that cultural activities hold any promise for the life to come, or have any connection to God's purposes for Adam, is to mingle the holy with the profane; worse, it confuses the grace of Christ with the works of Adam.[11] VanDrunen is quite explicit about this: "To understand our own cultural work as picking up and finishing Adam's original task is, however unwittingly, to compromise the sufficiency of Christ's work."[12]

All of this stems from a particular reading of Genesis (the stories of Adam, Noah, and Abraham), and it requires only a brief perusal of *Kingdom Prologue* to see that Kline is the source of the reading.

A Survey of Kline's Reading of Genesis

There's no place to start like the beginning, and Kline's view of Adam's pre-Fall situation illumines much of the rest of his work. Two major ideas stand out in his reading of Genesis 1–2, and it will be obvious that these parallel the two lines of argument noted above in VanDrunen's *LGTK*.

---

[11] This explains a strange and telling statement in *LGTK*: "Those who hold a traditional Protestant view of justification *consistently* should not find a redemptive transformationist perspective [such as one finds in Neo-Calvinism and in N. T. Wright] attractive. As some of the Reformers grasped, a two-kingdoms doctrine is a proper companion to a Protestant doctrine of justification." Ibid., 21 (emphasis in original). VanDrunen cites John Calvin's *Institutes of the Christian Religion*, 3.19, without specification. While Calvin does speak of "two kingdoms" in this section, the burden is on VanDrunen to show that Calvin's two-kingdoms doctrine bears any resemblance to the schema he is advocating.

[12] VanDrunen, *Living in God's Two Kingdoms*, 50–51. Cf. his conclusion in "Natural Law in Noahic Accent": [Noahic] natural law does not provide an ethic for the new creation, nor is it teleologically oriented toward the new creation. The kingdom of God proclaimed by Jesus represented a new work of God, grounded not in a covenantal act of preservation but in the new covenant in Jesus's blood, which promised not the maintenance of the present created order but the manifestation of a new created order of eschatological peace. The Christian gospel promises not the perfection of our life under the natural law but ultimately our liberation from life under the natural law in that it promises release from the confines of this present age. The ethic of the new covenant, in distinction from the Noahic covenant, is founded in an act of mercy and forgiveness, the love of God in giving the Son, which evokes an analogous merciful love in God's servants (1 John 4:9–11). Moral theologians face an ongoing challenge in seeking to define precisely the relation between natural law and a merciful, Christ-centered Christian ethic." They do, indeed!

First, Kline sees Adam's pre-Fall life as composed of two distinct dimensions: one *cultic* (or priestly), the other *cultural* (or kingly). The obligations of the creation covenant made with Adam, he says,

> were concerned with both the vertical and horizontal dimensions of covenant life. They dealt with man's cultural task, his commission with respect to his horizontal relationship to the world that was his environment and to all his fellow creatures. They dealt also with man's cultic role, his duties in his directly vertical relationship to his Creator-Lord. Man's theocratic commission involved a dual priest-king office.[13]

He then anticipates VanDrunen's "distinction argument" in this remarkable passage:

> Though man's total life and labor, his cultural and his cultic functioning, are religious, the distinction between the cultural and cultic dimensions, present from the beginning, *did provide a formal groundwork for the sacred-profane distinction that afterwards emerged in the fractured postlapsarian world.* With the exception of one or two notable situations, God's servants find themselves after the Fall in a common grace situation where their cultural functions are not holy but profane.[14]

Exactly how the pre-Fall cultic-cultural distinction could pave the way for a post-Fall sacred-profane distinction becomes clearer as we turn to a second major idea in Kline's reading of Genesis 1–2, the notion (cf. VanDrunen's "direction argument") that man's pre-Fall life was to unfold in three stages: "initial priestly reception of glory from God," a "middle stage" of kingship, and "an ultimate priestly return of glory to God."[15] Kline describes these stages elsewhere in different terms:

> As image of God, man also possessed the ethical glory of a state of simple righteousness, with the prospect of moving on to the greater glory of confirmed righteousness. And a

---

[13] Meredith G. Kline, *Kingdom Prologue: Genesis Foundations for a Covenantal Worldview* (Overland Park, KS: Two Age Press, 2000), 66. See the entire summary, ibid., 66–67; which is further elaborated, 67–90.

[14] Ibid., 67 (emphasis added).

[15] Ibid., 88.

further promise of man's image status was that of transformation into the likeness of the epiphanic light. Man was given the hope of an eschatological glorification that would change him into a transfigured glory-image of the radiant Glory-Spirit.[16]

The intended movement, then, was from (1) simple righteousness through priestly probation to the middle stage of (2) confirmed righteousness, to be finally consummated in (3) eschatological glory. Especially important is that Kline places kingly fulfillment of the creation mandate (cultivating and taking dominion over the earth) in the *second* stage (what he calls the "semi-eschatological" stage of man's existence), *after* Adam sustained a priestly probation in his encounter with the serpent.[17]

This is crucial: for Kline the creation/dominion mandate was to be fulfilled in the *post-probationary, "semi-eschatological"* stage of man's existence, in a state of confirmed righteousness. This introduces a problem: is there any equivalent of this "semi-eschatological" stage in the post-Fall (redemptive) context, or did the semi-eschatological prospect vanish with the Fall, and the creation mandate with it? The problem is compounded by the fact

---

[16] Ibid., 45. On the image of God, cf. Kline's *Images of the Spirit* (Grand Rapids: Baker, 1980; repr., Eugene, OR: Wipf and Stock, 1999).

[17] "The priestly charge to guard the sanctity of that garden-sanctuary in the hour of satanic encroachment, the critical probationary task, was man's first great historical assignment. This cultic-judicial encounter with the evil one was to precede the pursuit of the royal cultural commission to expand the sanctuary-kingdom-house of God from focus to fullness." *Kingdom Prologue*, 87. Bestowal of the blessings of the creation covenant "would occur over a lengthy span of history, including an extended semi-eschatological stage before the coming of the fully eschatological state of glory. Obedience with respect to the tree of knowledge would qualify man to avail himself of the invitation of the Logos-Life to partake of the sacramental tree of life. By that sacramental communion he would be confirmed in the beatitude of the covenant; the promise of glorified life would be sealed unto him. . . While the ethical glory of the *imago Dei* would at once be confirmed forever, the perfecting of the glory of dominion and the transfiguring realization of the physical glory would not be realized immediately. Though there would be at once a sabbatical fulfillment of rest from probationary work, entrance into the Sabbath as rest from and completion of the cultural commission of the covenant belonged still to the future. . . . [C]onsummation would await man's passage through a semi-eschatological stage of history devoted to the fulfilling of the assigned historical task of building the kingdom-city by filling and subduing the earth." Ibid., 96. Cf. Kline's description of Adam's probationary task, ibid., 121.

that, for Kline, the probation was a matter of strict merit ("pure and simple justice"[18]); which means that access to the semi-eschatological state was a matter of strict merit; which raises the possibility that, on a Klinean view, any efforts to fulfill the creation mandate post-Fall could be construed as a return to strict merit (works righteousness).[19] VanDrunen has straightforwardly said as much (see above).

Putting together the pieces of Kline's reading of Genesis 1–2, the following picture emerges: Adam *would* forfeit both semi-eschatological blessings (including the kingly prospect of cultivating and ruling the earth) and eschatological blessings if, as God's priest, he failed his probationary test in the encounter with the serpent. The possibility existed, however, that, because his cultural-kingly calling was distinct from his cultic-priestly calling, he might after the Fall be reinvested with cultural duties, not (we'll shortly hear from Kline) as a renewal of his creation mandate but as part of a profane order of life preserved by God's "common grace." What remains unclear in this picture is what benefits, if any, *redeeming* grace after the Fall might confer in the realm of man's cultural endeavors.

This brings us to Kline's description of the post-Fall situation in Genesis. We will briefly consider his reading of three episodes: the curse and blessing pronounced to Adam and Eve, the city of Cain, and the covenant made with Noah and all creation.

Grace to Adam and Eve

In his treatment of the mercies extended to Adam and Eve after the Fall, which were accompanied by "symbolic reinvestiture with the divine image" in the form of animal-skin garments,[20] Kline is silent about whether this reinvestiture entailed any renewal of the creation mandate. Part of the

---

[18] "A principle of works – do this and live – governed the attainment of the consummation-kingdom proferred in the blessing sanction of the creational covenant. Heaven must be earned. According to the terms stipulated by the Creator it would be on the ground of man's faithful completion of the work of probation that he would be entitled to enter the Sabbath rest. If Adam obediently performed the assignment signified by the probation tree, he would receive, as a matter of pure and simple justice, the reward symbolized by the tree of life." Ibid., 107.

[19] This would certainly be the case for the unredeemed, but what of the redeemed? Has Christ merited an entrance for them into something like the "semi-eschatological" state, and thus a renewal of the mandate? On this, see below.

[20] Ibid., 149–53.

reason for his silence seems to be that he regards the mercies extended to Adam and Eve as expressing both redemptive *and* common grace (in Genesis, of course, God's grace to them appears simply as grace, without distinction). He then places "the continuation, even though in modified fashion, of some important elements of the social-cultural order that had been established under the Creator's covenant with Adam" under the rubric of *common* grace. These elements included marriage, the propagation of human life, and dominion over the earth.[21] The question is why Kline makes this move. After all, Adam and Eve received God's promises as *believers* (Kline himself is clear about this[22]), so why are marriage, propagation, and dominion not viewed as foci of *redemption*?

Kline's unexpected partitioning of grace into redemptive and common compartments (and assigning cultural activities and institutions to the "common" compartment) is developed in his treatment of "The Holy and the Common."[23] Here he insists that "the political, institutional aspect of common grace culture is not holy, but profane," because God "did not attach his Sabbath promise to this common cultural order." "The withholding of the Sabbath sign from common grace culture is a clear indication," he says, "of the secular, nonholy character of that culture." Related to this, he insists that the common cultural order is *not* a continuation of the creation/dominion mandate:

> Common grace culture is not itself the particular holy kingdom-temple culture that was mandated under the creational covenant. Although certain functional and institutional provisions of the original cultural mandate are resumed in the common grace order, these now have such a different orientation, particularly as to objectives, that one cannot simply and strictly say that it is *the* cultural mandate that is being implemented in the process of common grace culture. It might be closer to the truth to say that the cultural mandate of the original covenant in Eden is being carried out in the program of salvation, since the ultimate objective of that mandate, the holy kingdom-temple, will be the consummate achievement of Christ under the Cov-

---

[21] Ibid., 154.

[22] Ibid., 149–50.

[23] Ibid., 155–60. Arguably, the exegetical framework for the entire "R2K" project lies exposed in these few pages.

enant of Grace. On the other hand, the genealogical and earthly aspects of the original cultural mandate that were to constitute its preconsummation history are not part of the redemptive program *per se*.[24]

For Kline, the problem with culture (man's kingly calling) post-Fall is that it is no longer oriented to production of the eschatological cult, the holy kingdom-temple. Cut off from this supernatural and eschatological end into which it was originally destined to be absorbed,[25] culture is not under divine wrath but neither is it a sphere of union and communion with the Holy One in this world or the next. The cultural enterprise cannot bear His name, it will not enter His eternal Sabbath-glory; its created purpose can be neither restored nor fulfilled (other than in the once-for-all work of Christ); it is, therefore, neither holy nor sinful; it is simply profane, irredeemable nature.[26] This may explain one of the more puzzling formulations at the end

---

[24] Ibid., 156–57 (emphasis in original).

[25] Kline states this in the strongest possible terms: "To produce the cult itself, the cosmic-human temple, was the ultimate objective in view in the cultural enterprise." Ibid., 89. "Man's external culture was intended to serve only a provisional purpose during man's preconsummation history. It was merely a temporary substitute for glorification, the real and permanent thing. . . . Prototypal culture performs its necessary function, then passes away at the advent of the heavenly antitype culture, which is not just a top-story superimposed on the earth-founded prototype but an eschatologically new reality through and through. And this metaculture, which renders all prototypes obsolete, comes down from heaven, from God, its Architect-Creator. . . . Nothing of earthly culture external to man enters [God's eschatological city]." Ibid., 99–100.

[26] A topic deserving further exploration is the similarity between Kline's cultural-cultic schema and the nature-grace schema in Roman Catholic protology. Herman Bavinck describes the Roman Catholic view as follows: "Rome does not abolish the natural order in Manicheaen fashion but suppresses it. It leaves marriage, family, possessions, earthly vocation, the state, science, and art intact and even permits them, in their own place, a greater space and freedom than Protestantism tends to do. Nonetheless it downgrades the natural by stamping it as profane and unhallowed. The contrast within which Rome operates is not that between holy and unholy but sacred and profane. This reduces the ethical to something material by regarding the natural realm not as ungodly because and insofar as it is unclean but because it is powerless to achieve the supernatural. Rome thus profanes the cosmos." Herman Bavinck, "The Catholicity of Christianity and the Church," trans. John Bolt, *Calvin Theological Journal* 27 (November 1992): 231. Related to this, see Peter Escalante's helpful analysis of the *donum superadditum* in "Two Ends or Two Kingdoms," http://calvinistinternational.com/2013/04/08/two-ends-or-two-

of "The Holy and the Common," where Kline posits that redeemed persons after the Fall *are* "to be conscious of doing all things, whether in the holy or common spheres, as a matter of thankful obedience to God and for his glory and thus as a religious service"; *but* the "religious integration of the believer's life as a comprehensive service of Christ does not mean that the distinction between holy and common spheres gets obliterated."[27] Is "integration" really an apt term here? True, grace restores nature, but only insofar as it restores holy motives and attitudes in the hearts of the redeemed; beyond that, nature and grace stand in parallel, all cultural labor and all fruits thereof being destined for apocalyptic obliteration.

The City of Cain

This leads us, secondly, to Kline's "tale of two cities": the original city of God that was intended in the creation covenant, and the common grace city built by Cain in Genesis 4.[28]

In the beginning, says Kline, Adam was to build Megapolis, the worldwide city of God, and in time Megapolis would be eschatologically transformed into Metapolis, the consummate antitype of which Megapolis was never more than a prototype.[29] (This is basically a picturesque restatement of the idea that, pre-Fall, human life was to unfold in stages, with fulfillment of the dominion mandate lying in the "middle" or "semi-eschatological" stage.)

After the Fall, Kline asserts, "God again appointed a city-structure for the benefit of the generality of mankind," but it "would not be the same city that the Lord established at the beginning."[30] In this post-Fall city, there would be no "institutional integration of culture and cult," but only "a divinely sponsored administration of justice among men," a barrier against "the formless void of the accursed wilderness" outside of Eden. There is, to be sure, a "formal, partial continuity . . . between the city of common grace and the city envisioned in the original cultural mandate, but the interim city

---

kingdoms/ (accessed 9 June 2014). It is difficult, reading Kline's formulations, not to conclude that he profanes the cosmos in much the same way Rome does.

[27] *Kingdom Prologue*, 160.

[28] Ibid., 162–89.

[29] Cf. ibid., 100–101; see also 269–78.

[30] Ibid., 163–64.

is so different from the city that would have emerged in a sinless history that we distinguish it from the latter by calling it the state."[31] The common grace city of man, then, is neither semi-eschatological (Megapolis), nor *per se* sinful (Babel), nor fully eschatological (Metapolis); rather, like everything else in the common grace order it simply lies outside the pale of God's redemptive purpose. It *cannot* be sacralized—God wills it.

A good deal more might be said about this "structural dualism" (Kline's term) in connection with the common grace city,[32] but nowhere are its implications better illustrated than in this passage where he describes life on "the other side of the fence" in the tents of Seth:

> Called to priestly mission by the altar, the Sethite saints were engaged in the priestly sanctification of culture to the Lord. . . . [W]hat would [this] entail with respect to the common city of man? Positively, it must be recognized that the whole life of God's people is covered by the liturgical model of their priestly identity. All that they do is done as a service rendered unto God. All their cultural activity in the sphere of the city of man they are to dedicate to the glory of God. *This sanctification of culture is subjective; it transpires within the spirit of the saints.* Negatively, it must be insisted that *this subjective sanctification of culture does not result in a change from common to holy status in culture objectively considered.* The common city of man does not in any fashion or to any degree become the holy kingdom of God through the participation of the culture-sanctifying saints in its development. Viewed in terms of its products, effects, institutional context, *etc.*, the cultural activity of God's people is common grace activity. Their city of man activity is not "kingdom (of God)" activity. Though it is an expression of the reign of God in their lives, it is not a building of the kingdom of God as institution or realm. For the common

---

[31] Ibid., 164, 165, 167. See also Meredith G. Kline, "The Oracular Origin of the State," in G. A. Tuttle, ed., *Biblical and Near Eastern Studies* (Grand Rapids: Eerdmans, 1978), 132–141 (available online at http://www.meredithkline.com/klines-works/articles-and-essays/the-oracular-origin-of-the-state/, accessed 9 June 2014).

[32] Particularly interesting is his insistence (against Dooyeweerd and his followers) that God's freedom is denied if we do not regard Him as "allowed to respond to the Fall with appropriate modifications of the institutional structuring of original creation" (i.e., institution of a holy/common distinction in the post-Fall order). *Kingdom Prologue*, 169–72.

city of man is not the holy kingdom realm, nor does it ever become the holy city of God, whether gradually or suddenly. Rather, it must be removed in judgment to make way for the heavenly city as a new creation.[33]

The structural dualism at the level of cultural institutions, activities, and products is absolute. All the "stuff" and "stuff to do" in the common grace realm is sealed off from God's original purposes, which are fulfilled now only in "the spirit of the saints" (certainly not in the fruit of their hands) and in the eschatological city of Metapolis to come. This brings us to Kline's reading of the Noahic narrative.

The Noahic Covenant

Kline rightly assigns pivotal significance to the Flood account in Genesis 6–9. So massive was the transition that occurred in the Flood that it divided world history into two major epochs: the first running from creation to the Flood (Kline, following 2 Peter 3:6, calls this "the world that then was"), the second running from the Flood to the *eschaton* ("the world that now is").[34] Given the epochal significance of the Flood, what sort of world emerged from its waters?

Kline believes that after the Flood God covenantally *reestablished* the common grace order initially established after the Fall.[35] As we have seen above, Kline absolutely denies that the character of this order is affected by whether culture building is done in obedience or disobedience to the Creator; the common grace order stands on its own, as a kind of "neutral zone" shared by the seed of the woman and the seed of the serpent alike. So we're not surprised to hear Kline posit that the Noahic covenant in Genesis 9 was "not an administration of redemptive grace but of common grace":

> It did not bestow the holy kingdom of God on an elect, redeemed people. The revelation of this covenant came to Noah and his family and the covenant is said to be made with them, but they are addressed here, as were Adam and Eve in the disclosure of common grace and curse in Gene-

---

[33] Ibid., 200, 201 (emphasis added).

[34] Ibid., 8–13.

[35] Ibid., 244.

sis 3:16–19, *not in distinction from but as representative of the generality of mankind.*[36]

This last phrase is curious. The covenant is made with Noah and his family "as representative of the generality of mankind," but Kline sees the grace extended here as entirely divorced from any sort of redemptive program. Why? Why could not this preserving grace extended to mankind-in-general be viewed as anticipating—indeed, organically connected to—the redeeming grace God later promised to mankind-in-general through Abraham and his seed (Gen 12:1–3). Why not see the preserving of mankind as an indicator of the scope of the redemptive program to come? The answer is that Kline has already committed himself to a rigid dualism of common and redeeming grace in his reading of the history leading up to Noah. His flow of thought concerning the Noahic covenant follows what we heard earlier in connection with Adam and Eve in Genesis 3:

> The covenant of Genesis 8:20ff. does not promise the restoration-consummation of the paradise order envisaged as the goal of redemption. It does not produce the everlasting perfection of the blessings of nature but merely provides for a partial and temporary limitation on the infliction of the curses of nature. *The sign of the Sabbath, prophetic symbol of consummated cosmic blessing, is conspicuously absent from it.* It does not culminate in the new heaven and earth; on the contrary it is terminated by the final cosmic cataclysm, which it only for a while postpones.[37]

The absence of the Sabbath sign may be significant; but it's curious that Kline doesn't mention in this context the altar built in Genesis 8:20, in response to which God announced His covenant (cf. Gen 8:21ff). Earlier, in connection with the Sethite genealogy in Genesis 5, Kline had this to say:

> Altars among the Sethites attested to the presence there of the holy assembly of the Lord. This sacramental link between the heavenly Lord of the covenant and his earthly servants was their identifying nucleus as a special covenant community. By its presence in their midst the people of the altar were constituted a priestly fellowship, a cultic congregation. Generation after generation this distinctive

---

[36] Ibid., 245 (emphasis added).

[37] Ibid., 248–49 (emphasis added).

altar-centered institution was the manifestation of the spiritual temple, the priestly people-house of God, in process of redemptive formation and destined to stand complete at the end of history, filled with the divine glory and filling all in all.[38]

What is different here? Why are those gathered about Noah's altar not a "priestly fellowship"? For Kline the absence of Sabbath trumps such questions, allowing him to preserve his structural dualism: the Noahic covenant is absolutely distinct from God's redemptive purposes in Genesis and beyond.[39]

One thing, at any rate, is now clear: there is an unmistakable link between the R2K position argued by VanDrunen and Kline's exegetical project in *Kingdom Prologue*. The former grows from the soil of the latter. This means that if Kline's work cannot sustain exegetical and theological scrutiny, the implications for VanDrunen's project, and for the R2K position as a whole, are considerable.

Exegetical-Theological Appraisal of Kline's Reading of Genesis

The remainder of this essay will explore the problems in Kline's reading of Genesis. Strange as it may sound at first, our critique will begin not with the text of Genesis but with the doctrine of Christ.

Orthodox Christology, following the witness of the New Testament, has long maintained (1) that God, having created human nature in His image, intends to restore it entirely and eternally in His image; (2) that to this end, for us and for our salvation, He assumed human nature such that no part of His humanity was replaced by His divine nature (against Apollinarius); (3) that in His assuming human nature no part of His humanity was absorbed into His divine nature (against Eutyches); and (4) that in His as-

---

[38] Ibid., 195.

[39] "The fact is that the specific character of the nature provision of the covenant of Genesis 8:20ff., a provision merely for the postponement of the final creational curse not for the consummation of the blessings of nature, contradicts any identification of this covenant with the covenant of Genesis 6:18 or with redemptive covenant in general and *demands that it rather be distinguished from all such administrations of saving grace and separately classified as a covenant of common grace*. To do otherwise is to introduce hopeless confusion into one's biblical-theological analysis and the resultant world-and-life view." Ibid., 249 (emphasis added).

suming our nature no part of His humanity was exempt from union with His divine nature (against Nestorius).[40] This Christological framework must inform our soteriological formulations, because what Christ did not assume He cannot save, and everything He assumed He fully redeemed. It must also inform our "protology" (our reading of early Genesis, especially the creation account), because, according to the New Testament (e.g., Col 1:15–20[41]), God's purposes for Adam and for humanity as a whole are to be understood in light of what He has accomplished, and will accomplish, through the redemption that is in Christ. Working from these Christological

---

[40] In an article well worth reading in connection with all of the issues raised in this essay, Torrance Kirby cites a masterful summary from Richard Hooker: "There are but fower thinges which concurre to make compleate the whole state of our Lord Jesus Christ, his deitie, his manhood, the conjunction of both, and the distinction of the one from the other beinge joyned in one. Fower principall heresies there are which have in those thinges withstood the truth, Arians by bendinge them selves against the deitie of Christ; Apollinarians by maiminge and misinterpretinge that which belongeth to his humane nature; Nestorians by rentinge Christ asunder and devidinge him into two persons; the followers of Eutiches by confoundinge in his person those natures which they should distinguish. Against these there have bene fower most famous ancient generall Councels, the Councel of Nice to define against the Arians, against Apollinarians the Councell of Constantinople, the Councel of Ephesus against Nestorians, against Eutichians the Chalcedon Councell. In fower words ἀληθῶς, τελέως, ἀδιαιρέτως, ἀσυγχύτως, *truly, perfectly, indivisibly, distinctly*; the fi8rst applyed to his beinge God, and the seconde to his beinge man, the third to his beinge of both one, and the fowrth to his still continuinge in that one both, wee may fullie by way of abridgment comprise whatsoever antiquitie hath at large handled either in declaration of Christian beliefe or in refutation of the foresaid heresies. Within the compasse of which fower heades I may trulie affirme, that all heresies, which touch but the person of Jesus Christ, whether they have risen in these later days, or in any age heretofore, may be with great facilitie brought to confine them selves." Richard Hooker, *Of the Lawes of Ecclesiasticall Politie*, 5.54.8; cited in W. J. Torrance Kirby, "The Paradigm of Chalcedonian Christology in Richard Hooker's Discourse on Grace and the Church," *Churchman*, vol. 114 (Spring, 2000): 24 (available online at http://www.biblicalstudies.org.uk/pdf/churchman/114-01_022.pdf, accessed 9 June 2014).

[41] In this remarkable text, Paul says Christ is the "firstborn" (in the position of preeminence as the πρωτότοκος) of all creation, because through Him (δι' αὐτοῦ) and for Him (εἰς αὐτὸν) all things were created. As the One to whom all things were united from creation, He is also the One in whom all things hold together (συνέστηκεν), and through Him (δι' αὐτοῦ) it is God's intent to reconcile all things (ἀποκαταλλάξαι τὰ πάντα) in heaven and on earth. In another place (Eph 1:10), Paul refers to God's plan to *unite* all things (ἀνακεφαλαιώσασθαι τὰ πάντα) in Christ.

premises, we will look again more closely at Kline's configuration of human life before the Fall.

An "Apollinarian" Turn: Kline's Reading of the Created Order in Genesis

Recall that for Kline Adam had two roles or tasks placed before him as one made in God's image. The first was a priestly role, a cultic task directed along a vertical axis of duties toward his Creator-Lord. The second was a cultural task, a kingly commission "with respect to his horizontal relationship to the world that was his environment and to all his fellow creatures." Both the cultic-priestly-vertical and the cultural-political-horizontal dimensions of Adam's life were "integrated into an institutional unity by the theocratic principle of the covenant kingdom."[42] The nature of this "institutional unity" is spelled out in the following two paragraphs, which are architectonic to *Kingdom Prologue*:

> *Priesthood is man's primary office.* It was with the priestly experience of beholding the Glory of the Creator in his Edenic sanctuary that human existence began. And the priestly charge to guard the sanctity of that garden-sanctuary in the hour of satanic encroachment, the critical probationary task, was man's first great historical assignment. This cultic-judicial encounter with the evil one was to precede the pursuit of the royal cultural commission to expand the sanctuary-kingdom-house of God from focus to fullness.
>
> Priesthood's primacy is not just a matter of historical priorities but of the *teleological subordination* of the kingly occupation to priestly-cultic objectives. In a theocratic context, kingship is *an adjunct of priesthood*, a middle stage between an initial priestly reception of glory from God and an ultimate priestly return of glory to God.[43]

---

[42] Kline, *Kingdom Prologue*, 66. Kline has earlier defined the "theocratic principle" as follows: "Theocracy involves something more than a general providential rule of God over men and nations. It denotes a particular kingdom realm that God claims in a special way as his own. . . . By making the Edenic kingdom his dwelling-place God sanctified it to himself; he imparted to it that holiness which is peculiar to theocracy." Ibid., 49–50.

[43] Ibid., 87–88 (emphasis added). Cf. this earlier passage: "In the kingdom in Eden there was an institutional coalescence of the cultic and the political in the identity of the head of the covenant-kingdom as God-King. This is entailed in the theocratic principle. At the level of the God-King the political and the cultic are not distin-

For Kline, there is a sort of "hypostatic union" between the cultic and cultural dimensions of human life prior to the Fall, but the cultic-priestly precedes the cultural-kingly both chronologically and as a matter of priority: only after man's perfect obedience in cultic probation is the cultural dimension activated; the cultural dimension operates only in the sinless, semi-eschatological context secured by initial cultic obedience (it is here in the "middle stage" of human existence that man is to partake of the tree of life which is, "in a figure, the Logos, the life of man"[44]); and so absolute is the "teleological subordination" of the cultural to the cultic that when, as the culmination of man's cultural labors, the cosmic temple-city of Megapolis (the cultic objective) is completed and eschatologically transfigured by the arrival from heaven of Metapolis, the cultural dimension of man's life is to be shed altogether as obsolete.[45] Whatever it may look like for man in glorified Metapolis to enjoy the cosmos "in joyous liberty in the unencumbered integrity of his own physical capabilities,"[46] it will look nothing like the cultural dimension of his earthly life.

There's something faintly "Apollinarian" about this "hypostatic union." Adam was created with the potential to fulfill a cultural commission, but this potential was not to be actualized until after he sustained his cultic probation. Thereafter, his cultural life would be animated entirely by the cultic spirit and oriented entirely to the cultic objective of producing a cosmic temple, such that kingship would be simply an "adjunct" to his priesthood, and a dispensable one at that, to be shed as obsolete in the *eschaton*. Culture, on this view, is disposable husk. Quite apart from sin, and with all

---

guishable. His palace is holy; his temple is royal. His temple and palace are one. At the human level of the theocracy the cultic and the political are distinquishable, but only as two theocratic functions. There is *the directly cultic priestly function* and there is *the royal function of culture, which is cult-oriented.*" Ibid., 51 (emphasis added). And this: "All culture in its spacial-temporal fullness was cult-oriented; *kingship was ancillary to priesthood.*" Ibid., 80 (emphasis added).

[44] Ibid., 95.

[45] "Nothing of earthly culture external to man enters Metapolis. . . . [T]o speak of glorified man entering Metapolis is to speak with a pronounced typological accent. For Metapolis is not a city that glorified man inhabits. It is rather the case that glorified man *is* Metapolis; in the redemptive dialect, the bride of the Lamb *is* the New Jerusalem (Rev 21:9, 10). In the Metapolis enterprise material and personnel coincide." Ibid., 100 (emphasis in original).

[46] Ibid., 98.

its semi-eschatological glory, it was never destined for enduring union with man's cultic purpose. It was from the beginning a mere means to an end; and in the end, like scaffolding, it would fall away.

It must be candidly said that none of this is required, or even strongly implied, by the text of Genesis 1–2. Nothing in Genesis indicates that Adam's cultural-royal calling stood in abeyance pending the outcome of his priestly probation and inauguration of a "semi-eschatological" stage of existence; nor does it indicate that his cultural-royal calling was "teleologically subordinated" to his cultic-priestly task, such that his cultural life had meaning, purpose, and value only until such time as he finished building the cosmic temple. Man's two callings were united in perfect integrity in his person; neither existed as a means to the end of the other. For Adam to do kingly work *was* priestly worship; and for him to worship and guard the temple-sanctuary *was* fulfilling his kingly calling—and both cult and culture, it must be emphasized, were constitutive of his being in the image of God. Humans worship because they are made for God, they work because they are made like God; and God said all of this, prior to any probation and apart from any semi-eschatological considerations, was "very good" – a glorious mirror of the knowledge, righteousness and holiness of Him in whose image man was made.

If Kline's view of the ordering of human life prior to the Fall is troubling, his view of human life after the Fall is even more so; and, as we will see, the latter worries stem directly from the former. In the post-Fall context, the tensions between Kline's formulations and those of orthodox Christology are especially pronounced.

A "Nestorian" Turn: Kline's Reading of the Redeemed Life in Genesis

By subordinating the kingly-cultural dimension of human life to the priestly-cultic, and by relegating kingly-cultural labors to the "semi-eschatological" stage of human existence, Kline opens the door for what is surely his most interesting structural move.

Those familiar with the traditional formulation that God in Christ is restoring humans in His image[47] might expect Kline to argue as follows:

---

[47] "The purpose of our redemption is the restoration of the original order of man's life. 'It is the glory of our faith,' says Calvin, 'that God, the Creator of the world, in no way disregards the order which He Himself at first established.' The work of Jesus Christ is to restore to man the image of God which was lost in Adam. 'Adam

Adam forfeited dominion over the earth by his disobedience; fallen humans continue to build culture because they're constituted to do so (and God allows them to do so by "common grace"), but the cultural mandate in its proper sense is now fulfilled among those restored to God's favor by the obedience of Christ, who sustained priestly probation on our behalf. By the grace of His perfect righteousness, the redeemed are secured in God's favor and will surely come to "Metapolis" (as God intended for Adam); and by the grace of righteousness worked in them by His Spirit, they imperfectly but faithfully worship and work as God's people in the world. All they possess, produce, and practice belongs to the Holy One; their whole lives are consecrated and are increasingly being sanctified. Together the redeemed are being corporately built up as the "Megapolis" of God by the Spirit (Eph 2:22) until the *eschaton*. Through them, all nations of the world will be discipled to worship God and devote their works to Him; and in them, God will fill the earth with His glory.

This is not, of course, how Kline proceeds. Recall again his priestly-kingly-priestly schema: the initial priestly work of Adam was to sustain his probation; the kingly-cultural work of building Megapolis was to follow; priestly-cultic consummation would arrive with the inbreaking of Metapolis. Christ, to be sure, obeyed in human flesh where Adam disobeyed, and earned Metapolis for the redeemed, but *in no sense* does this mean the mandate to build Megapolis is renewed among the redeemed.

The reason is simple: building Megapolis is a work of "confirmed righteousness"; it is not for sinners. Megapolis vanished forever the moment Adam sinned; nothing like it will appear again till Metapolis comes down out of heaven. With Adam and Eve, immediately after the Fall, God *institutionalized* the vanishing of Megapolis by establishing the "common grace order," in which the Sabbath (the sign of the perfect, consummated temple-cultus) was pointedly absent. This order was cemented as the "city

---

was first created after the image of God, and reflected as in a mirror the divine righteousness; but that image, having been defaced by sin, must now be restored in Christ. The regeneration of the godly is indeed . . . nothing else than the formation anew of the image of God in them. . . . The design contemplated by regeneration is to recall us from our wanderings to that end for which we were created.' The work of the Spirit in our hearts is to 'begin to reform us to the image of God' with a view to the complete restoration of that image both in ourselves and in the whole world." Ronald S. Wallace, *Calvin's Doctrine of the Christian Life* (Edinburgh: Oliver and Boyd, 1997; repr., Eugene, OR: Wipf and Stock, 1997), 107 (citations omitted).

of man" in the time of Cain. From then on, all cultural labors of the unredeemed and redeemed alike would belong to the common grace order and the city of man. The redeemed would work in this city as a way of honoring God, but the sanctity of their spirits would not extend to their works. If, before the Fall, holy Megapolis was destined to be absorbed into Metapolis, the profane city of man will be destroyed altogether at the coming of Metapolis. Human culture post-Fall is irredeemably profane (it is cut off from cultus); any attempt to re-sacralize it is an attempt to do the work of unfallen Adam or, worse still, the work of the perfect Last Adam. Then is grace no more grace.

An unavoidable question at this juncture is how the person and work of Christ fit into the redemptive framework Kline has proposed. Such an impenetrable wall has been erected between the cultic and the cultural, between the holy and the profane, that we must ask how this "structural dualism" can be squared with an orthodox understanding of the Incarnation and, by extension, with a Christologically informed understanding of the redeeming grace (*duplex gratia*) that flows from Christ to His people. We'll begin with the problem of how to square Kline's dualism with the Incarnation.

"Is Christ divided?" asks the apostle in his letter to Corinth (1 Cor 1:13)?[48] It seems a fair question in light of what we've heard from Kline so far. It is undeniable that when Christ assumed human nature He assumed its cultural dimension.[49] Following the logic of Kline's dualism, this must mean one of two things: either (1) the incarnate Christ Himself lived a divided life, partly holy and partly profane (i.e., His cultural activity was no more holy than that of any other human in the common grace city of man); or (2) His cultural activity was strictly a matter of priestly-probationary obe-

---

[48] A few years ago, Brad Littlejohn titled a blog post with this very question (see "Is Christ Divided? Christology and the Two Kingdoms," http://swordandploughshare.com/main-blog/2011/4/21/is-christ-divided-christology-and-the-two-kingdoms.html, accessed 9 June 2014), and addressed some of the same concerns about VanDrunen's project that I've put forward.

[49] Consider our Lord's labors in the carpentry shop as a boy; His learning to read, speak, and write; His turning water into wine at a wedding, feeding thousands with bread and fish, healing broken bodies and minds, savoring meals with His disciples, and teaching soldiers, scholars, and common folk (from a boat, no less). He wore clothes appropriate to the occasion, presumably trimmed His beard, and could recite Psalms by heart. What is all this but cultural activity?

dience by which He secured our redemption, and as a ground of redemption is as inimitable by the redeemed as His propitiatory death on the cross (a ground of redemption cannot be a fruit of redemption).

The first of these notions is absurd. It amounts to saying that Christ was not wholly sanctified. As the divine Logos, Christ is the One through whom all things (including every dimension of human life) came into being; and every part of the creation, and every dimension of human life, was "very good" because He made it. The pronouncement that all creatures (with their natures, properties, potentials, structures, relations, and operations) were "very good" was a divine affirmation that all things were "from Him, through Him, and to Him" for His glory—not in a semi-eschatological or eschatological future, but from the moment He gave them being. The Fall did not change the goodness of creation; what it brought into the world was sin and death; and when the Logos took flesh and dwelt among us, His human nature and everything done by Him in that nature partook of creational goodness (or He couldn't have assumed it) and was *sanctified* by indivisible union with His divine nature (by which He made all things) such that He was without sin (Heb 4:15; cf. Lk 1:35). To say that anything Christ did in the flesh was profane is to separate His humanity from the perfect holiness of His divine nature. Further, it denies that in Him the totality of human nature has been restored to its original union and communion with God. The ghost of Nestorius lives. In the words of Herman Bavinck:

> If even one essential constituent in the human nature of Christ is excluded from true union and communion with God, there is an element in creation that remains dualistically alongside and opposed to God. . . . Then God is not the Almighty, Creator of heaven and earth. Then the Christian religion is not truly catholic. For what is unassumable is incurable.[50]

---

[50] Herman Bavinck, *Sin and Salvation in Christ* (vol. 3 of *Reformed Dogmatics*; 4 vols.; ed. John Bolt, trans. John Vriend; Grand Rapids: Baker, 2006), 298. As noted above, the flip side of the ancient Christian formulation that "[what Christ] has not assumed He has not healed" is that "[what] is united to His Godhead is also saved." Gregory Nazianzen, *To Cledonius the Priest against Apollinarius* (vol. 7 of *Nicene and Post-Nicene Fathers: Second Series*, ed. Philip Schaff; available online at the Christian Classics Ethereal Library,
http://www.ccel.org/ccel/schaff/npnf207.iv.ii.iii.html, accessed 9 June 2014).

What then of the alternative: that Christ's cultural activity *was* holy, but only as part of the once-for-all priestly offering by which He earned eschatological glory for His people, and so the sanctity of His cultural life offers no basis for sanctification of cultural work or any renewal of the creation mandate among the redeemed? This is just Kline's pre-Fall "Apollinarianism" reintroduced at the level of the Incarnation: Christ's cultural life was a mere adjunct of His priestly-eschatological mission, so *what* He redeemed is only the priestly-eschatological dimension of the lives of His people (He is holy, but His offering does not sanctify the whole lives of the redeemed). "Apollinarian" Christology (Christ's natural life was holy only insofar as it merited supernatural glory) leads to a "Nestorian" soteriology.

This is consistent with Kline's system as a whole. We have observed that for him the cultural-kingly dimension of human life before the Fall was so absolutely oriented to (semi-)eschatological glory that after the Fall it vanished altogether except insofar as certain "functional and institutional provisions" resumed in the common grace order (later formalized in the Noahic covenant). The cultural-kingly dimension is *entirely absent* from the sphere of redemption (formalized in the Abrahamic covenant); only man's cultic-priestly calling remains in that sphere. Long before the advent of Christ, then, there was a limit to what He could redeem. The dualism in the lives of the redeemed is irreducible by God's design. The goodness of their good works and the holiness of their earthly callings extend only to the attitude or motive with which these things are performed. Their priestly spirits are holy; their kingly work is not. The kingly and priestly dimensions are never fully reintegrated in their persons; there is no "*communicatio idiomatum*" (we might say) between these aspects of their humanity.

The implications of Kline's views reach, however, far beyond individual sanctification. Because the cultural-kingly dimension of human life lies beyond the sphere of redemption, it follows that Christ redeemed *and rules over* nothing more than the cultic-priestly dimension of human life; all cultural-kingly affairs lie outside the sphere of His mediatorial reign in the common grace order, where He rules not as Christ-Redeemer but simply as Creator-Logos. This opens the way for a "two kingdoms" view in which Christ rules the cultic-priestly activity (the "spiritual" faith and worship) of the church, while the Logos rules everything else: not only the cultural but also the sociopolitical realm, not only *oeconomia* but also *politia*.[51] Here again, Christ is divided in "Nestorian" fashion.[52]

Division in the Person of Christ, division in the lives of the redeemed, division in the heavenly reign of the Son of God—something is very wrong with a protology that can produce such errors. Deep in the roots of Kline's protology lies what may be his most basic error: a dualism beneath all the others, a fancied dualism in the mind of God Himself with respect to creation and new creation. This fancy controls Kline's reading of the flow of redemptive history, nowhere more clearly than in the Noahic context—specifically, the impenetrable partition he erects between common and redeeming grace.

An Exegetical Crux: Kline's "Nestorian" Reading of the Noahic Covenant

At the heart of Kline's reading of Genesis is a pre-Fall structural distinction between the cultural and cultic dimensions of human life (and a radical subordination of the former to the latter), which gives rise after the Fall to an absolute and irreducible structural dualism between the holy and the profane, the priestly and kingly dimensions of humanity, God's redeeming grace and His common grace. This dualism was codified by God Himself in the establishment of a "common grace order" (Cain's city of man), and later in the emergence of two covenantal programs operating in parallel: the program of common grace in the Noahic covenant, and that of redeeming grace in the Abrahamic covenant.

It should not go unnoticed that this makes God of two minds in His dealing with the children of men. There is much that He made that He has no intention of redeeming, and He is content to let that part of His creation

---

[51] As an historical aside, this precisely parallels the thought of the English Disciplinarian Thomas Cartwright, Richard Hooker's brilliant opposition to which is chronicled in W. J. Torrance Kirby, *Richard Hooker's Doctrine of the Royal Supremacy*, Studies in the History of Christian Thought 43 (Leiden: Brill, 1990), 92–125.

[52] This gets "curiouser and curiouser." If the ascended Redeemer reigns *qua* Redeemer only over the "spiritual" faith and worship of His people, while as Logos He reigns over all purely earthly, cultural affairs, one wonders why it is the *incarnate* Lord who reigns over the spiritual realm, while the *spiritual* Logos rules the earthly realm. Then there are puzzles within the walls of the church, e.g., why spiritual worship should take the cultural form of singing and why the central emblem of Christ's eschatological presence with His people should be a meal consisting of cultural artifacts.

(and of human life particularly) carry on from the Fall to the *eschaton* as a temporary, provisional, and ultimately destructible thing that is somehow normed by His will and subject to His purpose yet in no sense imbued with either His holiness or the impurity of sin. It just is, "profanely."

What's deceiving about this is that many Reformed exegetes and theologians would agree with Kline that "common grace" operates after the Fall and that the Noahic covenant is a covenant of common grace.[53] But do these exegetes and theologians intend by "common grace covenant" anything like the profane realm of existence Kline has proposed? Would they accept the dualism he imposes between creation and new creation? We cannot pursue that historical question here, but we will look once more briefly at the substance of the Noahic covenant and ask whether it squares with Kline's reading.

Kline is insistent, first of all[54] (as is VanDrunen following him[55]), that God's covenant with Noah in Genesis 8:20–9:17 is *not* the covenant referred to before the Flood in Genesis 6:18. The redeeming grace promised to Noah and his family before the Flood is entirely distinct from the common grace extended to all creation after the Flood. The purpose of the former covenant was "salvation for a small remnant in the midst of a devastating and universal judgment," while the purpose of the latter was "preservation of the world while judgment is kept at bay."[56] As VanDrunen memorably puts it, "The promise of preservation *in the midst of* evil is not the same as the promise of salvation *from* evil."[57] Granting this distinction *arguendo*, is the preservation of the human race and the entirety of creation in 8:20ff. totally severable from the eschatological consummation—the attainment of new creation—that was the goal of the original creation covenant and which is bestowed by God after the Fall in the four redemptive covenants ("the Abrahamic, Mosaic, Davidic, and new"[58])?

---

[53] See, e.g., the list compiled by VanDrunen in *Divine Covenants and Moral Order*, 99, note 4.

[54] Kline, *Kingdom Prologue*, 231.

[55] VanDrunen, *Divine Covenants and Moral Order*, 107–14.

[56] Ibid., 110.

[57] Ibid., 112 (emphasis in original).

[58] Ibid., 114.

We have already heard Kline answer in the affirmative, and his disciple VanDrunen states the case succinctly in four points:

> First, in Genesis 8–9 God does not look upon his work as he completes it and declare it (very) good. Second, the description of God's rest in 8:21 (smelling an "aroma of rest") is muted, without the feel of a grand coronation scene as in 2:1–3. Third, 9:1–7 intentionally omits the language of dominion and subduing. Finally, 8:20–9:17 contains no conditional statements and gives no probationary command to Noah. These differentiating features are linked by a common theme that reveals a great difference between God's creating the world and his re-forming it. The original creation account directs readers toward consummation, both of God's work and of human work in God's likeness. . . . In Genesis 8–9, in contrast, God does not put his own work to the test and receive judicial approbation, or enjoy a grand coronation scene thereafter. It portrays human dominion in less glorious ways (hinting that postdiluvian human dominion will look different from that commissioned in Genesis 1), and sets forth no condition or probation that will bring about a particular response from Noah and thereby evoke a judicial decree and the attainment of a consummated new creation.[59]

This mode of argument is by now thoroughly familiar to us. The Noahic covenant does not promise eschatological glory; *ergo* it is merely common, merely profane, and could not possibly be organically related to God's eschatological (new creation) purposes in the sphere of redemption. Here, as in the doctrines of the Person, work, and reign of Christ, redemptive-historical "Apollinarianism" (the idea that anything not immediately oriented to earning/attaining eschatological glory is non-redemptive) has led to redemptive-historical "Nestorianism" (the segregating of all non-redemptive things into a merely profane sphere—a non-holy but not unholy realm—that will be obliterated at the *eschaton*).

Is it not possible that God's intentions in the Noahic covenant might have been more proximate than the attainment of eschatological glory, yet still organically connected to His intentions to bring His creation to eschatological glory? Perhaps God promised Noah that He would preserve the

---

[59] Ibid., 105–106.

creational order precisely because the world He made (and preserves) is the world He intends to restore and perfect through the seed of Abraham His friend. That is to say, perhaps creation was the object of Noahic preservation just because it would also be the object of Abrahamic redemption.[60]

This might be argued even more strongly concerning the human race. The Noahic covenant shows us the wideness of God's mercy to His human creatures. It issued in three lines of seed, in one of which redemption would begin but in all of which redemption will be realized. Even as the land promised to Abraham was a temporary focal point on the way to God's gift of the whole earth to His people, the seed promised to Abraham was narrow only so it might one day encompass all peoples of the world. The Jew-Gentile distinction created in the Abrahamic covenant was not to continue indefinitely. God set aside Israel in order to bring Messiah into the world, but the branches of Ham and Japheth would one day be grafted into the holy stump of Shem once again; the kings of earth would be drawn to the priestly light of Zion, and one King-Priest would rule them all. In Him, all nations of the earth, Jew and Gentile, would become "one new man in place of the two" (Eph 2:15), and those drawn from all tribes and tongues would be king-priests to God, a royal priesthood (1 Pt 2:9; Rev 1:6).[61] Preservation was *for* redemption, common grace *for* special grace. No one has expressed this better than Bavinck:

---

[60] E. J. Hutchinson has explored John Calvin's views of the restoration of creation (cf. Rom 8:19–22) in a series of essays at The Calvinist International: http://calvinistinternational.com/2014/03/26/john-calvin-new-heaven-new-earth/; http://calvinistinternational.com/2014/04/30/calvin-consummation-restoration/; http://calvinistinternational.com/2014/05/05/more-from-calvin-on-the-restoration-of-creation/; and http://calvinistinternational.com/2014/05/07/apocalypse-now/ (all accessed 9 June 2014).

[61] "The very last line of YHWH'S call to Abram (Gen. 12:3c) shows that there is something of a 'universal' purpose in Abram's election. The blessing given to Abram at this point in redemptive history has in view at some other point in time the rest of humanity ('all the families of the earth'). While it is true that Abram is the patriarchal head of Israel (one particular family/nation; cf. Gen. 15:13; Exod. 2:24; 3:6; etc.), and while it is true that the land Abram is promised is Canaan (again one particular part of the earth), this attention should never focus on 'the Jews in Palestine' question to the exclusion of the broad divine intentions: God's salvation is a restoration of His elect humanity along with the creation which is the home of this humanity." Mark D. Vander Hart, "Creation and Covenant: Part One," *Mid-America Journal of Theology* 6.1 (1990): 15–16.

[God's] *gratia specialis*, however, can be fully appreciated only when it is viewed in connection with its prevenient preparation from the time of earliest man onward. Christ is of Israel. The New Testament is the full-grown fruit of the old covenant. The portrait of Christ comes into sharp focus only against the tapestry of the Old Testament. And then we behold him clearly, full of grace and truth [cf. Exod. 34:6–7; John 1:14]. It is God himself, the Creator of heaven and earth, who in Christ fully reveals and gives himself to his people. But this grace, having fully appeared in Christ, is now intended for all men. Israel was chosen for the sake of all mankind. For a time the *gratia specialis* dug a channel for itself in Israel, only to flow out into the deep, wide sea of humankind, which had been maintained and preserved for it by the *gratia communis* [common grace]. Israel's election existed only to bring Christ into the world, as far as the flesh is concerned, so that the *gratia specialis* might be fully revealed, universal and superabundant. The stream of special grace swells and grows to overflow the banks of the nation Israel. It spreads itself across the face of the entire globe. This was the mystery of which Paul so often spoke with wonder and adoration, that the heathen are also fellow-heirs and members of the household of God [Eph. 3:6]. The two, special and common grace, separated for ages, once again combine. And thus united, they henceforth make their way together among the Christian peoples of the world. The wild olive tree is engrafted into the good olive tree. And in Abraham's seed all the families of the earth are blessed [Gen. 12:3].[62]

Everything about the Noahic covenant, from context to stipulations, agrees with this understanding of common grace. The altar and sacrifices in Genesis 8:20–22 must be viewed in light of preceding gatherings of the sons of Seth around God's altar (Kline himself sees these earlier altars as emblems of priestly holiness) and the subsequent history of atoning sacrifices in Israel. The Noahic covenant is filled with the aroma of God's re-

---

[62] Herman Bavinck, "Common Grace," trans. R. C. Van Leeuwen, *Calvin Theological Journal* 24 (April 1989): 44.

deeming purpose.⁶³ Against this sacrificial background, the covenant clearly renews the mandates given to Adam. It strains credibility to argue that what God has in view here is categorically different from what He intended for humans in the beginning. The conditions of dominion have changed (the evil of man's heart must be subdued, for one thing, 8:21; and thorns, thistles, and bloodshed will constantly threaten), but the substance of the mandate has not. True, the words "dominion" and "subdue" do not appear in 9:1–7, but there is no question that the commands to be fruitful, fill the earth, and rule the beasts are restated, albeit with acknowledgement of the real changes introduced by sin. God still intends for humankind to fill and rule the earth. Clearly hinted, however (and this supplies an organic link between preserving grace and redeeming grace), is that dominion will be achieved only in fellowship with God secured by sacrifice.⁶⁴ Ultimately, dominion will belong to those redeemed by Christ's blood, to whom, as fellow-heirs with the Heir of all things, it is the Father's good pleasure to give the world.⁶⁵ However, this full redemption through which the creation mandate would be fulfilled was not the immediate subject of Noah's covenant. His was truly a covenant of preservation, awaiting further developments in redemptive revelation. In keeping with this preserving purpose, not only did God promise to maintain the natural order, He also introduced civil order to provide "space" for His redemptive program to work—a barrier against potential chaos through human violence. Again, the "common grace" of preservation (the function of the state) is *for* the "special grace" of redemption (the mission of the Redeemer-God and of the people who bear His name and His Word in the world).⁶⁶

---

⁶³ Bavinck says that although the Noahic covenant "is not identical with" the covenant of grace, "it is rooted in God's grace and is *most intimately bound up with* the actual covenant of grace." Bavinck, *Sin and Salvation in Christ*, 218 (emphasis added).

⁶⁴ Remarkably, Kline can say of the Noahic covenant: "This covenant was concerned with natural life, *not with religious fellowship*, though it did take account of certain implications of the presence of the redemptive cultus for the common cultural area." *Kingdom Prologue*, 261 (emphasis added).

⁶⁵ On this see Vander Hart, "Creation and Covenant," 9–13.

⁶⁶ VanDrunen, predictably, is much more negative: "The Noahic covenant envisions no completion of the task of the dominion mandate. The covenant of creation held out the prospect that, like God, human beings would finish their work of dominion and would attain a state of eschatological consummation. The Noahic covenant envisions only the ongoing performance of the task in order to sustain

None of this is really controversial unless one has already committed oneself to a radical dualism of creation-cult-redemption-eschaton, on one hand, and creation-culture-profanation-obliteration, on the other. Both Kline and VanDrunen are committed to such a dualism, and thus are forced to read the Noahic covenant, and the rest of the Bible, in a way that comports with it.

Conclusion

Much exegetical and theological work remains to be done in response to Kline's reading of the early chapters of Genesis (and other portions of scripture). The purpose of this essay has been to suggest some lines along which responses might be directed. In particular, it has tried to show how the errors in Kline's protology are exposed by the light of Christological orthodoxy.

The essay has also tried to show the dependence of VanDrunen's "R2K" position on Kline's exegesis. To the extent it has succeeded, the problems pervading Kline's work raise significant concerns about the soundness of the "R2K" project.

Bavinck captures a number of the issues explored in this essay in his comments on a "Reformational view" of God's image in man:

> In Lutheran theology the image of God is restricted to original righteousness and was therefore totally lost when the latter was lost. In this theology the lines of demarcation between the spiritual and the worldly, between the heavenly and the earthly, are so sharply drawn that the result is two hemispheres, and the connection between nature and grace, between creation and re-creation is totally denied. The supernaturalist view [of Roman Catholicism] is still at work here; the image of God stands alongside nature, is detached from it, and is above it. The loss of the image, which renders man totally deaf and blind in spiritual

---

human existence and to maintain an uneasy and partial peace in society; animal-human tension is kept in check and human-human conflict is mitigated, but the conflict itself is not expunged. The dominion that Noah's descendants can achieve is but a shadow of the dominion that Adam and Eve were to achieve." VanDrunen, "Natural Law in Noahic Accent," 139. Such pessimism is possible only because he has already uncoupled the Noahic covenant from any organic connection with the Abrahamic program of redemption.

matters, still enables him in earthly matters to do much good and in a sense renders him independent from the grace of God in Christ. Reformed theology, on the other hand, by its distinction between the image of God in a broader and a narrower sense, has most soundly maintained the connection between substance and quality, nature and grace, creation and re-creation. . . . The whole being, therefore, and not *something in man* but *man himself*, is the image of God. Further, sin, which precipitated the loss of the image of God in the narrower sense and spoiled and ruined the image of God in the broader sense, has profoundly affected the whole person, so that, consequently, also the grace of God in Christ restores the whole person, and is of the greatest significance for his or her whole life and labor, also in the family, society, the state, art, science, and so forth.[67]

Regrettably, the "grace of God in Christ" portrayed in Kline's *Kingdom Prologue* falls far short of this beautiful and all-encompassing vision.

---

[67] Herman Bavinck, *God and Creation* (vol. 2 of *Reformed Dogmatics*; 4 vols.; ed. John Bolt, trans. John Vriend; Grand Rapids: Baker, 2004), 553–54 (emphasis in original). If it seems uncharitable to intimate that Kline would have any sympathy with the view that God's image in man "stands alongside nature, is detached from it, and is above it," one need only consider the opening lines from his *Images of the Spirit*: "When defining the *imago Dei* dogmatic theology has traditionally tended to engage in an analysis of what constitutes humanness. But to answer the general question 'What is man?' is not the same thing as answering the precise question 'What is the image of God?' If our objective is to discern what the biblical idea of the image of God is, it would appear necessary to abandon the traditional dogmatic wineskins, go back to the beginning of Genesis, and start afresh." Kline, *Images of the Spirit*, 13.

Bibliography

Bavinck, Herman. "Common Grace." Translated by R. C. Van Leeuwen. *Calvin Theological Journal* 24 (April 1989): 38–65.

———. "The Catholicity of Christianity and the Church." Translated by John Bolt. *Calvin Theological Journal* 27 (November 1992): 220–51.

———. *Reformed Dogmatics Vol. 2: God and Creation*. Edited by John Bolt. Translated by John Vriend. Grand Rapids: Baker, 2004.

———. *Reformed Dogmatics Vol. 3: Sin and Salvation in Christ*. Edited by John Bolt. Translated by John Vriend. Grand Rapids: Baker, 2006.

Calvin, John. *Institutes of the Christian Religion*, 2 vols. Edited by John T. McNeill. Translated by Ford Lewis Battles. Philadelphia: The Westminster Press, 1960.

Escalante, Peter. "Two Ends or Two Kingdoms." Available at http://calvinistinternational.com/2013/04/08/two-ends-or-two-kingdoms/.

Frame, John. *The Escondido Theology: A Reformed Response to Two Kingdoms Theology*. Lakeland, FL: Whitefield Media Productions, 2011.

Hutchinson, E. J. "John Calvin on the New Heaven and New Earth." Available at http://calvinistinternational.com/2014/03/26/john-calvin-new-heaven-new-earth/.

———. "Calvin on Consummation as Restoration, Again." Available at http://calvinistinternational.com/2014/04/30/calvin-consummation-restoration/.

———. "More from Calvin on the Restoration of Creation." Available at http://calvinistinternational.com/2014/05/05/more-from-calvin-on-the-restoration-of-creation/.

———. "Apocalypse Now, and Then." Available at http://calvinistinternational.com/2014/05/07/apocalypse-now/.

Kirby, W. J. Torrance. *Richard Hooker's Doctrine of the Royal Supremacy*. Studies in the History of Christian Thought 43. Leiden: Brill, 1990.

———. "The Paradigm of Chalcedonian Christology in Richard Hooker's Discourse on Grace and the Church." *Churchman* Vol. 114 (Spring, 2000): 22–39. Available at http://www.biblicalstudies.org.uk/pdf/churchman/114-01_022.pdf.

Kline, Meredith G. "The Oracular Origin of the State." In G. A. Tuttle (ed.), *Biblical and Near Eastern Studies*, 132–141. Grand Rapids: Eerdmans, 1978. Available at http://www.meredithkline.com/klines-works/articles-and-essays/the-oracular-origin-of-the-state/.

———. *Images of the Spirit*. Grand Rapids: Baker, 1980. Reprint, Eugene, OR: Wipf and Stock, 1999.

———. *Kingdom Prologue: Genesis Foundations for a Covenantal Worldview*. Overland Park, KS: Two Age Press, 2000.

Littlejohn, Brad. "Is Christ Divided? Christology and the Two Kingdoms." Available at http://swordandploughshare.com/main-blog/2011/4/21/is-christ-divided-christology-and-the-two-kingdoms.html.

McIlhenny, Ryan C. (ed.). *Kingdoms Apart: Engaging the Two Kingdoms Perspective*. Phillipsburg, NJ: P&R Publishing, 2012.

Nazianzen, Gregory. *To Cledonius the Priest against Apollinarius*. In Philip Schaff (ed.), *Nicene and Post-Nicene Fathers: Second Series Vol. 7*. Available at http://www.ccel.org/ccel/schaff/npnf207.iv.ii.iii.html.

Vander Hart, Mark D. "Creation and Covenant: Part One." *Mid-America Journal of Theology* 6.1 (1990): 3–18.

VanDrunen, David. *Natural Law and the Two Kingdoms: A Study in the Development of Reformed Social Thought*. Grand Rapids: Eerdmans, 2010.

———. *Living in God's Two Kingdoms: A Biblical Vision for Christianity and Culture*. Wheaton: Crossway, 2010.

———. "Natural Law in Noahic Accent: A Covenantal Conception of Natural Law Drawn from Genesis 9." *Journal of the Society of Christian Ethics* 30:2 (Fall–Winter 2010): 131–49.

———. "The Two Kingdoms and the Social Order: Political and Legal Theory in Light of God's Covenant with Noah." *Journal of Markets and Morality* 14:2 (Fall 2011): 445–62.

———. *Divine Covenants and Moral Order: A Biblical Theology of Natural Law*. Grand Rapids: Eerdmans, 2014.

Wallace, Ronald S. *Calvin's Doctrine of the Christian Life*. Edinburgh: Oliver and Boyd, 1959. Reprinted, Eugene, OR: Wipf and Stock, 1997.

Narrating Christian Transformationalism: Rousas J. Rushdoony and Christian Reconstructionism in Current Histories of American Religion and Politics

Dr. Brian J. Auten
Patrick Henry College

Introduction

In his comprehensive history of the evangelical right in the United States, *God's Own Party: The Making of the Christian Right*, Daniel K. Williams was comfortable with relegating the discussion of the overall influence of the Christian Reconstructionist movement and that of its progenitor, Rousas John Rushdoony, to a total of five short paragraphs near the end of the book.[1] Mentioned in the context of the late 1980s withering of the anti-abortion group Operation Rescue and its leader Randall Terry's political "disillusionment," Williams characterizes Rushdoony and Christian Reconstructionism – indeed Operation Rescue itself –as "fringe movements" that attracted the poor, tired, and politically-frustrated evangelical militants at the very end of the Cold War.[2] Yet, in a more popularly-written analysis of conservative evangelicalism's influence on the Republican Party published just one year before *God's Own Party*, journalist Max Blumenthal played the Rushdoony card within the first twenty pages of *Republican Gomorrah*, claiming, among other things, that Jerry Falwell had been attracted to Christian Reconstructionism and that Rushdoony and Francis Schaeffer, the late-20th century evangelical *philosophe* and cultural critic, had "mutually shaped the Christian Right's philosophy."[3] And three years before the release of *Republican Gomorrah*, Chris Hedges' *American Fascists: The Christian Right and the War on America* offered up within the first ten pages the idea of "dominionism,"

---

[1] Daniel K. Williams, *God's Own Party: The Making of the Christian Right* (New York: Oxford University Press, 2010), 225–26

[2] Ibid.

[3] Max Blumenthal, *Republican Gomorrah: Inside the Movement that Shattered the Party* (New York: Nation Books, 2009), 17–27

together with Rushdoony and Christian Reconstructionism, as the overall foundation for evangelical political engagement.[4]

Recently- or soon-to-be-published histories of American politics and religion which in some way address or reference Rushdoony and Christian Reconstructionism generally fall into three distinct categories, listed here by increasing volume or market share: (1) academically-oriented histories specifically centered on Rushdoony and Christian Reconstructionism; (2) academic histories of American evangelicalism, American conservatism, or the Religious Right in which the man and movement are addressed in some fashion; and, (3) popularly-written analyses of late 20th and early 21st-century conservative US politics and religion in which Rushdoony and Christian Reconstructionism are cited in the course of outlining the threat posed by evangelicals in politics and the threat of an alleged, underlying political program of Christian "dominionism."

In this paper, my aim is two-fold. First, I mean to highlight the ways select writers in the second category—academic historians of politics and religion who haven't specifically focused their work on Christian Reconstructionism—have or have not integrated the subject into their narratives, particularly while writing during (as Steven P. Miller has recently christened it) a "second great evangelical scare," characterized by the "phantasm" of "dominionism."[5] I will touch on a handful of recently-published histories, showing how the authors have chosen to talk about (or chosen *not* to talk about) Christian Reconstructionism. Next, I address the 'state of the evidence' for a long-standing historical assertion about the purported "transmission belt" of Rushdoony's and Christian Reconstructionism's ideas into "mainstream" evangelicalism – namely, that Rushdoony's ideas (as well as the ideas of other Reconstructionists) have made their way into the general population via the work of Francis Schaeffer.

---

[4] Chris Hedges, *American Fascists: The Christian Right and the War on America* (New York: Free Press, 2006), 10–14

[5] Steven P. Miller, The *Age of Evangelicalism: America's Born-Again Years* (New York: Oxford University Press, 2014), 141–42.

Christian Reconstructionism in Academic and Popular Literature
Category One – Authors Focused Directly on Rushdoony and Christian Reconstructionism

A few preliminary remarks about these literature categories are in order. The first category—academics who are specifically writing on Rushdoony and Christian Reconstructionism—constitutes a population of precisely two. Both are in the middle of completing their manuscripts for publication. The first is Michael McVicar, an assistant professor of religion at Florida State University. McVicar is nearly finished turning his Ohio State University doctoral thesis—the first archive-based history of Rushdoony and Christian Reconstructionism—into a book with University of North Carolina Press.[6] The second is Julie Ingersoll, a UC Santa Barbara-trained sociologist of religion and current assistant professor of religious studies at University of North Florida. Ingersoll, who comes at the subject via a handful of monographs and blog posts addressing the movement in light of her larger interest in gender battles within evangelicalism, is completing a draft of her own history of the movement, which is slated to be published by Oxford University Press sometime in 2015.[7]

McVicar and Ingersoll approach the subject of Christian Reconstructionism in different ways. One could reasonably label McVicar's project a revisionist one. That is, McVicar's primary interest, in light of all that has been written about the purported influence of Rushdoony and Christian Reconstructionism during the "second great evangelical scare," is to clear away the brush and build a clearer (and, in some aspects, more sympathetic) picture of the man and movement. Again, McVicar is the only scholar to date who has had access to Rushdoony's personal papers and notebooks held at Rushdoony's Chalcedon Foundation in Vallecito, California and who has also done additional spadework in the papers of the Institute for Humane Studies (George Mason University) and the William T. Couch Col-

---

[6] Michael J. McVicar, *Reconstructing America: Religion, American Conservatism and the Political Theology of Rousas John Rushdoony* (Ohio State University, Ph.D. dissertation, 2010); also see McVicar, *Christian Reconstruction: R. J. Rushdoony and American Religious Conservatism* (Chapel Hill: University of North Carolina Press; anticipated 2015)

[7] Julie Ingersoll, *Building the Kingdom of God: Christian Reconstructionism and the Religious Right in America* (New York: Oxford University Press; anticipated 2015); also see Ingersoll, "Mobilizing Evangelicals: Christian Reconstructionism and the Roots of the Religious Right," in *Evangelicals and Democracy in America (ii), Religion and Politics* (New York: Russell Sage, 2009), 179–208.

lection at the University of North Carolina at Chapel Hill. In contrast, judging from her articles, her posts at Religion Dispatches, and her previous books on the issue of gender, Ingersoll's take on Rushdoony and Christian Reconstructionism is comparatively more friendly to the theory of a "dominionism". That is, unlike McVicar, Ingersoll has cited approvingly many of noted authors in what has been called the "dominionist" interpretive camp. Such authors include Sara Diamond, Frederick Clarkson, Chip Berlet, Michelle Goldberg, Max Blumenthal, Jeff Sharlet, Chris Hedges and, most recently, Kathryn Joyce.

Category Three – The "Dominionist" Interpretive Camp

In a 2013 article for the *Journal of Religion and Popular Culture*, McVicar himself detailed much of the history behind the term "dominionism" and how Diamond's, Clarkson's and Berlet's analyses of the Christian Right have now become, in the last ten years, *the* dominant intellectual framework through which most journalists, pundits and academics evaluate Rushdoony's and Christian Reconstructionism's impact and influence on American evangelical political participation.[8] As McVicar explains, it is this third category of more popular accounts of American domestic policy, American politics and, to a lesser but growing extent, American foreign policy, that has, since Bush's re-election in 2004, become a veritable cottage subindustry.[9] He shows how these authors have been connected to one another through the work of Political Research Associates, the Boston-based advocacy think tank, and also through *The Nation* and (I would add) the *Nation's* funding arm for up-and-coming journalists, The Nation Institute.

From looking at the latter part of McVicar's above-referenced article and from culling the references and acknowledgments of many of the recently-published secular books addressing "dominionism," one sees in the "dominionism" camp two distinct generations of writers. The first generation cut its teeth by producing left-leaning analyses of the Christian

---

[8] Michael McVicar, "'Let Them Have Dominion': 'Dominion Theology' and the Construction of Religious Extremism in the US Media," *Journal of Religion and Popular Culture* 25.1 (Spring 2013): 120–45; also see Chip Berlet's, "How We Coined the Term 'Dominionism'," *Talk to Action*, 31 August 2011, http://www.talk2action.org/story/2011/8/31/17047/5683/ (accessed 21 June 2014) (which is also referenced in McVicar, "Let Them Have Dominion," 128)

[9] McVicar, "Let Them Have Dominion," 130–31.

Right during that movement's waning days in the late 1980s and early 1990s, with the typical 2-3 year lag that happens with book publishing. As already mentioned, the second generation began its work around 2004, with books being published up through the present. The second generation relies almost wholly upon the first generation's earlier reading of Rushdoony and Christian Reconstructionism. Indeed, if one scratches recent, more popular histories and/or blog posts dealing with the activities of the Christian Right in the United States and abroad, one generally finds one or more of the following first and/or second generation titles referenced (publication date listed, as well as author)[10]:

	First Generation
1989	*Spiritual Warfare: The Politics of the Christian Right* (Sara Diamond)
1992	*Confronting the Religious Right: The Activist's Handbook* (Frederick Clarkson)
1994	"Christian Reconstructionism: Theocratic Dominionism Gains Influence [Parts 1–4]," *Public Eye Magazine* (Frederick Clarkson)
1995	*Roads to Dominion: Right-Wing Movements and Political Power in the United States* (Sara Diamond)
1995	*Eyes Right! Challenging the Right Wing Backlash* (Chip Berlet)
1997	*Eternal Hostility: The Struggle Between Theocracy and Democracy* (Frederick Clarkson)
1998	*Not by Politics Alone: The Enduring Influence of the Christian Right* (Sara Diamond)
2000	*Right-Wing Populism in America: Too Close for Comfort* (Chip Berlet & Matthew Lyons)

	Second Generation
2006	*Kingdom Coming: The Rise of Christian Nationalism* (Michelle Goldberg)
2007	*American Fascists: The Christian Right and the War on America* (Chris Hedges)

---

[10] Ibid., 128–31.

2008	*The Family: The Secret Fundamentalism at the Heart of American Power* (Jeff Sharlet)
2009	*The Means of Reproduction: Sex, Power and the Future of the World* (Michelle Goldberg)
2009	*Republican Gomorrah: Inside the Movement that Shattered the Party* (Max Blumenthal)
2010	*C Street: The Fundamentalist Threat to American Democracy* (Jeff Sharlet)
2010	*Quiverfull: Inside the Christian Patriarchy Movement* (Kathryn Joyce)
2013	*The Child Catchers: Rescue, Trafficking and the New Gospel of Adoption* (Kathryn Joyce)
2014	*Blueprint for Theocracy: The Christian Right's Vision for America* (James C. Sanford)[11]

McVicar asserts in his article that the "dominionist" narrative is likely to continue into Obama's second administration, though at present, one sees more emphasis being placed on the export of "dominionism" abroad, particularly to sub-Saharan Africa.[12]

---

[11] One could argue about the inclusion of James Sanford's book in this category. First, it's self-published. Second, while Sanford cites Berlet and Lyons heavily, he, like Molly Worthen, takes much more seriously than others in the second generation "dominionism" camp the theological-philosophical origins of the movement. In Sanford's telling, as we will see with Worthen's, he argues for a direct intellectual line from John Calvin to Abraham Kuyper to Cornelius Van Til to Rushdoony and to Francis Schaeffer. One could be seeing in Sanford the beginnings of a third-generation of Category Three writers, who are still critical, but who are also comfortable with discussing and critiquing the movement's political theology-qua-theology.

[12] McVicar, "Let Them Have Dominion," 131. For the export of dominionism, see, for example, Kapya Kaoma's *American Culture Warriors in Africa: A Guide to the Exporters of Homophobia and Sexism* (Political Research Associates, May 2014). Kaoma is an ordained Anglican minister who wrote a 2009 report for Political Research Associates, *Globalizing the Culture Wars: US Conservatives, African Churches and Homophobia*, and who also participated in the 2013 documentary *God Loves Uganda*. It is interesting to note the existence of the "export of the Religious Right" argument during the latter years of the first "great evangelical scare," but focused on Southern Africa (i.e. Zimbabwe, Zambia, and Mozambique). See, as one example, Ecumenical Documentation and Information Centre for Eastern and Southern Africa

Category Two – Historians of American Evangelicalism and/or American Conservatism

Now, before starting the main thrust of this paper, I'd first like to highlight some observations about the current state of the study of American conservatism as offered by Kim Phillips-Fein in her "keynote" bibliographic essay in the December 2011 issue of the *Journal of American History*, "Conservatism: A State of the Field." Phillips-Fein's essay outlines the twenty-year renaissance in the academic study of Cold War- and post-Cold War-era conservatism. Reflecting on the changes that had taken place in the field since the publication of the infamous 1994 *American History Review* article in which Alan Brinkley and Leo Ribuffo lamented the lack of solidly-researched academic assessments of conservatism, Phillips-Fein celebrates the field's accomplishments and, at the same time, offers avenues for new research so as to bolster the spirits of those (read graduate students) who have been left fearing that the subject had been mined to such a degree that the only available option is the academic equivalent of fracking.[13]

The "Sunbelt" Argument

According to Phillips-Fein, the primary lens used for the academic exploration of the growth of American, Cold War conservatism can be summarized using a single phrase: reactionary, populist backlash. Up through the late 1990s, the dominant mode of study was aimed at understanding the political rise and underlying motivations of—using Susan F. Harding's terminology—"repugnant cultural Others" (including conserva-

---

(EDICESA), *Programme—Religion and Oppression: The Misuse of Religion for Social, Political and Economic Subjugation*, Symposium for General Secretaries of National Christian Councils and Church Leaders from Eastern and Southern Africa, 1–3 August 1989, most pointedly the contributions of Paul Gifford, Ove Gustafsson, Lawrence Jones, and Roger Arendse. The program can be found at http://www.disa.ukzn.ac.za/webpages/DC/pro19890801.026.009.726/pro198908 01.026.009.726.pdf (accessed 21 June 2014). Paul Gifford's contribution is especially noteworthy. Gifford, Emeritus Professor of Religion at SOAS, University of London, published multiple books in this genre in the late 1980s and early-to-mid 1990s, including *The Religious Right in Southern Africa* (Harare, Zimbabwe: University of Zimbabwe Publications, 1988), *The New Crusaders: Christianity and the New Right in Southern Africa* (London: Pluto Press, 1991); and *Exporting the American Gospel: Global Christian Fundamentalism* (London: Routledge, 1996).

[13] Kim Phillips-Fein, "Conservatism: A State of the Field," *Journal of American History* 98.3 (Dec. 2011), 723–43.

tive evangelicals).[14] Phillips-Fein outlines how, in order to understand the factors behind the apparently-sudden late 1970s political take-off of the "New Right" the late 1970s and Reagan's election in 1980, historians initially turned to the older, progressive historians, emphasizing the influence of money and elites on the general public, as well as to the 1950s "consensus" historians (like Richard Hofstadter), who offered up explanations involving "psychological anxiety" and resulting "backlash" politics. In essence, the growth of a populist, conservative movement was the result of "a fierce anxiety about their position in a prosperous, mobile consumer society of the postwar period."[15] Phillips-Fein adds that the positing of a *sudden* populist backlash in response to the rise of the New Left, Black Power, urban riots, abortion, and/or desegregation was merely a variant on the older "consensus" historians, particularly given its populist orientation.[16]

But, as Phillips-Fein suggests, how far back should one go for the backlash origin story? Should it really be thought of as a *sudden* backlash, or, riffing off the *Annales* school, is it wiser or more accurate to think in terms of a "*longue durée* backlash" beginning in the early Cold War, or maybe even earlier?[17] Though Phillips-Fein does not address it, I would argue that a "long backlash" approach also helps address the very real pressure of the historical guild to find material that has not been heavily picked-over, sources or archives not yet adequately addressed, or, in the case of a mature (or maturing field), the need to re-cast the "big story" through a blend of literatures and/or methodologies. Consequently, one sees a clear centering over the last ten years on the "Sunbelt" argument – a "long backlash" origin story, beginning in the late 1940s and early 1950s, which combines new urban/suburban history, social network analysis, women's history and women's studies, and political economy. In short, the Sunbelt was the geographic destination for large numbers of people, often from less-economically-advantaged areas, for employment during World War II and up through the defense spending of the Eisenhower years. These economic migrants carried with them their own regional (and, as we'll see in Darren Dochuk's

---

[14] Susan F. Harding, "Representing Fundamentalism: The Problem of the Repugnant Cultural Other," *Social Research* 58.2 (Summer 1991), 373–93.

[15] Phillips-Fein, 725–26.

[16] Ibid.

[17] Ibid,, 726–27, 735.

work, *denominational*) sensibilities and, over time, grew affluent and crafted a distinct political style—one revolving around a strong national defense (i.e. self-interest with respect to employment), anti-communism, limited state involvement in markets and, in most cases, neighborhood racial homogeneity.[18]

In her *Suburban Warriors: The Origins of the New American Right*, Lisa McGirr offered a study of conservative growth in defense industry-heavy Orange County, California in the 1950s and 1960s. Since McGirr—and particularly with the addition of Matthew Lassiter's *The Silent Majority: Suburban Politics in the Sunbelt South*—it is safe to say that the Sunbelt argument has been the primary arena of inquiry for the study of conservatism's rise for the last decade or so. Most recently-published academic histories play off the Sunbelt argument in some fashion – the role of Sunbelt housewives, fights over racial integration in Sunbelt cities, and the financial support of Sunbelt business/corporate leaders to conservative causes (which, one might argue, are merely a recent twist on the progressive historian decrying of elite influence).[19]

Take, as just one example, the study of the role and influence of suburban, Sunbelt housewives in the development of conservatism and right-wing politics. Taking McGirr's work in conjunction with Michelle Nickerson's recently-published *Mothers of Conservatism: Women and the Postwar Right*, the two focus attention on a much different type of Southern California housewife—mothers and spouses who ran "third space" coffee discussion groups on conservative and libertarian literature, organized local talks by conservative luminaries, and established and ran small, neighborhood-level conservative and "patriotic" bookshops.[20] Again, to reiterate, the Sunbelt argument, including the sub-stream about women in the Sunbelt, integrates political economy, urban history, and intellectual/movement history. It cen-

---

[18] For an overview of this argument, see Darren Dochuk, *From Bible Belt to Sun Belt: Plain-Folk Religion, Grassroots Politics and the Rise of Evangelical Conservatism* (New York: W.W. Norton, 2011), xv–xxiv, 171–89.

[19] Phillips-Fein, 728–29; 731–32.

[20] Phillips-Fein, 729; Lisa McGirr, *Suburban Warriors: The Origins of the New American Right* (Princeton: Princeton University Press, 2001); Michelle Nickerson, *Mothers of Conservatism: Women and the Postwar Right* (Princeton: Princeton University Press, 2012); also see Nickerson, "Politically Desperate Housewives: Women and Conservatism in Postwar Los Angeles," *California History*, 86.3 (June 2009): 4–21.

ters on the effects of national defense spending on (a) the urban/suburban landscape, (b) the disposable income of Sunbelt families, and, in turn, (c) local (and eventually national and international) politics. It is connected to the backlash thesis by virtue of what Sunbelt political mobilization was striking hard against.

Over the last decade, the Sunbelt argument has also directed the academic study of Cold War-era conservative evangelicalism and its influence over national politics. The debates still roll back and forth over a "sudden backlash" and the extent to which the immediate causes of the rise of the Religious Right can be found in the *Roe vs. Wade* decision versus fear and anger over desegregation—witness, for instance, Randall Balmer's late May 2014 article in *Politico* arguing emphatically for the latter[21]—but the bigger push in academia has been the search for the Religious Right's pre-1970s origins using the Sunbelt-oriented work of McGirr, Lassiter, Nickerson and others.

Enter Darren Dochuk's 2011 *From Bible Belt to Sun Belt: Plain Folk Religion, Grassroots Politics, and the Rise of Evangelical Conservatism*, followed in turn by Williams' *God's Own Party*. Williams and Dochuk cover similar ground, addressing the same personalities (both well-known and heretofore obscure), events, and regional and denominational distinctives. Williams himself says that his book is meant to provide a (very detailed) "chronological history of the Christian Right" and the Sunbelt argument definitely plays a role in it, particularly in his discussion of conservative evangelicalism during and after Nixon.[22] Dochuk, however, offers an explicitly-Sunbelt-oriented thesis. In *From Bible Belt to Sun Belt*, he shows how a distinct, populist brand of Protestantism from the "Western South," or what Dochuk labels the "burned-over district of Southern evangelicalism," was carried to Southern California during the Dust Bowl, World War II and the early Cold War.[23] In Southern California, economic migrants from the "Western South" planted churches, built neighborhoods, increased their personal wealth (largely as a result of national defense spending), established vibrant parachurch minis-

---

[21] Randall Balmer, "The Real Origins of the Religious Right," Politico, 27 May 2014, www.politico.com/magazine/story/2014/05/religious-right-real-origins-107133.html (accessed 21 June 2014).

[22] See Chapter Five of Williams, *God's Own Party*.

[23] Dochuk, *From Bible Belt to Sun Belt*, 9–10; 13–17

tries, and, through the Goldwater and post-Goldwater years, helped to build a Christian conservatism in the California Southland.[24] The appearance of conservative evangelicalism on the national scene in the late 1970s was, Dochuk argues, an export of Southern Californian evangelicalism to Texas, Virginia, and further afield, particularly with Reagan's post-Goldwater rise in the GOP.[25]

Rushdoony and Christian Reconstructionism in Academic Histories: Daniel Williams, Darren Dochuk, and Molly Worthen

How, then, have these academic historians of 20th and early 21st century American politics, social relations and religious movements, writing during this 20-year renaissance of "conservative studies," addressed Christian Reconstructionism and Rushdoony? I noted earlier the extent of Williams' discussion about the influence of Rushdoony and Christian Reconstructionism in *God's Own Party*—a bare reference in the context of Randall Terry and Operation Rescue. Two other points should be made about Williams' take on Christian Reconstructionism. First, even though he talks about Francis Schaeffer throughout the book, Williams chose not to use a common argument or assertion addressed in more depth later in this paper—the assertion that Rushdoony and Christian Reconstructionism were brought through the backdoor via Schaeffer's writings.[26] Second, it is strange, given the context of anti-abortion activity, that Williams chose not to reference the one example with the closest connection to Christian Reconstructionism—Paul Hill. Those familiar with the literature about Hill's murder of an abortion doctor and his bodyguard in July 1994 know that Hill (a) took classes with the theonomist scholar Greg Bahnsen at Reformed Theological Seminary in Jackson, Mississippi (RTS-Jackson) in the late 1970s, (b) attended St. Paul Presbyterian, a theonomist/ Reconstructionist congregation in Jackson, (c) followed A. Michael Schneider, the minister at St. Paul Presbyterian, to Trinity Presbyterian in Valparaiso, Florida

---

[24] Ibid, 167ff.

[25] Ibid., 321ff.

[26] Williams, *God's Own Party*, 137–42, 154–56, 158, 173–74

and (d) remained a member of Trinity Presbyterian up through his status as an excommunicate in 1993.[27]

What about Darren Dochuk? For a book covering the growth of the California conservative evangelical scene from the 1940s through the 1970s, including that community's interaction with the myriad of conservative think tanks, publishers, funders and sponsors, one would expect that Rushdoony and Christian Reconstruction to have appeared somewhere in the book. Surprisingly, there are no references—none. And that is unfortunate because Rushdoony would fit extraordinarily well into Dochuk's overall storyline. In 1958–1959, having moved to the Orthodox Presbyterian Church (OPC) in Northern California and having secured funding under the libertarian-oriented Volker Fund, Rushdoony was busy re-working draft material for what later became his book *Intellectual Schizophrenia*, a study of the philosophical underpinnings of American education. In Dochuk's narrative, education was, in late 1958, a hot-button issue in California in light of William Knowland's run for governor against Pat Brown and a fight over Proposition 16 (which involved the taxing of private schools).[28]

Another way Rushdoony could be integrated with Dochuk's work (as well as with McGirr and Nickerson) can be seen by McVicar's and Rushdoony's estranged son-in-law Gary North's descriptions of how Southern California housewives and the conservative Betsy Ross Book Shop in Westwood financed and sponsored Rushdoony's activities, particularly in the wake of his termination from the Volker Fund's follow-on Center for American Studies in Burlingame.[29] And then, after Rushdoony was able to

---

[27] Gary North, *Lone Gunners for Jesus: Letters to Paul J. Hill* (Tyler, TX: Institute for Christian Economics, 1994), 2, 39–40; Tomilola Adewale, "Paul Hill's Journey: The Analysis of a Former Minister's Path to Violent Anti-Abortion Extremism," (BA Senior Thesis, Duke University, 2010), 51–52; 127–29; http://www.tomiadewale.com/thesis.pdf (accessed 28 June 2014); Douglas Wilson, *Black and Tan: A Collection of Essays and Excursions on Slavery, Culture War and Scripture* (Moscow, ID: Canon Press, 2005), 62–63. Adwale's thesis relies heavily on material from Jim Risen and Judy Thomas, *Wrath of Angels: The American Abortion War* (New York: Basic Books, 1998), 345ff. Michael Schneider continued to serve at Trinity Presbyterian Church and was scheduled to retire in 2012. See http://www.crechurches.org/documents/minutes/2010_spring_AthanasiusMin.pdf.

[28] Dochuk, 191–95; McVicar, *Reconstructing America*, 118–19.

[29] See McVicar, *Reconstructing America*, 210, 214–19. McVicar cites Michelle Nickerson's work in this section, including her original Ph.D. dissertation. Nickerson's *Mothers of Conservatism* actually mentions a 1960s-era conservative bookshop in Van

solidify his speaking base in Southern California, conservative philanthropist William Knott – a significant figure in Dochuk's narrative – paid for Rushdoony's move down to Woodland Hills. Indeed, McVicar and North also explain how it was Knott's non-profit educational arm, Americanism Education, Inc. which served as the umbrella organization for the Chalcedon Foundation until it was able to secure its own status.[30]

In light of this, I would argue that there's room for looking at Rushdoony as a consummate *California* figure, which makes his absence in Dochuk's narrative peculiar. Part of this may simply be that Rushdoony himself wasn't a "Western South" transplant, which means he simply did not fit Dochuk's overarching theory. The problem with this, as I've demonstrated, is that Rushdoony was nonetheless very involved with many of the people Dochuk highlights. One other possibility is that Rushdoony was involved in California's conservative Presbyterian circles rather than with the Baptists and Pentecostals Dochuk emphasizes. Comparatively, Presbyterians receive less air time in Dochuk's narrative, but, as he is willing to address Carl McIntire's influence among California evangelicals, it is not as if he completely ignores the conservative Presbyterian side of the story.[31] All in all, Rushdoony—not to mention the other Southern California-centered Christian Reconstructionists (i.e. Gary North, Greg Bahnsen and David Chilton)—is missing in action in Dochuk's work. And though it borders on pop-psychology, one final California angle on Rushdoony (particularly giv-

---

Nuys, California named "Betsy Ross Book Shop," but given that North and McVicar both place the bookstore in Westwood, it appears that the two are likely different. Nickerson, *Mothers of Conservatism*, 149, 175. Dochuk's discussion of the "Sunbelt housewives" issue is limited. See Dochuk, *From Bible Belt to Sun Belt*, 187, 201, 352. Gary North discusses the relationship between Rushdoony and Betsy Ross Book Shop in *Tithing and the Church* (Tyler, TX: Institute for Christian Economics, 1994), 152, 156.

[30] McVicar, *Reconstructing America*, 193, 217, 288; Dochuk, *From Bible Belt to Sun Belt*, 7, 206, 247; North, *Tithing and the Church*, p. 152.

[31] See Dochuk, 151–52; 241, 271-72. Dochuk talks about the McIntire-Southern California connections, including, for example, how Strom Thurmond, for example, would talk at McIntire's East Coast conferences, and then head to rally the crowds in Christian events in Southern California (241–42). It's important to note that, unlike Rushdoony, McIntire *does* fit Dochuk's "Western South" theory, growing up in the faith as he did in Oklahoma. For McIntire's early years in Oklahoma, see Chapter 1 of Gladys Titzck Rhodes and Nancy Titzck Anderson, *McIntire: Defender of Faith and Freedom* (Xulon Press, 2012), 3-15.

en his emphasis on education reform and Biblically-based law and order) might be found in his relationship to his undergraduate alma mater, University of California at Berkeley. A traveler in right-wing and libertarian circles, Rushdoony, along with everyone else in California starting around 1964, watched as his alma mater became ground zero for nationwide, left-wing campus rebellion. On this subject, Seth Rosenfeld's *Subversives: The FBI's War on Student Radicals and Reagan's Rise to Power*[32] makes for a great tandem read with Dochuk, as it fleshes out the extent to which the events in Berkeley served as an energizing force for the post-Goldwater Right in California, of which Rushdoony, his Chalcedon Foundation, and other Southern California-based Christian Reconstructionists were part and parcel.

Out of the three academic historians of American evangelicalism under evaluation in this section of the paper, Molly Worthen, an assistant professor of history at University of North Carolina – Chapel Hill, is the only figure to have addressed Rushdoony's thought and the Christian Reconstructionist movement in any detailed fashion. She examined them in a 2008 article in *Church History*, and then re-used (and corrected) that material for one of the latter chapters in her recently-published *Apostles of Reason: The Crisis of Authority in American Evangelicalism*. Unlike Williams and Dochuk, both of whom are distinctly interested in explaining the *power-political* rise of conservative evangelicalism in the later 20th century, Worthen's larger project is centered on American evangelicalism's intellectual undergirding. *Apostles*, as she explains it, is meant to focus attention on the "intellectual authority provid[ing] the framework, the rules and [the] logic" for evangelicalism's past, current and future activity.[33]

This makes *Apostles*, as I've labeled it in another venue, one of the first "post-revisionist" treatments of American evangelicalism, *Apostles* outlines how the neo-evangelicals of the mid-20th century and their progeny used the intellectual constructs of inerrancy and "Christian worldview" as

---

[32] New York : Farrar, Straus and Giroux, 2012.

[33] Molly Worthen, *Apostles of Reason: The Crisis of Authority in American Evangelicalism* (New York:Oxford University Press, 2013), 10-11; Worthen, "The Chalcedon Problem: Rousas John Rushdoony and the Origins of Christian Reconstructionism," *Church History*,77.2 (June 2008): 399–437. When one compares the references in Worthen's 2008 article to those involving Rushdoony and Christian Reconstructionism in *Apostles*, the only significant difference is the addition of McVicar's dissertation in *Apostles* (the use of which helpfully corrects a few timeline errors in her earlier article).

the ideological glue to forge a larger cultural-theological bulwark against modernism and secularism.[34] Worthen's tale is one of decline—by the mid-1970s, this glue had lost its potency, the alliance was in tatters, and an "intellectual civil war" fully underway within evangelicalism over the Bible's overarching authority for private and public life.[35] Her discussion of Rushdoony and Christian Reconstructionism, therefore, should be evaluated in light of her interest in conservative evangelicalism's thought structures (*vice* its political history), in conjunction with her treatment of "Christian worldview" as but one, Christianized version of what she notes to be a larger 1940s-1950s-era "presuppositionalist vogue [on the rise] in the West."[36]

In Worthen's view, how then should one think about the role played by Rushdoony and Christian Reconstructionism in American evangelicalism intellectual history? First, Worthen makes it clear that she has little patience with the apocalyptic tone of scholars and writers in the "dominionist" interpretive camp. In her opinion, Frederick Clarkson's 1990s work on Christian Reconstructionism was "sloppy" and exemplified the type of "pop analysis" which over-inflates the political threat posed by evangelicals in the public sphere.[37] Worthen's 2008 article was precipitated by her observation that very little scholarly work had been done on the subject, and therefore what was needed was not simple "caricature" but a willingness to look seriously at Rushdoony and Christian Reconstructionism as representing one of a number of active streams of thought within late 20th-century conservative evangelicalism seeking to demarcate the boundaries of Christian conscience, the church, and the state in a period of increasing secularization.[38]

---

[34] Brian J. Auten, review of *Apostles of Reason*, Canon and Culture, Ethics and Religious Liberty Commission, 4 February 2014, http://www.canonandculture.com/apostles-of-reason-the-crisis-of-authority-in-american-evangelicalism/ (accessed 12 July 2014). Also see Worthen, *Apostles*, 203–207, and her interview with Tiffany Stanley, "The Intellectual Civil War within Evangelicalism: An Interview with Molly Worthen," *Religion and Politics*, 3 December 2013, http://religionandpolitics.org/2013/12/03/the-intellectual-civil-war-within-evangelicalism-an-interview-with-molly-worthen/ (accessed 12 July 2014).

[35] Worthen, *Apostles*, 200, 202.

[36] Ibid., 260.

[37] Worthen, "Chalcedon Problem," 400.

[38] Ibid., 400–401.

Worthen's approach begins to make up for the shortcomings in both Williams and Dochuk narratives. Worthen agrees with Williams that the Christian Reconstructionist movement was known more for its being filled with odd characters and, as Worthen puts it, "disgruntled PhDs and ex-seminarians" than for its actual theological positions or for its significant influence over the Religious Right.[39] Unlike Williams, however, Worthen argues that, huge influence or not, Rushdoony and Christian Reconstructionism are still worth examining in greater detail because they represent a "radical[ization]" of already-extant "trends of thought [regarding reason, the state and pluralism] long present in the Presbyterian and libertarian traditions."[40] Worthen goes so far as to argue that Rushdoony's overall project was the crafting of a political theology connecting the reigning *theophilosophical* stance of the Orthodox Presbyterian Church (OPC) of the 1950s and 1960s—i.e. Cornelius Van Til's presuppositionalism—to the economic and cultural libertarianism of the California post-Goldwater Right.[41] And whereas Dochuk overlooks Rushdoony completely in his analysis of post-Goldwater California conservatism, Worthen does try to place Rushdoony in his immediate social and political context.[42] The post-1964, disillusioned, Southern California conservatives (including evangelical conservatives) described so well by Dochuk constituted, as Rushdoony's son Mark explained to Worthen, the very target audience Rushdoony looked to inculcate with "a more theological view, a moral view of culture [and/or] civilization."[43]

Christian Reconstructionism, Worthen suggests, can be categorized as a hardened, Reformed Protestant variation on a larger *Weltanschauung* and "worldview" theme popularized by liberal hawks and political conservatives—religious and secular—in the early-to-mid Cold War. In *Apostles*, she

---

[39] Ibid, 399.

[40] Ibid, 404.

[41] Ibid., 404–406.

[42] Ibid, 403–404. In her article, Worthen mistakenly states that Rushdoony started the Chalcedon Foundation in Vallecito (in Northern California) —a point she later corrected in *Apostles*. It's an important distinction, given that it puts Rushdoony in the very midst of the Southern California post-Goldwater ferment, rather than at its outskirts.

[43] Ibid., 403.

references the growing interest in the 1940s and 1950s among foreign policy experts and pundits in ideas surrounding the intellectual Cold War and the perceived need for effective counter-narratives with which to combat Marxism-Leninism. She cites, for example, George Kennan's views on the importance of understanding the Soviet worldview, but one can easily turn to the writings of James Burnham or to the literature on the Congress of Cultural Freedom or Radio Free Europe-Radio Liberty (RFERL) to observe her point about the Cold War weaponization of *Weltanschauung*.[44] And, as Worthen notes, this Cold War interest in *Weltanshauung* took on flesh in Christian circles, Catholic and Protestant alike. In Worthen's hands, the mid-century Thomist revival is interpreted as the creation of an "intellectual fortress" to protect Catholic youth against the barbarian secular hordes.[45] In the same fashion, says Worthen, Abraham Kuyper's "world and life view" and Van Tillian philosophy were wielded defensively in Protestant circles.[46] What Rushdoony and other Christian Reconstructionists attempted to do, therefore, was to take this stab at crafting a Reformed Protestant *Weltanschauung*, mix it with aspects of Austrian School economics, and offer what they considered to be "Biblically-based blueprints" for positive law and the reorganization of civic life.[47]

---

[44] *Apostles*, 27-28. James Burnham, *The Coming Defeat of Communism* (John Day Company, 1949). For a biography of Burnham, see Daniel Kelly, *James Burnham and the Struggle for the World: A Life* (ISI, 2002). For work on the Congress of Cultural Freedom (CCE), one can consult Peter Coleman, *The Liberal Conspiracy: The Congress for Cultural Freedom and the Struggle for the Mind of Postwar Europe* (Free Press, 1989), and Frances Stonor Saunders, *The Cultural Cold War: The CIA and the World of Arts and Letters* (New Press, 2001). Lastly, for the role played by Cold War radio broadcasting, one should look to Arch Puddington, *Broadcasting Freedom: The Cold War Triumph of Radio Free Europe and Radio Liberty* (University Press of Kentucky, 2000), Richard H. Cummings, *Cold War Radio: The Dangerous History of American Broadcasting in Europe: 1950-1989* (McFarland, 2009), and A. Ross Johnson, *Radio Free Europe and Radio Liberty: The CIA Years and Beyond* (Cold War International History Project, 2010).

[45] *Apostles*, p. 28.

[46] Ibid., 27, 29-30.

[47] Regarding the influence of the Austrian school of economics on Rushdoony, see, for instance, Worthen, "Chalcedon Problem," p. 406. McVicar has a great deal more to say about this, including the fact that the Volker Fund, which supported Rushdoony, also provided the money to bring Friedrich Hayek to the University of Chicago and Ludwig von Mises to NYU. See McVicar, "Reconstructing America," p. 112. McVicar takes this information from Kim Phillips-Fein, *Invisible Hands: The*

It is Worthen's contention that Rushdoony and his associates failed *prescriptively*, but succeeded (or, perhaps better put, *partially* succeeded) *diagnostically* and *descriptively*. She believes the overall project to have been "quasi-Burkean" in its character. It was Burkean in its concerns about state power and the need for authority, tradition, and "law and order," particularly during the revolutionary period of the late 1960s and early 1970s. But it could only be "quasi" given Christian Reconstructionism's dismissal of natural law and its belief that authority and tradition proves to be mere "humanism" unless tethered to God.[48] To be sure, Worthen doesn't brush over Rushdoony's more unsavory aspects—his racist language and his use of Holocaust Denial materials—and she demonstrates how the movement's offering of Mosaic law as the basis for "blueprints" for the refashioning of American law fell flat.[49] Yet, at the same time, she insists that Rushdoony and his followers nonetheless represent some of the tougher interlocutors when it comes to what she calls the "fundamental challenge" for Christians in the late 20th (and early 21st century) – the related problems of tolerance in the public square and "[the] reconciliation [of] the Bible with true pluralism."[50] In the end, Worthen neither inflates Rushdoony's or Christian Reconstructionism's influence over conservative evangelicalism writ large, nor suggests the group was of no consequence, but instead situates Rushdoony and his movement as one, small part of an overall debate in American con-

---

Making of the Conservative Movement from the New Deal to Reagan (W.W. Norton and Company, 2009).

[48] On Worthen's description of Rushdoony's quasi-Burkean thought, see Worthen, "Chalcedon Problem," 422–23.

[49] Ibid, 417; 423–25. For additional arguments regarding Rushdoony's use of Holocaust Denial materials, see Carl Trueman, *Histories and Fallacies: Problems Faced in the Writing of History* (Wheaton, IL: Crossway, 2010), 30, esp. fn. 4. Also see Trueman's earlier blog posts at Reformation 21, "Rushdoony, Historical Incompetence, Racism and Lunacy," Reformation21blog, 20 December 2006, http://www.reformation21.org/blog/2006/12/rushdoony-historical-incompete.php (accessed 5 August 2014); "Rushdoony Revisited," Reformation21blog, 21 December 2006, http://www.reformation21.org/blog/2006/12/rushdoony-revisited.php (accessed 5 August 2014); "Rushdoony once again—for the last time," Reformation21blog, 31 December 2006, http://www.reformation21.org/blog/2006/12/rushdoony-once-again-for-the-l.php (accessed 5 August 2014).

[50] Worthen, "Chalcedon Problem," 436—37.

servative Christianity over political and religious authority and the role of believers in the public realm.

The Mediation of Rushdoony's Thought and Christian Reconstructionism via Francis Schaeffer

If one takes as true that Rushdoony and Christian Reconstructionism had some influence over mainstream American evangelicalism, then how did such influence come about? One of the more common arguments offered by academic and popular historians goes something like this: over the course of his life, Rushdoony had a fairly small audience for his writing and speaking, but his ideas had a much wider distribution and influence because of their adoption and dissemination by Francis Schaeffer. According to this line of assertion and argument, Schaeffer served as the mediator or transmission belt between Rushdoony and Christian Reconstructionist thought and the wider public. Restated, Schaeffer's popularity—particularly among English-speaking evangelical youth between the early 1960s and early 1980s—provided, over time, a platform by which Rushdoony's work was legitimated, given a much wider hearing, and, consequently, influenced larger numbers of pastors, scholars and political activists.

On the whole, this assertion is constructed on a rather limited evidentiary foundation. One may begin by consulting Gary North's essay regarding Schaeffer in *Tactics of Christian Resistance* ("Apologetics and Strategy"), parts of which are repeated in his later book, *Political Polytheism* (in the chapter entitled "Halfway Covenant Social Criticism"). In "Apologetics and Strategy," North claims that Schaeffer "[had] been reading [Rushdoony] for twenty years" and Rushdoony had been "a major influence" on Schaeffer. After this, North compares passages from Schaeffer's *A Christian Manifesto* to Rushdoony's *The One and the Many*, accusing Schaeffer of lifting Rushdoony's work without attribution.[51] Later in *Political Polytheism*, North again questions the identities of Schaeffer's theological and philosophical sources, and, as before, asserts Schaeffer borrowed extensively (and without attribution) from both Cornelius Van Til and Rushdoony.[52] He once more relates

---

[51] Gary North and David Chilton, "Apologetics and Strategy," in North (ed.), *Tactics of Christian Resistance* (Tyler, TX: Geneva Divinity School Press, 1983), 124–26.

[52] On the questioning of Schaeffer's theological and philosophical fountainheads, see Gary North, *Political Polytheism: The Myth of Pluralism* (Tyler, TX: Institute for Christian Economics, 1989), 169.

his earlier points about Schaeffer's unattributed use of Rushdoony's *The One and the Many* and what he sees as citation problems in Schaeffer's *A Christian Manifesto*, the latter of which also included, according to North, word-for-word liftings from two essays in the Winter 1978–1979 issue of the *Journal of Christian Reconstruction* (including some of David Chilton's work).[53]

What other evidence does North use to support his claim that Schaeffer's used Rushdoony's material? In *Tactics of Christian Resistance* and *Political Polytheism*, North also references one of Schaeffer's taped lecture series on the subject of relativism which, he says, was based on material from an "early," "unpaginated" and "spiral-bound" edition of Rushdoony's *This Independent Republic*. In North's telling in *Tactics of Christian Resistance*, no citation is provided, but when offering the same story in a footnote in *Political Polytheism*, he cites a contribution made by Calvin College's Donald A. Wells to a 1986 monograph on Schaeffer. According to the footnote in *Political Polytheism*, Wells's monograph chapter relates how, during a visit to L'Abri in the early-to-mid 1960s, he asked about Schaeffer's views of US history and was directed to the set of tapes based on *This Independent Republic*.[54]

The contention over attributed versus unattributed "borrowing" aside, North nonetheless concludes both of his essays by outlining what he sees as a litany of differences between the Christian Reconstructionist agenda and, what in *Political Polytheism*, he calls Schaeffer's "premillenialism-based, anti-theonomic, pro-pluralism, silently Calvinistic, Christian protest movement."[55] Indeed, North asserts that it was the decline and ultimate demise of Schaeffer's project in the mid-1980s that brought about the "watershed" moment for Christian Reconstructionism by creating a void forcing Christian intellectuals across the political spectrum to choose sides between it and liberation theology.[56] In short, North complains time and time

---

[53] Ibid., 194–96; North and Chilton, "Apologetics and Strategy," 126. McVicar makes it clear, however, that there were also footnotes in *A Christian Manifesto* which did properly cite articles from the *Journal of Christian Reconstructionism*. See McVicar, *Reconstructing America*, 353fn189.

[54] North, *Political Polytheism*, pg. 175, 175f34; North and Chilton, "Apologetics and Strategy," p. 126.

[55] North, *Political Polytheism*, 206, 218–19

[56] Ibid., 213–14

again that Schaeffer stole his ideas from Rushdoony, but then proceeds to take Schaeffer to task for not sticking to the Reconstructionist project.

In the pages of *First Things* in August 2001 ("The Passing of R.J. Rushdoony"), Westminster Theological Seminary's William Edgar related a similar—a very similar—story about Schaeffer's mid-1960s interaction with Rushdoony's *This Independent Republic* during a seminar he [Schaeffer] offered on political revolutions. Edgar says that Schaeffer centered a 1964 seminar around the book.[57] Edgar and his wife, Barbara (who were former L'Abri participants) appear to have related this very story to Schaeffer's recent biographer, Barry Hankins. In the one section of Hankins' *Francis Schaeffer and the Shaping of Evangelical America* where Rushdoony is mentioned, Hankins uses much more emotive language to describe Schaeffer's purported interest in Rushdoony's work ("enamored with Rushdoony's writings in the 1960s"), admits that it was "quite likely" that Schaeffer adopted Rushdoony's position on the United States's "Christian" founding, and relates how visitors to L'Abri could remember Schaeffer's "excite[ment]" about Rushdoony. In the end, however, Hankins does not provide sources for these claims beyond a single 2005 interview he had with the Edgars. According to Hankins, Schaeffer's excitement about Rushdoony waned over time, which he attributes to Schaeffer's hesitancy over Rushdoony's postmillennialism, non-separation of church and state, and concrete, current-day applications of Old Testament law, but the reader gets no sense for the evidence supporting the claim of Schaeffer's decreased interest.[58]

Unfortunately, these assertions of "Schaeffer-as-a-stalking-horse-for-Rushdoony" and/or "Schaeffer-as-Rushdoony's-mediator-to-the-public"

---

[57] William Edgar, "The Passing of RJ Rushdoony," *First Things*, August 2001, http://www.firstthings.com/article/2001/08/the-passing-of-r-j-rushdoony (accessed 28 June 2014).

[58] Barry Hankins, *Francis Schaeffer and the Shaping of Evangelical America* (Grand Rapids: Eerdmans, 2008), 193–94. Hankins talks much more (194–200) about Rushdoony's influence on John Whitehead, and then Whitehead's relationship with Francis and Franky Schaeffer. In addressing the Founding Fathers and the non-separation of church and state in *A Christian Manifesto*, Hankins says that the "influence of Whitehead and Rushdoony is unmistakable" but then doesn't elucidate whether such influence arose from both individuals, or whether the influence was primarily through Whitehead. In the latter case, one would then have an interpretation where Rushdoony was mediated through Whitehead to Schaeffer, and then mediated to the general public via Schaeffer.

still continue with very little work being done to compare and contrast their respective *oeuvres* closely.[59] Julie Ingersoll, in one of the endnotes for her chapter-length outline of Christian Reconstruction, states that Rushdoony and Schaeffer were "aware of one another" and that when she visited L'Abri in the late 1980s—which would have been after Schaeffer's death— "the staff and the other guests readily discussed the Reconstructionist movement."[60] In his just-published history of late 20th-century American evangelicalism, Schaeffer's is the very first name Steven Miller drops to support his contention that "softer versions of Rushdoony's ideas had filtered into the broader evangelical right" through the work of some who were "sympathetic" to Christian Reconstructionism, but then he does not offer any concerted analysis along this front.[61] And in their 2011 analysis of the role of evangelical experts, Randall J. Stephens and Karl W. Giberson argue similarly. They reference Schaeffer's study of Rushdoony's work, hearkening back to Schaeffer's talks on *This Independent Republic* (i.e. the fact that Schaeffer "based a L'Abri seminar on one of [Rushdoony's] books on American history"). Additionally, Stephens and Giberson contrast what they see as Schaeffer's moderation compared to Christian Reconstruction's "extreme form."[62]

In recent years – particularly among the "dominionist" interpretive camp – Schaeffer's reliance on *This Independent Republic* and his use of other Rushdoony materials (whether attributed or not) has morphed into the claim that Schaeffer was one of Rushdoony's close followers, a prize Rushdoony student and/or a devoted Rushdoony acolyte. In a May 2006 *Salon.com* article about "Christian nationalism," Michelle Goldberg follows the

---

[59] Indeed, at the conclusion of her section about presuppositional thought in *Apostles of Reason*, Worthen asserts that it is Schaeffer who "deserves more credit [than Rushdoony] for teaching evangelicals to reclaim culture and speak the language of presuppositionalism." Worthen, *Apostles of Reason*, 227–28.

[60] Ingersoll, "Mobilizing Evangelicals," 204fn8.

[61] Miller, *Age of Evangelicalism*, 142.

[62] Randall J. Stephens and Karl W. Giberson, *The Anointed: Evangelical Truth in a Secular Age* (Cambridge, MA: Harvard University Press, 2011), 79. In fact, the authors argue that it was D. James Kennedy, the minister of Coral Ridge Presbyterian Church in Fort Lauderdale, more so than Schaeffer, who brought Rushdoony's ideas to the general public. The authors specifically say that Kennedy "carried Rushdoony's ideas about history, politics and providence" to a wider audience (80–81).

standard line that Schaeffer was "reading and holding seminars" on Rushdoony's writing "as early as the 1960s" and that *A Christian Manifesto* "[drew] on Reconstructionist ideas of America as an originally Christian nation,"[63] However, later that same year in the pages of *Harper's*, Jeff Sharlet called Schaeffer "Rushdoony's most influential student."[64] This single phrase set off a spirited back-and-forth in Christianity Today's *Books and Culture* between Sharlet and Wheaton literature professor Alan Jacobs. In his initial salvo, Jacobs conceded that Schaeffer "read and cited [Rushdoony] approvingly," but then argued, given their respective educational and career paths, that there was "no conceivable sense" that Schaeffer was a student to the "Dark Armenian-American Lord [sitting] on his dark Californian throne."[65] Sharlet backpedaled and dropped the "most influential" moniker but maintained that Schaeffer should indeed be considered a Rushdoony student because, as others had argued, Schaeffer read and taught Rushdoony's ideas and used Rushdoony's work in *A Christian Manifesto*.[66] The Sharlet-Jacobs exchange concluded with Jacobs continuing to criticize what he saw as Sharlet's original, and intentional, misdirection of his *Harper's* readers with the "most influential student" language but registering skepticism over Rushdoony's larger influence ("if [Rushdoony's political] theology had significantly more influence than the ideas of the Flat Earth Society I might be worried about it").[67]

What about the biographical and autobiographical writings of Schaeffer's son, Frank? Might they provide any additional insights into the

---

[63] Michelle Goldberg, "Kingdom Coming: The Rise of Christian Nationalism," *Salon.com*, 12 May 2006; http://www.salon.com/2006/05/12/goldberg_14/ (accessed 28 June 2014).

[64] Jeff Sharlet, "Through a Glass, Darkly: How the Christian Right is reimagining US History," *Harper's* (December 2006), 36.

[65] Alan Jacobs, "The Know-Nothing Party," Christianity Today *Books and Culture*, February 2007; http://www.booksandculture.com/articles/webexclusives/2007/february/070205.html (accessed 28 June 2014).

[66] Alan Jacobs and Jeff Sharlet, "Some Fanged Enemy of Christendom," Christianity Today *Books and Culture*, February 2007; http://www.booksandculture.com/articles/webexclusives/2007/february/070212.html (accessed 28 June 2014).

[67] Ibid.

relationship between Rushdoony, Christian Reconstructionism and Francis Schaeffer's own work? Part of the difficulty of turning to Frank Schaeffer is that, since the early 1990s, he has been engaged in his own critical re-appraisal of his family's legacy, his Christian activism in the late 1970s and 1980s, and the whole of conservative evangelicalism. Historians therefore need to be cautious about taking Frank Schaeffer's self-narratives at face value. For example, in *Crazy for God*, Frank Schaeffer claims that he and his father "to [their] lasting discredit, [never] went public with [their] real opinions of the religious-right leaders" with whom they cooperated because they were worried about the impact of such criticisms to their personal reputations and to the pro-life movement. [68] Frank Schaeffer's references to his father's relationship with Rushdoony and Christian Reconstructionism in *Crazy for God* takes place in a larger discussion about John Whitehead and the Rutherford Institute. In 1979, Frank Schaeffer represented Whitehead in the publishing arena, and was subsequently asked to come on board as one of the founders of the Rutherford Institute. Frank Schaeffer highlights Gary North's participation in Rutherford Institute planning meetings, describing how his father considered North "a nutty gold-standard fruitcake" and thought Rushdoony to have been "clinically insane."[69] Frank Schaeffer adds that his father "never had liked John Calvin" and that the Christian Reconstructionists, including North, were using Schaeffer's name and brand parasitically, so as to improve the movement's public image.[70]

In Frank Schaeffer's *Sex, God and Mom*, the chapter devoted to Rushdoony and Christian Reconstructionism is even more problematic, particularly when it comes to the question of how much of his father's thought was based on Rushdoony's earlier work. Unlike *Crazy for God*, the description here relies much more heavily on writers in the "dominionist" interpretive camp. Dismissing Rushdoony the "patron saint to gold-hoarding haters of the Federal Reserve" while at the same time over-exaggerating Rushdoony's stature as the "creator of the modern [e]vangelical homeschool movement," Frank Schaeffer, citing Frederick Clarkson's 1994 *Public Eye*

---

[68] Frank Schaeffer, *Crazy for God: How I Grew Up as One of the Elect, Helped Found the Religious Right, and Lived to Take All (or Almost All) of It Back* (New York: Carroll and Graf, 2007), 300.

[69] Ibid, 301, 315–16, 332–35.

[70] Ibid, 334.

series, gives his readers a quick overview of Christian Reconstructionism. He also posits that the movement's origins and goals could be considered akin to those of the *ikhwan* (Muslim Brotherhood), both arising out of the same, late 20th century religious critique of modernism and perceived moral breakdown.[71] The chapter relates Frank Schaeffer's introduction to Rushdoony and Southern California philanthropist Howard Ahmanson in the late 1970s during planning sessions for the anti-abortion film series, *Whatever Happened to the Human Race?* Repeating the "insanity" descriptor (but this time in reference to the entire Christian Reconstructionist agenda), Frank Schaeffer does little to show the ways in which his father's work might or could have been based, even in part, on Rushdoony's. In contrast, he argues—in line with Gary North's arguments from the 1980s—that it was Rushdoony's belief that Francis Schaeffer was never willing to go far enough when it came to the civic introduction of Biblical law. Rushdoony, according to Frank Schaeffer, did not think that the senior Schaeffer was "consistently Calvinist" or offered the "full[y] Reformed solution" to the threat of secular humanism.[72]

In addressing this overall question in his dissertation and his 2013 article on "dominionism," McVicar tries to navigate some middle ground. Hearkening back to North, Wells and Edgar, McVicar agrees that Schaeffer "relied" on Rushdoony's ideas, shared sources and used Rushdoony's books in his L'Abri seminars.[73] Schaeffer and Rushdoony also exchanged letters, some of which McVicar was able to dig up at Chalcedon; however, the correspondence McVicar cites does not lend much to the debate over intellectual influence. Both men, argues McVicar, had a deep appreciation for Kuyper and Dutch philosopher Herman Dooyeweerd, and while McVicar says that *A Christian Manifesto* was "clearly [influenced]" by Rushdoony and "pulse[s] with the force of Christian Reconstruction[ism]," he concludes that the book is "more deeply Kuyperian and Van Tillian than it is Rushdoonian."[74] In the end, McVicar shares the opinion of Canadian scholar

---

[71] Frank Schaeffer, *Sex, Mom and God: How the Bible's Strange Take on Sex Led to Crazy Politics—and How I Learned to Love Women (and Jesus) Anyway* (Cambridge, MA: Da Capo Press, 2011), 100–107.

[72] Ibid., 107–10.

[73] McVicar, *Reconstructing America*, 308fn62.

[74] Ibid, 308fn62, 351–53; McVicar, however, also argues in "Let Them Have Dominion" that Schaeffer "explicitly dismissed" key aspects of Rushdoony's thought

Irving Hexham who, writing about Rushdoony and Schaeffer in the early 1990s, insisted that critics of both men often conflate the two so as to "turn Schaeffer into a derivative Reconstructionist."[75] All-in-all, when it comes to historians of American evangelicalism, or journalists on the evangelical beat, the claim that one is getting Rushdoony when reading Schaeffer is still an under-developed one, and one that requires a much deeper, concerted, text-based comparison of the two thinkers.

Conclusion

In conclusion, to tweak John Lewis Gaddis' phrasing, "we now know" through scholars like Daniel Williams (or, in a more condensed format, Steven Miller) much more than we did a mere decade ago about the contours of American conservative evangelicalism's *power-political* rise in the late 1970s and 1980s. We also now know, specifically through Darren Dochuk, much more than we did about the early Cold War-era political economy and regionalism behind conservative evangelicalism's national political debut. What I would argue is lacking, and what Molly Worthen's *Apostles* begins to address, is a much deeper engagement with the actual theologies—dare I say political theologies—driving evangelical public engagement in the Cold War and beyond. And this is why, I would add, Rushdoony and Christian Reconstructionism have been topics of inquiry which are ignored and dismissed, or else captured and used as a generalized, shorthand-caricature (under the "dominionism" flag) for conservative Christians who want to organize civic life along Biblical lines. The upcoming histories by Michael McVicar and Julie Ingersoll will go far in providing an academically-sound foundation for the public's understanding of Rushdoony, theonomy and Christian Reconstructionism, but what will be needed in the near future is for scholars to build on McVicar and Ingersoll's work, integrating it with other studies of American conservatism and American religious history. Along this vein, one hopes to see at some point the publication of a larger academic history of theonomy from the 1970s through the present.

---

in *A Christian Manifesto*. He names Rushdoony's penchant for conspiracy theory and Rushdoony's theocratic vision. McVicar, "Let Them Have Dominion," 132–33. Hence, there appears to be a bit of disconnect.

[75] McVicar, *Reconstructing America*, p. 351fn184; McVicar, "Let Them Have Dominion," 132–33.

Bibliography

Adewale, Tomilola. "Paul Hill's Journey: The Analysis of a Former Minister's Path to Violent Anti-Abortion Extremism." B.A. Senior Thesis, Duke University, 2010, http://www.tomiadewale.com/thesis.pdf (accessed 28 June 2014).

Auten, Brian J. Review of Molly Worthen, *Apostles of Reason: The Crisis of Authority in American Evangelicalism*, in *Canon and Culture* [Southern Baptist Convention's Ethics and Religious Liberty Commission], 4 February 2014, http://www.canonandculture.com/apostles-of-reason-the-crisis-of-authority-in-american-evangelicalism/ (accessed 12 July 2014).

Balmer, Randall, "The Real Origins of the Religious Right." *Politico*, 27 May 2014, www.politico.com/magazine/story/2014/05/religious-right-real-origins-107133.html (accessed 21 June 2014).

Berlet, Chip, "How We Coined the Term 'Dominionism'" *Talk to Action*, 31 August 2011, http://www.talk2action.org/story/2011/8/31/17047/5683/ (accessed 21 June 2014).

Blumenthal, Max. *Republican Gomorrah: Inside the Movement that Shattered the Party*. New York: Nation Books, 2009.

Dochuk, Darren. *From Bible Belt to Sun Belt: Plain-Folk Religion, Grassroots Politics and the Rise of Evangelical Conservatism*. New York: W.W. Norton, 2011.

Ecumenical Documentation and Information Centre for Eastern and Southern Africa (EDICESA). *Programme—Religion and Oppression: The Misuse of Religion for Social, Political and Economic Subjugation, Symposium for General Secretaries of National Christian Councils and Church Leaders from Eastern and Southern Africa*. 1–3 August 1989. http://www.disa.ukzn.ac.za/webpages/DC/pro19890801.026.009.726/pro19890801.026.009.726.pdf (accessed 21 June 2014).

Edgar, William. "The Passing of R.J. Rushdoony," *First Things*, August 2001, http://www.firstthings.com/article/2001/08/the-passing-of-r-j-rushdoony (accessed 28 June 2014).

Goldberg, Michelle. "Kingdom Coming: The Rise of Christian Nationalism," *Salon.com*, 12 May 2006, http://www.salon.com/2006/05/12/goldberg_14/ (accessed 28 June 2014).

———. *Kingdom Coming: The Rise of Christian Nationalism*. New York: W.W. Norton and Company, 2006.

Hankins, Barry. *Francis Schaeffer and the Shaping of Evangelical America*. Grand Rapids: Eerdmans, 2008.

Harding, Susan Friend. "Representing Fundamentalism: The Problem of the Repugnant Cultural Other." *Social Research* 58.2 (Summer 1991), pp. 373-393.

Hedges, Chris. *American Fascists: The Christian Right and the War on America*. New York: Free Press, 2006.

Ingersoll, Julie. "Mobilizing Evangelicals: Christian Reconstructionism and the Roots of the Religious Right." In Steven Brint and Jean Reith Schroedel (eds.), *Evangelicals and Democracy in America: Religion and Politics*, 179–208. New York: Russell Sage, 2009.

Jacobs, Alan. "The Know-Nothing Party," Christianity Today *Books and Culture*, February 2007, http://www.booksandculture.com/articles/webexclusives/2007/february/070205.html (accessed 28 June 2014).

Jacobs, Alan, and Jeff Sharlet. "Some Fanged Enemy of Christendom," Christianity Today *Books and Culture*, February 2007, http://www.booksandculture.com/articles/webexclusives/2007/february/070212.html (accessed 28 June 2014).

Joyce, Kathryn. *The Child Catchers: Rescue, Trafficking and the New Gospel of Adoption*. New York: PublicAffairs, 2013.

———. *Quiverfull: Inside the Christian Patriarchy Movement*. Boston: Beacon Press, 2009.

McVicar, Michael J. "'Let Them Have Dominion:' 'Dominion Theology' and the Construction of Religious Extremism in the US Media." *Journal of Religion and Popular Culture* 25:1 (Spring 2013), 120–45.

———. *Reconstructing America: Religion, American Conservatism and the Political Theology of Rousas John Rushdoony*. Ph.D. dissertation, Ohio State University, 2010.

Miller, Steven P. *The Age of Evangelicalism: America's Born-Again Years*. New York: Oxford University Press, 2014

Nickerson, Michelle. *Mothers of Conservatism: Women and the Postwar Right*. Princeton: Princeton University Press, 2012.

North, Gary. *Lone Gunners for Jesus: Letters to Paul J. Hill*. Tyler, TX: Institute for Christian Economics, 1994.

———. *Political Polytheism: The Myth of Pluralism*. Tyler, TX: Institute for Christian Economics, 1989.

———. *Tithing and the Church*. Tyler, TX: Institute for Christian Economics, 1994.

North, Gary, and David Chilton. "Apologetics and Strategy." In Gary North (ed.), *Tactics of Christian Resistance*. Tyler, TX: Geneva Divinity School Press, 1983.

Phillips-Fein, Kim. "Conservatism: A State of the Field." *Journal of American History* 98:3 (December 2011), 723–43.

Rhodes, Gladys Titzck and Nancy Titzck Anderson. *McIntire: Defender of Faith and Freedom*, Xulon Press, 2012.

Risen, Jim and Judy Thomas. *Wrath of Angels: The American Abortion War*. New York: Basic Books, 1998.

Rosenfeld, Seth. *Subversives: The FBI's War on Student Radicals and Reagan's Rise to Power.* New York: Farrar, Straus and Giroux, 2012.

Sanford, James C. *Blueprint for Theocracy: The Christian Right's Vision for America.* Providence, RI: Metacomet Books, 2014.

Schaeffer, Frank. *Crazy for God: How I Grew Up as One of the Elect, Helped Found the Religious Right, and Lived to Take All (or Almost All) of It Back.* New York: Carroll and Graf, 2007.

———. *Sex, Mom and God: How the Bible's Strange Take on Sex Led to Crazy Politics—and How I Learned to Love Women (and Jesus) Anyway.* Cambridge, MA: Da Capo Press, 2011.

Sharlet, Jeff. *C Street: The Fundamentalist Threat to American Democracy.* New York: Little, Brown and Company, 2010.

———. *The Family: The Secret Fundamentalism at the Heart of American Power.* New York: Harper Perennial, 2008.

———. "Through a Glass, Darkly: How the Christian Right is reimagining US History," *Harper's*, December 2006, http://jeffsharlet.com/content/wp-content/uploads/2008/09/through_a_glass.pdf (accessed 21 September 2014).

Stanley, Tiffany. "The Intellectual War within Evangelicalism: An Interview with Molly Worthen." *Religion and Politics*, http://religionandpolitics.org/2013/12/03/the-intellectual-civil-war-within-evangelicalism-an-interview-with-molly-worthen/ (accessed 12 July 2014)

Stephens, Randall J., and Karl W. Giberson. *The Anointed: Evangelical Truth in a Secular Age.* Cambridge, MA: Harvard University Press, 2011.

Trueman, Carl. *Histories and Fallacies: Problems Faced in the Writing of History.* Wheaton, IL: Crossway Press, 2010.

———. "Rushdoony, Historical Incompetence, Racism and Lunacy," *Reformation21 blog*, 20 December 2006, http://www.reformation21.org/blog/2006/12/rushdoony-historical-incompete.php (accessed 5 August 2014).

———. "Rushdoony once again—for the last time," *Reformation21blog*, 31 December 2006, http://www.reformation21.org/blog/2006/12/rushdoony-once-again-for-the-l.php (accessed 5 August 2014).

———. "Rushdoony Revisited," *Reformation21blog*, 21 December 2006, http://www.reformation21.org/blog/2006/12/rushdoony-revisited.php (accessed 5 August 2014).

Williams, Daniel K. *God's Own Party: The Making of the Christian Right*. New York: Oxford University Press, 2010.

Wilson, Douglas. *Black and Tan: A Collection of Essays and Excursions on Slavery, Culture War and Scripture*. Moscow, ID: Canon Press, 2005.

Worthen, Molly. *Apostles of Reason: The Crisis of Authority in American Evangelicalism*. New York: Oxford University Press, 2013.

———. "The Chalcedon Problem: Rousas John Rushdoony and the Origins of Christian Reconstructionism." *Church History* 77:2 (June 2008), 399–437.

Nature and Grace, Visible and Invisible: A New Look at the Question of Infant Baptism

Joseph Minich
University of Texas at Dallas

I. Introduction

Imagine a pastor who has recently received a call to a struggling church. This pastor wants to speak the word of God to the needs of this congregation. But further imagine that within a year of his ministry he discovers open sexual immorality among the members of the congregation (which is not being dealt with by the elders of the church), petty divisions over trivial matters, disorderliness in the church's worship, questioning of central tenets of the Christian faith, and what might seem most personal to the pastor, factions which question his right to tend to the congregation in these situations.

You have just imagined something of the relationship Paul had with the congregations of the city of Corinth. What does this have to do with infant baptism? Simply put, I want to argue that the way that we speak to adults in our churches is integrally related to the way that we speak to our covenant children. More to the point, the way *God* speaks through His public words to the adults in the congregation is integrally related to the way He speaks to His little ones. This is, in part, because the ambiguities that attend the confession of our children attend the confession of adults. How then does God speak, through the apostle Paul, to the congregations at Corinth? It is worth noticing that he does not overtly question the integrity of their confession until the very end of (what is probably more than) two epistles (2 Cor. 13:5). We get a glimpse of Paul's general long-term pastoral strategy in 2 Corinthians 2. Explaining why he has not visited the congregations for a while, Paul writes, "I determined this for my own sake, that I would not come to you in sorrow again. For if I cause you sorrow, who then makes me glad but the one whom I made sorrowful" (v.1-2)?[1] Instead of visiting

---

[1] All Bible quotations are from the *New American Standard Bible* (1995). For an analysis of the unity of Paul's Corinthian correspondence, see Carson & Moo, *Introduction to the New Testament* (Grand Rapids: Zondervan, 2005), pgs. 415-55.

the congregations at a time when they were spiritually weak, Paul decided to refrain from visiting so that they could deal with their spiritual problems—that his visit might be one of joy rather than of correction. But notice how Paul explains the motivation for his sorrow over their spiritual condition. "Out of much affliction and anguish of heart I wrote to you with many tears; not so that you would be made sorrowful, but that you might know the love which I have especially for you" (v. 4). His intimate love for the congregation spilled over into expectancy that they would respond to his ministry. While he wrote that his letters were a test of their obedience (v. 9), he spoke of his "confidence in you all that my joy would be the joy of you all" (v. 3). The confidence Paul has toward these congregations is expressed continually in the epistle. "Great is my confidence in you; great is my boasting on your behalf" (7:4). It is important for us to remember that Paul's words were also the words of *God* for this congregation. It was not Paul who established grace and peace toward them, but God (1:1-2). Paul defended the apostolic ministry (especially His activity of speaking) as containing the very words of God, working through Paul in the effective ministry of the new covenant (chapters 3 and 4).

I have stated already that the way we speak to adults will become the way we speak to children, but it also works the other way around. Indeed, in Reformed churches, it most often works this way. The ambiguity which attends our speech toward covenant children often spills over into an ambiguity concerning covenant adults. This leads many to abandon a Reformed theology of children altogether. But this is wrong. There are good reasons to speak confidently about God's disposition toward children in His covenant.

> Herman Bavinck eloquently captures precisely why this is so:
> It [the covenant of grace] pronounces the deep and beautiful truth that Adam has been replaced by Christ, that the humanity that fell in the person of the first is restored in the second; that not just a few separate individuals are saved but that in the elect-under-Christ the organism of humanity and of the world itself is saved…For that reason the covenant of grace does not leap from individual to individual but perpetuates itself organically and historically…It is never made with a solitary individual but always al-

so with his or her descendants.[2]

Indeed, what is perhaps most persuasive about the Reformed practice and theology of infant baptism is that it maintains the Biblical connection between nature and grace, between creation and new creation. The goal of this essay is to briefly state how the connection between nature and grace warrants infant baptism (section 2), to entertain the objection that this collapses the difference between God's disposition to the elect and to the reprobate within the covenant (section 3), and to state what I think is a satisfying answer to the objection (section 4). It is appropriate to ask the reader to be patient with the development of this argument, because its persuasive power lies in its totality, not in its isolated piecemeal claims (even though these could be defended individually). In the end, I want to argue that there are resources within an orthodox doctrine of God to most effectively resolve the theological tensions in our practice of speaking kindly and favorably (on behalf of God) to our children.

II. Nature And Grace: An Argument For Infant Baptism
Nature and Grace

Perhaps the most obvious bookends of the grand story of redemption are the bookends of creation and new creation. The Bible begins with God creating the world in Genesis 1 and ends with His renewing the world in an act of new creation in Revelation 21-22. But it is clear in the Bible that while the eschatological era will be different from the present age, the new grows out of the old. The new is not new "stuff," but the old stuff renewed to be what it was always meant to be. Grace does not replace nature, but renews it by conquering sin and death and takes it into its always-intended *telos*.[3] The body of Jesus is the first-fruits of the new creation harvest (1 Cor. 15:23). But the resurrected body of Jesus exists in continuity with the body He possessed in His state of humiliation. The tomb is empty. Jesus did not escape death in the flesh, but conquered it and entered into His glory (Luke 24:26, 1 Pet. 1:11).

Now some object that this undervalues the difference between pre-

---

[2] Herman Bavinck, *Reformed Dogmatics Vol. 3: Sin and Salvation in Christ* (Grand Rapids: Baker, 2006), 231.

[3] See the discussion of Bavinck in *Reformed Dogmatics Vol. 4: Holy Spirit, Church, and New Creation* (Grand Rapids: Baker, 2008), chapter 18.

eschatological creation and the eschatological state. Scripture is clear that our identity in Christ is not essentially tied to our identities as male or female, slave or free, for instance (Gal. 3:29). And it is clear that our bodies and social relationships will be somehow different in the *eschaton* (Mat. 19:29-32). But all of these things (marriage, family, gender, etc) have an eschatological goal and analogue. They are all creational goods and even if their current form is meant to "perish with use" and to be crowned with the fitting eschatological corollary at the end, it is *they* who are brought to that eschatological state to be so changed. Certainly there is discontinuity between our current state and the "state of glory," but it is precisely in redeeming creation *as such* that grace saves, because all of the structures of creation are taken up into glory and crowned fittingly for the final state which was always their *telos*.[4] That is to say, creation "as it exists" is redeemed and taken to its goal. Grace does not replace but restores creation to achieve its destiny. Human labor, for instance, is highlighted as having eschatological significance in Revelation 21–22.[5] Similarly, in Ephesians 5, the institution of marriage is shown to have an eschatological analogue in the eternal union of Christ and the church.

Infant Baptism

The biblical and logical implication of this is that grace renews nature as nature actually exists. And in nature, my visible identity and the visible (historical, narrative, etc) identities of my children are wrapped up in one another.[6] The public identities of my children are given to them before they

---

[4] In his recent *Living in God's Two Kingdoms* (Wheaton: Crossway, 2010), 66, David VanDrunen goes so far as to say that "Our earthly bodies are the only part of the present world that Scripture says will be transformed and taken up into the world-to-come." VanDrunen has recently clarified that he only meant to claim that this is the only continuity that Scripture is clear about, not that this is the only continuity that will obtain in the new heavens and earth. But, I would argue that (a) Scripture itself does say more than this and that (b) one can still articulate principles of continuity (i.e. the "substance" of creation remains, etc) without being speculative about all the specifics. See Bavinck, *Reformed Dogmatics* Vol. 4, chapter 18.

[5] See particularly the discussion of Andy Crouch in *Culture Making* (Downers Grove: InterVarsity Press, 2008), chapter 10.

[6] Joachim Jeremias, *Origins of Infant Baptism* (Eugene: Wipf and Stock, 2004), 12-32, is probably the best argument that the "household" passages of the New Testament strongly support infant baptism. But my argument seeks to get to the root of

are ever actors on the world-stage. Their name is given to them.[7] Their tasks are given to them. Their race and gender are given to them. Most of their relationships are given to them. Their language is given to them. Outside of Western attempts to protect an individuals' development of values, their religion and philosophy are given to them.[8] James K.A. Smith helpfully defines human beings as "liturgical animals."[9] Our identities are formed in cultural liturgies, habits, thoughts and practices. In contrast to those who give primacy to human thought, Smith argues that reflexive (for most of us, pre-cognitive) cultural practices are so imbedded in our engagement with the world that they function as a tacit evaluative filter. Through them we judge whether or not certain ideas or practices seem plausible or implausible (ideas), wise or foolish (practices). Even our 21st century individualism, for example, makes it very difficult for us to think in terms of group primacy. More traditional views of human societal relations (i.e. the primacy of the organism over the individual, corporate identity, etc) simply do not *feel* persuasive. Even if more traditional views are deemed to be correct, the problem is that our cultural habits almost coerce us to relate to the world primarily as individuals—and so it is extremely difficult for corporate ways of imagining the world to become an ideological or practical reflex. The point here is not to criticize Western culture, but to make the point at hand by way of irony: even the individualism of Western culture shows that our identities are anything but individualistic. This simply reflects what human beings are, or more generally, what humanity is.

Given the connection between nature and grace, it is worth asking what we would expect if God were to redeem a creation that looks precisely like this. How does God address us in redemptive speech? How does He grant new identity? Peter Leithart argues that the track of redemption cannot move along a different track than that of creation. If the visible "unit" of redemptive "selection" (to borrow a phrase from evolutionary biology) is

---

this. What is it about the nature of creation and redemption that would make us expect this?

[7] See James V. Brownson, *The Promise of Baptism* (Grand Rapids: Eerdmans, 2007), 102, for the baptismal analogue.

[8] Of course, this is just a way of insuring that they have Western values and a Western mode of being religious.

[9] *Desiring the Kingdom* (Grand Rapids: Baker, 2009).

the "individual" while our religious and ethical identities in creation are anything but individualistic, then God is not redeeming creation as it actually is. He is, in fact, redeeming something other than creation.[10] As we will see below, this does not mean that individual identity does not exist, but it does mean that it does not exist apart from communal identity. In anticipation, visibly communal identities in creation remain visibly communal in redemption – and invisibly particular identities in creation remain invisibly particular in redemption. Balancing these two perspectives with respect to God's redemptive favor is a major task of this essay.

Preliminary Clarifications
Arbitrary Definitions?

One objection to this line of reasoning is that the boundaries of corporate solidarity seem to be arbitrarily located by Reformed theologians. In Meredith Kline's discussion of human solidarity, for instance, he seeks to avoid the implication that the baptism of infants might imply the baptism of unbelieving wives and family servants (in continuity with the Old Testament order).[11] In truth, we need not avoid the implications of covenantal continuity the way Kline does. A spouse or a servant could have refused to participate in the liturgical life of Israel in the old covenant and they would have been cut off from the people of Israel. Infants, however, have not refused the covenant, whereas an unbelieving husband or wife might automatically refuse God's offer of grace. This objection overlooks, furthermore, how God seems to actually work in history. God often saves in families. In cultures where the social imaginary[12] of the people includes elements

---

[10] I often disagree with Peter Leithart on issues related to baptism (as the rest of this essay will make clear), but I think that his appendix, "The Sociology of Infant Baptism," in *The Baptized Body* (Moscow: Canon, 2007), is very helpful along these lines. For the ubiquity of the biblical notion of corporate solidarity, see J. de Fraine, *Adam and the Family of Man* (Staten Island: Alba House, 1965).

[11] This is clear at the end of *By Oath Consigned* (Grand Rapids: Eerdmans, 1968), chapter 6, and it is becomes a point which his critics, like Duane Garrett, "Meredith Kline on Suzerainty, Circumcision, and Baptism" in Thomas R. Schreiner and Shawn D. Wright (eds.), *Believers Baptism: Sign of the New Covenant in Christ* (Nashville, B&H, 2006), 257-84, use against him.

[12] See Taylor's *A Secular Age* (Cambridge: Harvard, 2007), 159-211 as well as his genealogy of the modern concept of the self in his *Sources of the Self* (Cambridge: Harvard, 1989).

of tribalism or empire, religious decisions made by cultural "heads" often have automatic effects on the religious identity of those over whom they exercise their lordship.[13] And this is just natural. One could argue that these structures are simply modes of the original creation family unit, and as such the structural changes that exist within those contexts follow the nature-grace pattern. This is precisely what we see in Scripture and in history.[14]

In the history of God's speech, God's call always includes all that belongs to us. When God first commissioned our human parents, He commissioned them together (Gen 1:28). When God called Noah, Abraham, and all the leaders of Israel, He called all that belonged to each of them, including their households—the public identities of which were represented in their respective visible heads. God addresses us and relates to us as we actually live in history. Household members may reject our corporate calling (as in the case of unbelieving spouses above), but this does not change the corporate dimensions of God's covenantal address.[15] Instead, it highlights that this address does not overcome but rather creates the space where human beings respond in freedom and own their identities.[16] And, in a prelim-

---

[13] Interestingly, Anthony Lane's argument for a dual-practice view of infant baptism in the early church must be rooted in the early church's notion of corporate solidarity (See his "Did the Apostolic Church Baptize Babies? A Seismological Approach" *Tyndale Bulletin* 55.1 (2004), 109-30). That is to say, even if the evidence for their actual practice can be confusing, this is only because the pressure to baptize particular children might have been (perhaps wrongly!) small given the perception that the sacramental status of children was "taken care of" by the baptism of the head of a family.

[14] Frame's discussion of the way human government is rooted in the creational institution of family is instructive in this regard; see *The Doctrine of the Christian Life* (Phillipsburg, NJ: Presbyterian and Reformed, 2008), chapter 32.

[15] As William Shedd, *Dogmatic Theology* (Philipsburg: Presbyterian & Reformed, 2003), 818, writes, "The question that confronts them [covenant children] at the period of discretion is not 'Will you join the visible church?' but 'Will you go out of it?'"

[16] Bavinck writes, "In the creation of humanity, God himself chose this way of freedom, which carried with it the danger and actually the fact of sin as well, in preference to forced subjection. Even now, in ruling the world and governing the church, God still follows this royal road of liberty. It is precisely his honor that through freedom he nevertheless reaches his goal, creating order out of disorder, light from darkness, a cosmos out of chaos," *Reformed Dogmatics Vol 1: Prolegomena* (Grand Rapids: Baker, 2003), 479.

inary way, this makes clear that we are talking about *objective* identity, the kind by which we are addressed in dialogue. I am not "Joseph Minich" apart from being the "father of Sam" or the "employee of the University of Texas at Dallas." As Leithart writes, these are not pins stuck into the "pincushion" of the "real me."[17] It is true, of course, that I also cannot be reduced to the identities by which I am able to be publicly addressed in dialogue. To address me by virtue of my identities, there is a "me" in which the relations subsist.[18] But as I live and move in history, I relate to others by virtue of my identities. At the most fundamental level, there are aspects of my identity which are essential properties of my being at all (i.e. the capacity to be spoken to by God and to answer back, etc).[19] But these essential identities only subsist in the contingent identities of our historical location. And the point here is that God does not address us behind these contingent identities, but precisely in them.

As in creation, so in redemption. The sacraments are God's promises with our name written on them. They are "visible words," His address to us. They call us to live a certain way (Romans 6). They are attached to promises (Genesis 17, Acts. 2:38). They are a claim in which God declares that He will be our God and we shall be His people. And this claim is also a claim upon all that belongs to me, including my children. Infant baptism is rooted in a more fundamental theology of children.[20] God's promise belongs to them (Acts 2:38-39).[21] As a promise, baptism functions very much

---

[17] Leithart, "Trinitarian Anthropology: Toward a Trinitarian Re-casting of Reformed Theology" in Calvin E. Beisner (ed.), *The Auburn Avenue Theology* (Fort Lauderdale: Knox Theological Seminary, 2004)., 68.

[18] Kevin Vanhoozer argues against the modern reduction of all things to relations by arguing that things must be logically prior to relations in order to *be* in relation, *Remythologizing Theology* (New York: Cambridge, 2010), 140-49.

[19] Michael Horton, *Lord and Servant* (Louisville: Westminster/John Knox, 2005), part 2, discusses our creational identity as our being "spoken to" by God. Similarly, in *People and Place* (Louisville: Westminster/John Knox, 2008), chapter 2, he describes the church as the "worded community."

[20] This point is made especially well by Douglas Wilson, "Baptism and Children: Their Place in the Old and New Testaments," in Gregg Strawbridge (ed.), *The Case for Covenantal Infant Baptism* (Phillipsburg, NJ: Presbyterian and Reformed, 2003), 286–302

[21] For a competent exegesis of this passage, see Joel R. Beeke's "Unto You, and to Your Children" in *The Case for Covenantal Infant Baptism*, 49–69, in conjunction with

like my wedding ring. It is often assumed that my wedding ring represents my commitment to my wife, but in point of fact, the relation is precisely the converse. It represents my wife's commitment to me. She put this mark on me at our wedding and attached it to the words, "With this ring, I thee wed." More colloquially, baptism is analogous to a branding on a cow. If I found a cow in the wilderness roaming around in the wild, a branding on that cow would be a mark by which the owner told those who found it, "Mine!" Baptism is an operative ceremony wherein God says "Mine!" to all the baptized. He commits Himself to them and calls for their faith.[22] Coordinated with the argument above, God relates to us in baptism in conjunction with our created identities, and all that is implied in them. Said more simply, He relates to the real (both essential and contingent) us. It is *we* who are baptized.

But just what is this baptismal relation? This is actually a matter of intense debate. Though my reasons will become clearer as this essay progresses, I would argue that baptism needs to be understood as God's objective relation of favor and blessing. His filial love (adoption), judicial regard (justification) and vitalizing presence (sanctification) are all implied here, *but it is all of these things in the form of promissory speech in Christ.* Baptism situates one into a formal relationship with Christ (to whom all the benefits proper belong), and they are ours by virtue of our organic relation to our head. *But a legal right to all the blessings of Christ does not imply a vital possession of these benefits.*[23] The initiatory address of Christian baptism can only result in vital union through the response of faith. That the benefits are offered and given (in Christ) does not necessarily imply that they are received and enjoyed.

Marshall's observations concerning Luke's use of the Joel 2 prophecy in "Acts" in *Commentary on the New Testament Use of the Old Testament*, G.K. Beale & D.A. Carson (Eds.) (Grand Rapids: Baker, 2007), 543.

[22] Peter J. Leithart, *Priesthood of the Plebs* (Eugene: Wipf and Stock, 2003), chapter 4.

[23] Francis Turretin, *Institutes of Elenctic Theology* 3 Vols. (Phillipsburg, NJ: Presbyterian and

Reformed, 1992), 15.16.29, and Herman Witsius, *The Economy of the Covenants Between God and Man* (Escondido: del Dulk Christian Foundation, 1990), 3.13.4, both speak of a sort of formal union with Christ, but they do so in stark contrast to the union possessed by the elect, which is alone redemptive. C.A. Schouls, *The Covenant of Grace* (Vineland: Niagara Ligonier Study Center, 1996), offers a very helpful survey about how the Reformed tradition has struggled to articulate this.

They might be as unopened Christmas presents under the tree with one's name written on them.

What About Faith?

And this helps to clarify the scriptural emphasis on the response of faith. The New Testament attributes all the benefits of redemption to their being received by faith (John 1:12–13, Rom. 3:25). Surely baptism does not guarantee a right relation between God and the saint without the response of faith. And so baptism is not just an identity, but a calling. Said better, baptism is a promise that is meant to evoke a response.[24] God covenantally binds Himself to the baptized[25] in such a way as to produce the response of faith. In the case of adults outside the covenant community, we do not know that the promise belongs to them until they believe, and so baptism follows confession. But in the case of infants inside the covenant community, the promise belongs to them in *anticipation* of their coming to faith. Baptism is never disconnected from faith, but neither does it represent faith any more than my wedding ring represents my commitment to my wife. Baptism is God's promise given in a visible form, whether given before or after the response of faith. As in creation, God first speaks in promise and commission to mankind and calls for their response.[26] Our fundamental task as both created and redeemed persons is to "answer back" to God's initiatory speech.[27]

---

[24] Oscar Cullman, *Baptism in the New Testament* (London: SCM Press, 1950), insists on this point. Beasley-Murray, in a book also titled *Baptism in the New Testament* (Grand Rapids: Eerdmans, 1962), exegetes 1 Pet. 3:21 to relate baptism essentially to Christian confession, 361–62. But the "appeal" spoken of in the passage is predicated of the sign itself, not of the person using the sign. The contrast with "removal of dirt from the flesh" suggests that it is the sign-as-instrument which is in question (i.e. what is this good for?) rather than the relation between the sign and faith *as such*.

[25] Peter Lillback, *The Binding of God: Calvin's Role in the Development of Covenant Theology* (Grand Rapids: Baker, 2001), shows the ubiquity of this theme in Calvin.

[26] G.C. Berkouwer, *The Sacraments* (Grand Rapids: Eerdmans, 1981), chapter 8, is especially insistent on the priority of promise, even before the exercise of faith. Bavinck's discussion of covenant conditions, *Reformed Dogmatics* Vol. 3, 229–30, is particularly instructive on this issue. Kline's argument that the covenant signs might just as much be a seal of death as of life will be discussed below.

[27] Horton's discussion in *Lord and Servant* (Section 2) defends this well.

Even in the case of children, baptism is never separated from faith. It is normative for covenant children to confess their faith. In creation, if we are taught to speak English, we will speak English. In redemption, if we are taught to say "Our Father" and "Jesus is Lord," we will say "Our Father" and "Jesus is Lord." Now, this raises all sorts of objections which will be dealt with throughout the rest of this essay, but it is important to realize at the outset that this sort of confession is meaningful in the New Testament. The suspicion we might have toward the verbal confession of a seven year old will often become precisely the sort of suspicion we have toward the verbal confession of a twenty-seven year old. But Paul's confidence and affirmation to a church which might have seemed very "non-credible" should teach us something about how we are to treat visible confession. Paul speaks of children as being "in the Lord" in Ephesians 6:1. In Matthew 19:14, Jesus does not highlight the children who came to Him as an analogy of faith but as an instance of it.[28]

Thesis: Maintaining *Visible* and *Invisible* Perspectives

This focuses the argument here. The simple thesis of this paper is that visible confession is real and that God relates to it *as such*. But, it will further be argued that the visible does not exhaust God's relation to each individual. In my judgment, the solution to so many of the battles that have been fought in Reformed churches over the last decade is to reflect theologically from the perspective of God's objective and historical covenant speech (which is His visible relation to us), rather than from the *res* of the individual benefits of being in Christ. Said differently, we must learn to le-

---

[28] A. Andrew Das, *Baptized into God's Family* (Milwaukee: Northwestern Publishing House, 2008), 33–38, nicely exegetes these passages. Lusk's article, "God of My Youth: Infant Faith in the Psalter" in Gregg Strawbridge (ed.), *The Case for Covenant Communion* (Monroe: Athanasius Press, 2006), 89–110, is also quite helpful. One need not agree with everything Lusk writes about infant faith to be persuaded that the Bible tends to predicate faith of infants, even if only in anticipation of their future confession. Expectation of faith, however, is still not the ground of baptism. But it helps to emphasize this so that baptism is not disconnected from faith (as the two are so often seen together in Scripture). Vern Poythress' "Indifferentism and Rigorism in the Church: With Implications for Baptizing Small Children" in *Westminster Theological Journal* 59.1 (1997), 13–29, and "Linking Small Children with Infants in the Theology of Baptizing" in *Westminster Theological Journal* 59.2 (1997), 143–58, comprise perhaps the most nuanced treatment of this issue of which I am aware.

gitimately predicate the categories of the *ordo salutis* to the manner in which God speaks objectively to individuals in the covenant rather than reducing them to something which is true of individuals *in themselves*. The latter is an appropriate and biblical perspective, but it is not the only way the Bible speaks. This is not precisely the same thing as the "sacramental relation" between the sacraments, faith and Christ. The emphasis is not on the way that we may *notionally* connect what is said of one thing to what is said of another.[29] Rather, we must account for the fact that Paul can speak so confidently and objectively concerning God's relation to individuals without having access to information concerning their inner relationship to Christ. In short, he can do so because God's visible relationship is not hidden. And this real visible relationship can be spoken of in all the terms of the *ordo salutis*, so long as we understand that the visible is proximate and partial in its relation to the whole. Or, what can be said of one aspect of a relationship might or might not correspond to what can be said of a relationship in its entirety.[30]

III. The Challenge of Apostasy

The theological tensions in the previous section are very apparent. While theological tension does not make a position wrong,[31] we should feel the pressure to show that the Bible is coherent in its claims.[32] For Reformed Christians, the problem here is that we find it difficult to say that God relates redemptively to a person when that person doesn't have vital (as opposed to simply apparent) faith. Anyone who has been a Christian long enough has known baptized professors who apostatized. Given the fact that Paul speaks very confidently about the salvation, faith, justification, etc. of the baptized in his epistles, there are at least two ways Reformed Chris-

---

[29] Herman Bavinck, *Saved by Grace* (Grand Rapids: Reformation Heritage Books, 2008), 132-40.

[30] We have often known this in relation to marriages, for instance. The public face of a marriage or particular instances of love and affection sometimes (tragically) do not correspond to the often publicly unperceived brokenness of a marriage taken as a whole.

[31] John Murray, *Christian Baptism* (Phillipsburg: Presbyterian and Reformed, 1980), 54–55, rightly insists that divine warrant trumps our need to know.

[32] See James Anderson's *Paradox in Christian Theology* (Eugene: Wipf and Stock, 2007), for an intelligent approach to this issue.

tians have attempted to reconcile these statements with the reality of apostasy.

"Judgment of Charity": An Insufficient Answer

One answer is to say that we simply cannot be certain of God's favorable regard for visible confessors. Consistent with this is the contention that baptism is mainly a "sign" of the "content" of the gospel. Baptism is seen as God's commitment to justify those who have faith. Many Reformed theologians point out that while the benefits of the sign depend upon faith, the sign itself is administered before faith.[33] The covenant is then seen as a place where faith is created and sustained, but it does not *necessarily* imply favor.[34] Some might think of God as well-disposed to give grace to our children (in the sense that He is well-disposed to give grace to any), but His disposal towards the reprobate baptized infant in the covenant community is difficult to distinguish from the reprobate non-baptized infant outside the covenant community. Reducing God's favor to His secret disposition has sometimes led to a lack of confidence in God's favor even for adults. The Puritan and American Presbyterian tradition, in particular, are well known for ecclesiastical rigor in judging congregants' confessions of faith (and for consequently needing to write voluminously about assurance).[35]

The Scriptures in which Paul speaks confidently about the justification of persons in the visible church (some of whom would likely aposta-

---

[33] This demonstrates that the absence of faith does not preclude baptism, but it understates the significance of baptism itself. Mark Ross, "Baptism and Circumcision as Signs and Seals" in *The Case for Covenantal Infant Baptism*, 85–111, is especially dissatisfying. The sign becomes indistinguishable from God's general promise to all persons and, in the end, turns out to be primarily God's communication of information rather than a unique covenantal bond of favor. As will be argued in this essay, God's covenant promising to us is more than just a presentation to our minds of the relationship between redemption and faith.

[34] Kline states, "covenant is no longer identified with election and guaranteed blessing, and especially when the baptismal sign of incorporation into the covenant is understood as pointing *without prejudice* to a judgment ordeal with the potential of both curse and blessing," *By Oath Consigned*, 50 (emphasis mine). J.V. Fesko's recent book on baptism, *Water, Word and Spirit* (Grand Rapids: Reformation Heritage Books, 2010), makes this a central point of his treatment and it becomes his primary tool used to resolve tensions in Reformed baptismal theology.

[35] On this, see Edmund S. Morgan's fascinating volume, *Visible Saints: The History of a Puritan Idea* (New York: The New York University Press, 1963).

tize), on this view, are taken as "general" statements or as a judgment of charity. Since the *res* of the benefits (mystical communion with Christ) is invisible, we can only judge someone based on their confession. And since we cannot see into the heart, we judge with charity those who confess. Paul's statement that the Corinthians were "justified" should not be taken as a confident "head for head" sort of a statement, but rather as his receiving the confession of individual church members on a judgment of charity and ascribing redemptive benefits to them on that basis.

This view has several problems. First, Kline and Fesko's argument that baptism does not essentially imply blessing or curse is not well supported by Scripture. Even if baptism might result in curse, God's intention in baptizing is to bless.[36] Fesko's point that all of the Old Testament baptismal allegories included an element of judgment (against the world in Noah's day and against the Egyptians in Moses' day) overlooks the fact that these aspects of the events are not called "baptism" in the New Testament. It is Noah and his family (in 1 Peter 3) and Israel (in 1 Cor. 10) who are baptized in these events, not the enemies of God. Certainly Kline and Fesko are right that these various baptisms point to judgment, but it is ultimately to the judgment of Christ. But, inasmuch as baptism is related to union with Christ (and our dying and rising with Him), one cannot reduce the meaning of baptism to a "maybe, maybe not" sort of contract. And so, even if our baptism increases our judgment, it is objectively intended for and means *blessing*.

Second, this view reduces all aspects of the individual elements of the application of redemption to our actual possession of them. Though more fully argued in the next section, we can assert preliminarily that all of these elements can also be predicated of God's visible relationship to covenant-members proper. More specifically, they can be predicated both of the to-

---

[36] P. Richard Flinn, "Baptism, Redemptive History, and Eschatology: The Parameters of Debate" in James B. Jordan (ed.), *The Failure of American Baptist Culture* (Tyler: Geneva Divinity School Press, 1982), 111–51, makes this point powerfully in response to Kline. Analogously Mark A. Garcia, *Life in Christ: Union with Christ and Twofold Grace in Calvin's Theology* (Colorado Springs: Paternoster, 2008), 180, notes that Calvin goes to great lengths in his treatment of 1 Corinthians 11 to say that the condemning element of unworthy participation in the sacrament of the Lord's Supper is not to be found in the elements themselves (they are always objectively intended for blessing), but in the unbelieving refusal to take what is offered in the sacrament.

tality of our relationship with God and the particularity of His visible covenantal speech. Effectual calling, for instance, co-opts an objective calling in the preached word. Reprobate covenant members visibly receive this preached word. God's justifying disposition toward us is communicated in liturgy. God's faithfulness and love are communicated to us in the fellowship of the Christian community. Reprobate covenant members participate in all of these visible corollaries to the elements of the *ordo salutis*.

Third, this view overlooks the way in which the sacraments function according to the well-established indicative/imperative pattern of biblical ethics. It is precisely because of God's promises and grace that we are encouraged not to apostatize (1 Cor. 10:1–13). A major motivation to remain faithful to Christ is that He loves us and is faithful to us (Heb. 4:14–16). Our faithfulness is not to prove that we are already loved (though it does that), but to respond to the love already received. If apostasy demonstrates that Jesus never loved us in any redemptive sense, then the rejection of His divine and gracious speech could not be a basis for condemnation, because it never applied to the apostate in the first place (Heb. 2:1–4).

Fourth, our judgment of charity is not with respect to the identity of the baptized (they are part of the house and family of God), nor with whether or not baptism is God's gracious speech (it is such objectively). Our judgment of charity has to do with the confessor receiving the baptism. Our judgment of charity is not with respect to God's speech, but man's. Even more precisely, the judgment of charity does not concern the Christian's profession as such (that is also objective), but whether or not such profession reflects the heart. By analogy, when we observe a wedding ceremony, we have no doubt that a marriage occurred or that vows were publicly made, even if we must judge the exchange of vows charitably. If God is the groom, however, we have absolute assurance of the integrity of *His* promises.

Finally and most importantly, this view threatens the authenticity of God's speech. Again, the epistles of Paul are not just Paul's guessing what God thinks about the congregation based upon their profession. The epistles of Paul are *God's* words to the congregation. God's intention in inspiring Paul to write these words might be *more* than Paul's own intention, but it cannot be *less*.[37] Like the Old Testament prophets, Paul is really communi-

---

[37] John Frame, *Doctrine of the Word of God* (Phillipsburg: Presbyterian and Reformed, 2010), chapter 15.

cating God's feelings towards His people (note God's speech concerning "my children" in Eze. 16:21). That speech *is* a relation, a regard, revealing a real disposition toward a visible people. God really and objectively speaks comfort to His people.

These objections notwithstanding, perhaps a grain of truth can be salvaged from this view. What if we argued that, by way of accommodation and condescension, God Himself participates in the judgment of charity towards professors? What if God rejoices with every single baptized "as though" it were a real conversion? This brings us close to what will be argued in the next section as a solution to this problem.

"We Don't (Can't?) Know the Difference": Another Insufficient Answer

Another solution to the problem of apostasy in the covenant is to either collapse baptism and election or to say that we are unable to distinguish the relationship of the elect and reprobate to Christ and all of His benefits. This is argued in a myriad of ways. James Jordan simply says that there is no difference except for perseverance.[38] Peter Leithart implies that there is a difference, but is vague about what it is. Employing the analogy of marriages which end in divorce as opposed to those which do not, he states that "the conclusion of the marriages reveals that there was something fundamentally and permanently different in the two marriages. The differences are never merely differences at the end, because the end reveals the shape of the whole story-line."[39] Similarly, Rich Lusk writes, "The blessings the reprobate covenant member receives may be phenomenologically and covenantally identical to those received by the elect covenant member. Grace is undifferentiated from a covenantal perspective…but from God's perspective, these blessings are at most only analogous to what the elect receive. They belong to the 'common operations of the Spirit' (WCF 10.4), but the lack of perseverance colors and shades even that commonality."[40] Lusk is not precise, however, concerning *what* the similarity and dissimilarity

---

[38] James B. Jordan, "Thoughts on Sovereign Grace" (Biblical Horizons Occasional Paper, 2003).

[39] Leithart in his first Pacific Northwest Presbytery written examination, available at http://www.federal-vision.com/pdf/pacific_nw_leithart.pdf.

[40] Lusk, "Baptismal Efficacy and Baptismal Latency: A Sacramental Dialogue," in *Presbyterion* (2005), no pagination.

(i.e. "analogy") is between the blessings as enjoyed by the elect and the reprobate.

This is problematic, in my judgment, because the Bible is clearer about the difference between the elect and reprobate's relation to redemptive benefits than these authors imply. The reprobate can be said to have "never had" the benefits (Mat. 7:23, 1 John 2:19).[41] In Romans 4, Paul speaks about Abraham's justification (in Genesis 15:6). But Paul is clear that Abraham's perseverance later in his life (in Genesis 17 and 22) is inseparable from the justification earlier in his life. After going over Abraham's life of faithfulness, Paul concludes, "*therefore* it was credited to him as righteousness" (v.22 emphasis mine). Implied in this logic is that if Abraham had not persevered in Genesis 17 and 22, we could not speak of his justification in Genesis 15. Clearly, Paul is not arguing that Abraham's justification is caused by his perseverance, but He is arguing that no other faith (even initially!) justifies than the faith which perseveres.[42]

This view also fails to appreciate, in my judgment, that while God's covenantal speech is real and authentic, it is also conditional and provisional (sometimes called sacramental).[43] God's promising to be our God and calling us to be His people is one thing, but the mystical union enjoyed in the response of faith is another. Once again anticipating the argument of the next section, God condescends to relate to us according to our visible confession, but this is not the entirety of His relation to us. In the totality of that relation, Scripture speaks not only of the future but also the *present* enjoyment of the benefits of Christ as ultimately inseparable from our final perseverance (Rom. 11:22, Col. 1, Heb. 3). While we cannot distinguish between one confession and another, the final judgment will make us manifest (2 Cor. 5:10). The presence or absence of our redemption will be "revealed" (1 Peter 1:5, cf Gal. 5:6).

Perhaps the greatest theological problem with this view is that it casts

---

[41] 1 John 2:19 is certainly a debated text. See the discussion of Robert Yarbrough, *1-3 John* (Grand Rapids: Baker, 2008), 145-8.

[42] Of course, it is not the persevering quality of faith which makes it justifying. It is simply *that without which* it cannot justify. Scholastics call this "concomitant conditionality."

[43] Turretin, *Institutes* 17.1.22, states that we can speak of remission of sins in baptism "conditionally and sacramentally" but "absolutely" only in those with true belief.

doubt upon the faithfulness of God. In the New Testament, it is clear that the redemption which God begins in us will be completed (Phil. 1:6). Part of our assurance is rooted in the certainty of His activity (1 Thes. 5:23). We can *know* that God will certainly be faithful to the end. This is especially apparent in Romans 8:29–39. Note especially verses 28 and 38 where Paul can speak of "knowing" and "being convinced." His assurance is rooted in the very character of God and the nature of His redeeming acts. In creation, God's special activity of making the world is integrally connected to His providential activity of preserving the same.[44] Similarly in new creation, God does not breath into existence the "new man" who believes the gospel (2 Cor. 3-5) and then fail to sustain the same in being. In Colossians 1, Paul claims that Christ is both the world's creator and sustainer (v. 16-17). Paul then goes on to claim that in redemption, Jesus is also the firstborn of new creation and the reconciler of things in heaven and on earth (analogous to His sustaining activity in creation). Paul then declares the Colossians to be reconciled to God, qualifying his statement with a call to perseverance (v.23). Is it any more imaginable that one reconciled to God in the new creation order can fail to remain reconciled than it is possible that the created order can cease to be?[45] Perseverance, then, is not the cause of preservation, but rather the human corollary to God's preservation of His new creation in Christ.[46]

This underscores the eschatological character of saving faith. It is not just a receptacle for receiving the "last things" in Christ in the present. It simply is the presence of the "new man."[47] That is to say, "faith" is not merely a medium of receiving eschatological benefits or the subjective evidence of some eschatological "prior" in the human subject. The presence of

---

[44] I know of no better discussion of the connection between creation and providence that Bavinck, *Reformed Dogmatics, Vol. 2: God and Creation* (Grand Rapids: Baker, 2004), chapter 14.

[45] Think also of Hebrews 1:3 in relation to the epistle's concern with perseverance and assurance.

[46] G.K. Beale makes an extensive argument for the eschatological character of justification and for the essential connection between justification now and not yet, *A New Testament Biblical Theology* (Grand Rapids: Baker, 2011), 469–526.

[47] Mark Seifrid's discussion of faith in *Christ our Righteousness: Paul's Theology of Justification* (Downers Grove: InterVarsity Press, 2000), chapter 5, is the best treatment of which I am aware.

faith is virtually identical with initial eschatological transformation (John 5:24). While it is true that the Bible can speak of a visible sort of faith which perishes (Luke 8:13 and the "temporary" or "historical" faith that some of the Reformers spoke about), there is a sort of faith which simply is the content of new creation (James 1:18, 2:14).[48] Paul parallels faith-response to gospel proclamation with Genesis' portrayal of the existence of light as an effect of God's speech (2 Cor. 4:6). Faith can be said to "arrive" in history in Christ (Gal. 3:23). Christ and faith are so intimately connected in the New Testament that union with the former simply looks like the latter (Gal. 2:20). Jesus is the substance of the preached word, and the effect of both is the response of faith (Rom. 10:5–15). Faith's dependence on proclamation is its dependence of God's power (1 Cor. 2:5). The response of faith is the word performing its work (1 Thes. 2:13). The reason new birth and faith are so hard to distinguish (see especially Col. 2:12–13) is because faith simply is the form new creation takes in the human subject. Abraham's response of faith in Romans 4 is an effect of God's promise. He was "made strong" in faith (v. 20). The point here is simply that as the "and there was" of God's gospel's "let there be" is certain, the Christian's continuance in faith is no more in question than God's preservation of the created order in His providential activity.[49]

What shall we say then? Are we left with a hopeless contradiction? Must we say that God is favorable and not favorable towards the baptized reprobate? Must we increase ambiguity that the truth of Scripture may abound? May it never be!

---

[48] This is not to be confused with the similar-sounding language used by the recent "Finnish" school in Luther interpretation, for which see William W. Schumacher, *Who Do I Say That You Are?* (Eugene: Wipf & Stock, 2010). My exclusive point here is to argue that faith does not just receive (though it does that!) but is part—indeed, is the primary subjective instance of the new creation order in the individual Christian. It represents the intersection of human *pistic* faculties and the initial renewing activity of the Holy Spirit. In this sense, the debate over the priority of regeneration and faith might be called redundant.

[49] Cf. Vanhoozer's discussion of "middle-voiced" dialogue, which is a doing which can also be spoken of as a "done to," *Remythologizing Theology*, 426–33. The New Testament description of faith (especially in its connection with the word) might be illuminated from this perspective. Cf Ridderbos, *Paul: An Outline of His Theology* (Grand Rapids: Eerdmans, 1975), 231–36.

IV. Addressing the Challenge: The Doctrine of God and God's Speech

The Visible and the Invisible (Church, Man, Cosmos, and Salvation)

The solution to the tension inherent in the Reformed practice and theology of infant baptism is found at the intersection of the Church's (and the Christian's) visible and invisible nature and the manner in which God condescends distinctively to each aspect of that nature. The Bible speaks of realms which are visible and invisible (Col. 1:16). While distinguishing aspects of the created order generally, similar language is used of human persons particularly. Paul's famous dictum, "We walk by faith, not by sight" (2 Cor. 5:7) is said in the context of two chapters (2 Cor. 4–5) where Paul is (in part) discussing the outward and inward aspects of our human nature.[50] Arguably, Scripture underdetermines the ontological nature of the invisible realm,[51] but what is important for our purposes is to emphasize that the invisible is not fully *manifest* to the senses. This is precisely Paul's point in the famous statement repeated above, and is consistent throughout his discussion in 2 Corinthians. While the new creation is manifest in our endurance through suffering and in our faith, our bodies are outwardly decaying. The final judgment makes manifest the hidden things (See especially 1 Cor. 4:1–5, 2 Cor. 5:10, Heb. 4:12–13). What is unseen is believed and known by faith (not in contrast with reason, but in contrast with *seeing*). In terms of Christian belief, faith is related to the unseen the way Christian profession is related to the seen. We cannot know if someone believes, but we can know if they profess. Similarly, in a marriage ceremony, the saying of the vows is a visible thing while the intentional state and resolve to bind one's self to another in all the psychological and emotional dimensions represented by the vows is invisible. While we cannot see faith, hope, and love directly, we can see them indirectly through confession, good cheer, and Christian charity. It is precisely for this reason that the *eschaton* can be manifest in our dying bodies, even before the resurrection day. And yet it is a dim reflection (1 Cor. 13:12, 2 Cor. 4:11).

What is the relationship between the visible and the invisible aspects

---

[50] See Bavinck's discussion in *Reformed Dogmatics* Vol. 2, chapters 9–10.

[51] Cf Ridderbos, *Paul*, 114–26.

of creation, human beings and the church?[52] In certain modern contexts, one often gets the impression that the invisible church is the "real" church while the visible church is the "proximate" church.[53] Leithart has cleverly called this "Nestorian ecclesiology."[54] It is better, in my judgment, to think of the visible and invisible church as dual aspects (or better, *modes of being*) of the one church. This is why I have chosen to relate the language of visibility and invisibility to human anthropology and creation generally. The soul and the body are not two independent entities within a human being, but each is an aspect of the whole. It is not the "real" versus "our approximation of reality" or worse, "the church as we see it" versus "the church as God sees it." Clarifying this helps us to anticipate and argue that God relates distinctly to each aspect of the church generally and human beings particularly. In short, God relates visibly to what is visible and invisibly to what is invisible.

Once we realize that we are talking about two aspects of the whole or two modes of the one, we open up space to think of the various elements of the *ordo salutis* from both perspectives. And here we must think particularly of God's covenantal speech. What is an invisible and unbreakable relation between God and the elect in Christ (i.e. justification) takes the visible form of Scriptural promises and the public proclamation of forgiveness. What is an invisible bond of union and love between Christ and His people takes the visible form of Christian charity and communion (Mat. 25, 1 Cor. 10–11). God's speech to the baptized in the covenantal canon[55] and in the

---

[52] The best treatment of which I am aware on the Reformers' doctrine of the church is Paul D.L. Avis, *The Church in the Theology of the Reformers* (Eugene: Wipf and Stock, 2002). See also Jonathan D. Trigg, *Baptism in the Theology of Martin Luther* (Leiden: Brill, 1994).

[53] R. Scott Clark in particular, "Baptism and the Benefits of Christ: The Double Mode of Communion in the Covenant of Grace," in *The Confessional Presbyterian* Vol. 2 (2006), 3–19, makes distinctions between being in the covenant internally and externally, participating in the substance versus the administration of the covenant, etc. While these distinctions have Reformed precedent, Clark is very careful to put every redemptive aspect of the covenant on the invisible/substance side of the dialectic. While similar distinctions are made in this essay, my attempt is to show that these distinctions pertain to aspects of the baptismal benefits themselves as well as to participation in the covenant.

[54] Leithart, *The Baptized Body*, 69–74.

[55] This is important. We do not want to reduce God's speech to His people to His liturgical actions. The Scriptures belong to each individual confessor and God's speech is as direct to them in the pages of Scripture as it is in the sound of the min-

liturgy as well as His activity embodied in Christian service are all really His visible speech and activity toward His visible people.

Reformed theologians have often seen all the elements of the *ordo salutis* as aspects of the saint's singular union with Christ.[56] But there is certainly a visible aspect of this union as well (John 15, Romans 11). Christ relates to us publicly and audibly in calling and promise. He does this in word, sacrament, and community. As the one in Whom all the benefits of redemption inhere relates to us visibly, so we participate in all the *visible* forms that the benefits of redemption take in actual history. He speaks *publicly* to the church as to His bride, extending all the benefits of Himself.

In my judgment, this is why Paul can say to those who might fall away, without apparent qualifiers (i.e. "if you *really* believe," etc), that they were certainly washed, sanctified, and justified in the name of Christ (1 Cor. 6:11). Their objective visible relation to God was one of receiving promises. In the words of Paul, in the word and sacraments, and in the fellowship of the saints, God *at least* visibly spoke to the Corinthians favorably. The *ordo salutis* can be spoken of as visible in its manifestation because *we* are visible persons (who relate to things through the visible) and it is precisely to *us* that they relate.

Certainly this is not all that Paul means when he speaks in this manner. The benefits of redemption cannot be reduced to their visible corollaries. In the fullest proper sense, justification and forgiveness are, indeed, essentially invisible things. Bavinck can even provocatively write that "unbelievers...no more constitute the essence of the visible church than of the invisible church." [57] But note that it is the "essence" of the visible church (which just is the invisible church) that Bavinck refers to. And since calling and justification (etc.) have accidental properties (visible historical corollar-

---

ister's voice. Some recent trends in emphasizing "the role of the minister," in my judgment, threaten this reality. For the role of the minister as a "particular office" deriving from the church's "general office" and priesthood in Reformed thought, see Geddes MacGregor, *Corpus Christi: The Nature of the Church According to the Reformed Tradition* (Philadelphia: The Westminster Press, 1958), 197–226, and Avis, *The Church*, 81–108.

[56] Recently, Richard Gaffin, *By Faith, Not by Sight: Paul and the Order of Salvation* (Waynesboro: Paternoster, 2006).

[57] *Reformed Dogmatics* Vol. 4, 306. His discussion of the visible and invisible church here is quite valuable.

ies), they can be predicated (visibly!) of the visible church without qualification. Again, the focus here is not on the *res* of the benefits, but on their public attribution to individual participants in their non-essential public analogues. Like Turretin, we may speak of the baptismal remission of sins in a sacramental and conditional fashion, while reserving these things "absolutely" for genuine persevering faith alone. The visible is conditional in relation to the whole, but it is no less real—and that makes all the pastoral difference in the world.

Likewise, our relation to Christ and His benefits also cannot be *reduced* to the visible any more than *we* can. Rooted in this point is the argument upon which this essay hinges. Specifically, the visible and invisible do not always cohere or reflect one another. In the ways that this marks different boundaries around the visible and invisible church, theologians have often reflected on the "mixed character" of the church. When it comes to individual human beings, this is (in some of its manifestations) called "hypocrisy." One might visibly profess faith and yet not believe in their heart. One can, in a word, lie (whether consciously and overtly or in the form of self-deception). It is key to realize then that this tension between the visible and invisible is not a tension rooted in creation, but in the Fall. And it is not until the final judgment that heaven and earth, body and soul, and the visible and invisible church will be brought together in perfect harmony.

What I want to argue here is that even when this is the case, God still relates to the visible visibly. God's gifts really are given *visibly* in the mode of covenant speech. The relation established in God's word of promise is real because His speech is real. When a person visibly responds to God's real speech (i.e. relation) in the word, sacraments, and liturgy, the poor condition of their soul does not negate the fact that they have really dialogued in a favorable exchange with the living God at the *public* level.

This does not amount to two parallel "soteriological tracks" (one for the elect and another for the reprobate). Rather, what is described here are two ways of relating to the one Christ *and* the two aspects (hidden and revealed) of each relation. The elect are united to Christ in both the visible and invisible aspects of that union. The reprobate can only be spoken of in terms of union with Christ in a visible, public and sacramental manner.[58]

---

[58] Howard Griffith, "'The First Title of the Spirit': Adoption in Calvin's Soteriology" in *Evangelical Quarterly* 73.2 (2001), 142–44, has an excellent discussion of this in Calvin's language concerning adoption.

The point here, however, is that the latter is still a mode of union and it is real (even if not ultimately savingly effective). All confessors have a visible connection to Jesus and, as such, have a visible connection to all the benefits of redemption. God's covenantal speech in word and sacrament is the visible form that God's justifying and sanctifying speech-acts take in history, but the effects of God's public speech-acts are different in the case of the elect and the reprobate. Only in the elect is the "new man" brought about in faith.

How God Speaks to His Children

It is at this point that we must deal with an objection arising from a classical doctrine of God and provide replies rooted in the very same classical doctrine of God: how can this argument be right if we confess that God knows all things? How can God's visible speech in word and sacrament really be addressed to persons when God knows that their profession lacks vitality? It is not hard to see why a church leader might treat a hypocrite as a Christian (since they cannot see the heart), but God *can* see the heart. Am I arguing for a sort of schizophrenic or perhaps a dishonest God who relates to us one way in public but really might not like us behind our back?

The first thing that needs to be answered to this is that God seems to do precisely this, whether or not we understand how or why. But I don't think we are left with that. First, God is often, in Scripture, portrayed in a real give-and-take dialogue with other persons. The stunning dialogue between God and Abraham in Genesis 18 is a case in point. While God does not have any lack in His being and knowledge, He postures His speech toward us in lisps mediated to our location in space and time. This often takes the form of responding to limited pieces of information as though He were "standing here with us." The God of creation does this ultimately in the person of Christ, who experiences in our very nature the give-and-take of *human* reaction and response.

One helpful analogy can be found in the way parents, in some circumstances, communicate with their children.[59] Many of us have had the childhood experience of being asked whether or not we committed a certain crime. And, many of us have lied to our parents in such circumstances. In some cases, we later discovered that our parents "saw us in the very act"

---

[59] Thanks very much to my wife, Rebecca, for this helpful illustration.

of performing the crime but nevertheless gave us an opportunity to fess up to our mischief. Furthermore, they did not necessarily call us out on our dishonesty. For various reasons, our parents might have authentically and wisely "played along" as though our confession were true. Even though they knew our actual deeds, they visibly related to us as though we had not performed those deeds. In doing this, they were not intending to dismiss the truth, but to allow us to engage with the invisible pangs of conscience for the sake of our moral development. A similar form of non-deceptive but not fully revealing external relation can be found in Luke 24:28 when Jesus, with His Emmaus road companions, acted "as if" (says Luke) he was going to walk further than His friends, only to be stopped and invited to dine with them.

God as Author and Character

Similarly, Kevin Vanhoozer has extensively argued that God is related to His creatures as both an Author and as the main Character in the book (i.e. the world) that He authors.[60] God's relation to His creatures can be seen from the perspective of His authorial holistic perspective or from the perspective of His give-and-take dialogue in the middle of the story. It is Vanhoozer's contention that God's speaking role "dialogically consummates" the human characters in the story.[61] By this, he means (in part) that God as Author develops His characters precisely through engaging them as a Character in the play (especially through Scripture). His public speech often reveals the true nature of the characters in question as well. God's favorable speech in history is not His final word, but a word He speaks to bring about a variety of effects (creating faith in the elect, exposing the reprobate, etc). God's visible speech reveals election as His church-characters respond to His real gracious interaction. Some of His characters are complicated enough, however, that their hypocrisy is not revealed until the final act. But this does not change the reality of God's gracious speech-relation to them throughout the entire narrative. Clearly, then, God relates differently to such reprobate covenant members as transcendent Author than as imminent Character.

---

[60] Vanhoozer, *Remythologizing Theology* (Part 3).

[61] Ibid., 329–31. The issue of visible judgments could be dealt with in a similar fashion to that of visible blessing. Daniel's participation in Israel's visible judgment did not correspond to the whole of his relationship with God.

Narrow-lens vs. Broad-lens

There is an analogy between God's visible and invisible relation to individuals and the distinction that the Reformed tradition has made between God's hidden and revealed will. Though we are not precisely sure how both wills fit together, we confess that God's will is *one*.[62] But despite the unity of God's will, God declares His *value* for certain things which He does not ordain to occur in history. Similarly with God's relation to individuals: While God's relation to each person is a *single* relation, His visible communion with a person does not always correspond to mystical union and an experiential knowledge of Jesus' preserving high priestly ministry. Bavinck argues that we can only speak of the decree as God's ultimate will, but this does not mean that His revealed will is an unimportant access point to our understanding of His "ultimate" will.[63] John Piper has argued that we must speak of God's will from both a "narrow-lens" and a "broad-lens" perspective. Considered apart from the relationship of the whole nexus of God's values, God's revealed will can be said to be in tension with His decree. God elects only some (Romans 9) but desires the salvation of all (1 Tim. 2:4, 2 Peter 3:9). God takes no pleasure in the death of the one who dies (Eze. 18:23), but He does delight in justice (Deut. 28:63). Piper's solution is to argue that from the narrow-lens of the suffering of the wicked (considered in itself), God takes no pleasure in their suffering. But from the broad lens of the relation of that event to the affirmation of His created order and the maintenance of divine justice, the event (broadly considered) does please God.[64] Another way of saying this is that God's decree is God's will concerning a particular object in that object's relationship to all other things in space and time. For instance, God's decree concerning this paper is His will for it in this paper's relationship to every particle, substance, person, moment in time (etc.), in the universe. But we can also speak of God's will concerning a particular object as pertaining to what God values with respect to that object *as such*. With respect to this paper, God's revealed will is His evaluation of it, in itself, in its relation to His whole character. Is it

---

[62] See Muller's excellent discussion of the history of the Reformed understanding of God's will in his *Post-Reformation Reformed Dogmatics, Vol. 3: The Divine Essence and Attributes* (Grand Rapids: Baker, 2003), 432–75.

[63] Bavinck, *Reformed Dogmatics* Vol. 2, 242–49.

[64] Piper, "Are There Two Wills in God?" in Thomas R. Schreiner and Bruce A. Ware (eds.), *Still Sovereign* (Grand Rapids: Baker, 2000), 107–31.

true? Is it edifying? Does it glorify Him?

This is precisely the sort of argument I want to make about God's relation to the reprobate covenant member. God's visible relation (analogous to God's revealed will) does reflect a real disposition and a real personal engagement of mercy and grace. But it does so at the isolated level of the visible. As stated above, God relates publicly (at times) apart from all that He knows, precisely because it is through that scripted role that God accomplishes His intention as the Author of history. But from the perspective of His authorship (analogous to God's will of decree), God's relation takes into account all the facts of history (manifest and non-manifest). As such, God's relation to the reprobate covenant member (at this level & on the whole) is one of enmity. The former takes into account only man as a public actor in history. The latter takes into account the totality of who a person is as only God can know it.

God's "Emotions"

Another tool Vanhoozer contributes to our theological toolbox is his discussion concerning God's emotions. His account illuminates both our treatment of the dual-aspect of God's relation to each individual and the Reformed Scholastic treatment of the dual-aspect of God's will. After a technical discussion of what emotions are (concern-based construals of certain facts), Vanhoozer argues that God's emotions are His construal of situations according to His covenantal concern. God's emotions are how He "value-perceives" certain facts according to His interpretation of them in relation to His will (for Vanhoozer, His theo-drama).[65] While Vanhoozer's argument occurs in the middle of his discussion of divine impassibility (i.e. God's inability to be "moved" by the world), his treatment of the issue is particularly helpful to my argument. Why? Because it is not difficult to see how the argument of this essay might lead to an objection that goes something like the following: "Maybe you can account for a tension between

---

[65] Vanhoozer, *Remythologizing Theology*, 398–416. It should be noted that Vanhoozer's self-described "Post-Barthian Thomism" (and the analogues in this paper) could all be put in more traditional Thomist language without sacrificing coherence or innate explanatory power. This is not to speak of persuasive power, which is very much audience-dependent. A fantastic, and I believe persuasive, recent exposition of God's relation to the world in a traditionally Thomist voice is James Dolezal, *God Without Parts: Divine Simplicity and the Metaphysics of God's Absoluteness* (Eugene: Pickwick, 2011).

God's public vs. spiritual relation to a person, but given that justification and forgiveness involve His inner emotions (i.e. His favorable dispositions), wouldn't at least His emotions be schizophrenic given the potential dissimilarity concerning His disposition towards someone visibly and invisibly?" The answer to this is that God's construal of a situation, co-opting Piper's language, can be understood from both a narrow-lens and a wide-lens perspective. God's justifying speech in word and sacrament really does reflect His feelings and emotions as it reflects His construal of a certain *subset* of information, namely, the visible things. It reflects God's entire character related to an isolated object. God knows all things, but His revelation is an accommodation to *us*, and this involves His disposition toward the visible realm with appropriate value-perceptions for the set of factors which are only visible (or perhaps some other combination of facts which He appropriately construes in relation to His drama). Thus we can be confident that God really participates in our joy at the conversion of every new confessor. Even if that person will apostatize in the future, God interacts with us as though He knew only what *we* did about that confessor. The difference is that God also knows if that person is a hypocrite, and so His relation to that person is more complex than ours, and this includes more complex emotions. From the narrow lens of His revealed relation, He is favorable toward that person in word, sacrament and Christian fellowship. From the broad lens of both the visible and invisible information concerning that person, God is not favorably disposed toward that person.

Having set up a theological foundation of theology proper, we may now construct a theological edifice based on an intuition that has always existed in the Reformed tradition, and which is essential for the argument of this essay to be made relevant to the Christian life— namely, that we relate *invisibly* to God through the *means* of the visible. Analogous to the point about dialogical consummation above, our invisible character formation occurs through visible encounters with God in word, sacrament, and community. God's speech reaches into our finitude and we are called to answer back. Of course, our speech might be a lie whereas God's speech can never be.[66] God responds to our visible faith the same way we respond to other confessors. In His public acts, He inhabits a "judgment of charity"

---

[66] Vanhoozer has a fascinating discussion on lying in *Remythologizing Theology*, 342–45.

along with us. God does know hypocrites, but the issue here is not the extent of His knowledge, but of *how* God relates (often taking into consideration an isolated visible set of factors). Certainly He need not do this, and certainly this does not negate His essential omniscience, but God takes on a relation similar to the sort that we have with one another (as in the Incarnation), precisely because He is relating to us. And so God speaks visibly with forgiveness and favor to the visible church (usually through the rest of the church) and it is presumed that the confession of the visible saints is not hypocritical. But it is precisely *through* His visible speech that He invisibly communicates and effects new creation. In any case, Scripture is clear that the preached word is powerful and that through it God works invisible and eschatological effects (2 Cor. 3–5).[67] The invisibility of our justification, however, will become the visibility of our glorification at the final hour (Rom. 8:28–30 in context).[68]

God's Visible Covenant

God's secret decree is accomplished through the visible means of the covenant. Romans 9 is a key text in this regard. Paul begins with a lament over Israel's rejection of Christ and he lists all of their covenantal benefits. They are children, called, chosen (vs. 15). But then there is an election within an election (vs. 6–29). There is a special calling within their general calling. There is a special grace within covenantal grace. Abraham had two sons, but Isaac was his "only son" (Gen. 22:1–2). But these distinctions are created precisely within the covenant. It is through the general and public speech-act of calling that God accomplishes His secret calling (Romans 10). Election is ultimate, but it is accomplished through history.[69] We should reject, however, the notion that this represents two callings or two justifications. Rather we see the public *aspect* of all the elements of the *ordo*. In the

---

[67] On the way in which Christian proclamation can be said to be the word of God, see Stephen H. Webb, *The Divine Voice: Christian Proclamation and the Theology of Sound* (Grand Rapids: Brazos, 2004), and Michael Horton, *The Christian Faith* (Grand Rapids: Zondervan, 2011), 751–63.

[68] On the connection between justification and glorification, see Horton, *Covenant and Salvation: Union With Christ* (Louisville: Westminster/John Knox, 2007), chapter 12.

[69] Richard Gaffin's lectures on Hebrews 6 (available on Westminster Theological Seminary's i-Tunes page) make this very clear.

language of speech-act theory, God's locution and illocution are singular. But the secret perlocutionary effects of His covenantal speech-acts are varied in the subject (faith or hardening).[70]

Invisible effects are accomplished by God's visible acts in history. His invisible relation with each individual is accomplished through His visible relation with them. They do not always correspond in history, but the final judgment will make all things clear. The point of this essay, however, is that God nevertheless relates to us according to our confession. Perhaps the most poignant scriptural example of this is that of Jesus' relationship with Judas. In particular, the gospel of John is clear that Jesus was aware of Judas' heart (John 6:70, cf v. 64 and the apostle's narrative commentary in 12:6). On the one hand, Jesus' invisible relation to Judas must have been affected by this. Jesus cannot have been disposed toward Judas invisibly in the same way He was disposed to Peter. And yet we have no evidence that Jesus spoke differently (in any objective sense) to Judas until his apostasy was manifest in John 13. Indeed, Jesus' relation to Judas was clearly so similar (on a visible level) to that of the other disciples that they actually misunderstood what was going on *when* Judas publically left the upper room to betray Jesus. They thought Judas was going to buy bread (John 13:29) right after Jesus explicitly stated that Judas was going to betray Him.

This reflects the way that God speaks to us in the covenant. Remember that Paul's epistles are *God's* own speech to the congregations. Indeed, Paul often has a sort of "you'll make it" attitude to a congregation (some of whom would likely apostatize). The texts from 2 Corinthians quoted at the beginning of this essay are a case in point. This is similar to the author of the epistle to the Hebrews who is persuaded that, despite his warnings, "better things" were in store for the recipients of his letter (Heb. 6:9). These are not simply the exhortations of Paul and the author to the Hebrews, but of God Himself. And they cannot but apply to individuals. It is individuals who must persevere. It is individuals who receive promises. And yet this anticipation of victory will not, in the end, be true of some individuals. But God's speech-acts are never inauthentic. He is not being dishonest by encouraging some who will never make it. Rather, these speech-acts are to evoke a response. Through the ministry of the Holy Spirit, they are the very

---

[70] For an excellent explanation and discussion of speech-act theory as applied to these issues, see Kevin J. Vanhoozer, *First Theology: God, Scripture & Hermeneutics* (Downers Grove: InterVarsity Press, 2002).

means of encouragement by which the elect *will* make it. They are the very means by which God establishes and confirms the mystical union with Christ that sustains the elect.[71] The reprobate are truly spoken to, but they do not respond in faith. There is a relation between God and the reprobate, but not persuasion (even if there is visible confession). The history of Israel reveals the extent to which sin disenables us from being shaped after the pattern of God's will for humanity. Even the final Word is rejected (John 1:11), the "final" speech-act of God in Christ. It takes resurrection power (effective dialogue) to overcome this (2 Cor. 4:6).[72]

Conclusion: Jesus Loves The Little Children—And Us Too

In the end, it seems to me that the persuasive power of this argument is that it predicts precisely the pastoral dynamics we find in Scripture. Taking visible confession so seriously might run the risk of forgetting about the heart. And it is precisely for this reason that Scripture is so insistent that our confession reflect our hearts. But it also does this in precisely the way that this model would predict. It does not say, "make sure you are really related to God in a favorable manner…and then His visible speech-acts are really yours." It says, "Because He speaks to you visibly and you have responded visibly, make sure that your heart reflects your confession" (See Hebrews 3:12). And it is *because* of the visible encouragements and the confidence that God really is speaking to and loves us that we are enabled to respond. Furthermore, this view helps us to see why apostasy is a real loss of some visible relation to God. In sum, if this view is correct, we cannot just ac-

---

[71] My "functional view" of promises and warnings is pastorally similar to that of Thomas R. Schreiner and Ardel B. Caneday, *The Race Set Before Us: A Biblical Theology of Perseverance and Assurance* (Downers Grove: InterVarsity Press, 2001), but they focus on a "functional" view of warnings *alone*. Understanding how promises also "function" in God's accomplishing His decree in history helps us to see how He can relate to the reprobate publicly in a favorable way, even as He is acting to bring out their hypocrisy.

[72] Reformed Baptists often struggle to see how a Reformed view of the new covenant squares with Jeremiah 31, and its seeming promise that all of the members of the new covenant will savingly believe and persevere. In my judgment, Richard L. Pratt's analysis of this passage is persuasive in "Infant Baptism in the New Covenant" in *The Case for Covenantal Infant Baptism*, 156–74. His already/not-yet view of the fulfillment of Jeremiah 31 is echoed even by some non-Reformed scholars of the covenant in biblical theology. See Paul Williamson, *Sealed With An Oath* (Downers Grove: InterVarsity Press, 2007), 208–11.

count for the fact *that* God speaks to us in promise and warning, but also account for the precise *way* in which He does so.

Does the fact that God's public speech-acts might not correspond to His invisible operations make us question our own status as we draw encouragement from the liturgy? Certainly not. Our assurance is not rooted in ourselves, even our own faith, but it is found only by looking to Christ.[73] We do not gain assurance by having a look at God's book of decrees. Those whom He has chosen to justify can never lose that justification. But we know our election in Christ.[74] It is true that we cannot have assurance apart from faith, but this is true of any Christian view of assurance. A Reformed theology of the tension between the already and not-yet highlights our being situated in a mixed assembly and also the partial character of our knowledge (concerning others and ourselves).[75] Assurance is ultimately, then, an invisible thing communicated through visible means. Calvin summarizes the biblical position best when he says, "Christ, then, is the mirror wherein we must, and without self-deception may, contemplate of our own election."[76]

Finally, the major pay-off of this model is pastoral. Ordinary believers may hear the Word of God without a filter. I wrote at the beginning of this essay that the way that we speak to children is the way that we will inevita-

---

[73] Seifrid, *Christ our Righteousness*, 149–50, writes, "For Paul 'assurance' cannot arise from a present assessment of our works...Paul does not even speak of 'assurance' in psychological terms, but in an active sense, as 'boasting.' This boasting, as we have seen, is found solely in Christ and in faith in him...It is this 'certitude' of hope and not a present 'security' which belongs to the believer, according to Paul." The Scriptures do teach, of course, that self-examination may *confirm* our faith. An excellent treatment of assurance can be found in Schreiner and Caneday, *The Race Set Before Us*, chapter 7.

[74] Again, the tension with infants is the same as that with adults. The visible church is like Israel in the wilderness undergoing a period of testing (Heb. 3). Scripture teaches that testing is revelatory as our external activities reveal the internal effect of the word in our heart (1 Pet. 1:7). In this respect, 2 Peter 1:10 is less a call to subjective analysis than a call to activity, which then *confirms* our identity as called and chosen.

[75] On the already/not-yet tension in Scripture (as applied to redemption and knowledge), see Michael Horton, *Covenant and Eschatology: The Divine Drama* (Louisville: Westminster/John Knox, 2002).

[76] *Institutes of the Christian Religion*, 2 vols., ed. John T. McNeill, trans. Ford Lewis Bttles (Philadelphia: The Westminster Press, 1960), 3.24.5.

bly speak to adults. If we are suspicious of the visible confession of children, it is almost inevitable that we will be suspicious of the confession of others and (ultimately!) of our own confession. But recall how affirming Paul is to the congregations at Corinth. His warnings occur in the context of tremendous affection, affirmation, love and *confident encouragement*. We *need* this to persevere. We *need* to hear God's words of affection and promise and know that they are spoken to *us*. In my argument, we can take the pronouncement of the liturgy at face value. We can take God's care for us in the Christian community at face value. Even if they are not ultimate and even if they can be rejected, it is precisely when I know that they are really addressed *to me*, precisely when I know that God speaks favorably *to me*, that I am driven to faith, perseverance and love. We and our children must not doubt that we really do belong to God, that His revealed *intention* is to bless us, or that He is well disposed toward us. Certainly assurance cannot be had without the response of faith. But faith cannot be created or sustained unless I can hear God's kindly speech. God's speech-acts to His covenant people are His promises with our names written on them. He intends that we enjoy them. He bids us come. He speaks kindly to Jerusalem. We can know this as surely as we know anything, and it is because of this that we can respond in faith and love.

Bibliography

Anderson, James. *Paradox in Christian Theology*. Eugene, OR: Wipf and Stock, 2007.

Avis, Paul D.L. *The Church in the Theology of the Reformers*. Eugene, OR: Wipf and Stock, 2002.

Bavinck, Herman. *Reformed Dogmatics Vol. 1: Prolegomena*. Grand Rapids: Baker, 2003.

Reformed Dogmatics Vol. 2: God and Creation. Grand Rapids: Baker, 2004.

Reformed Dogmatics Vol. 3: Sin and Salvation in Christ. Grand Rapids: Baker, 2006..

Reformed Dogmatics Vol. 4: Holy Spirit, Church, and New Creation. Grand Rapids: Baker, 2008.

———. *Saved by Grace*. Grand Rapids: Reformation Heritage Books, 2008.

Beale, G.K. *A New Testament Biblical Theology*. Grand Rapids: Baker, 2011.

Beeke, Joel R. & Ray B. Lanning. "Unto You, and to Your Children." In Gregg Strawbridge (ed.), *The Case for Covenantal Infant Baptism*, 49–69. Phillipsburg, NJ: Presbyterian and Reformed, 2003.

Berkouwer, G.C. *The Sacraments*. Grand Rapids: Eerdmans, 1981.

Beasley-Murray, G.R. *Baptism in the New Testament*. Grand Rapids: Eerdmans, 1962.

Brownson, James V. *The Promise of Baptism*. Grand Rapids: Eerdmans, 2007.

Calvin, John. *Institutes of the Christian Religion*, 2 vols. Edited by John T. McNeill. Translated by Ford Lewis Battles. Philadelphia: The Westminster Press, 1960.

Carson, D.A. and Douglas J. Moo. *An Introduction to the New Testament.* Grand Rapids: Zondervan, 2005.

Clark, R. Scott. "Baptism and the Benefits of Christ: The Double Mode of Communion in the Covenant of Grace." *The Confessional Presbyterian* Vol. 2 (2006): 3–19.

Crouch, Andy. *Culture Making.* Downers Grove: InterVarsity Press, 2008.

Cullmann, Oscar. *Baptism in the New Testament.* London: SCM Press, 1950.

Das, A. Andrew. *Baptized into God's Family.* Milwaukee: Northwestern Publishing House, 2008.

de Fraine, Jean. *Adam and the Family of Man.* Staten Island: Alba House, 1965.

Dolezal, James E. *God Without Parts: Divine Simplicity and the Metaphysics of God's Absoluteness.* Eugene, OR: Pickwick, 2011.

Fesko, J.V. *Water, Word, and Spirit: A Reformed Perspective on Baptism.* Grand Rapids: Reformation Heritage Books, 2010.

Flinn, P. Richard. "Baptism, Redemptive History, and Eschatology: The Parameters of Debate," in James B. Jordan (ed.), *The Failure of American Baptist Culture*, 111–51. Tyler, TX: Geneva Divinity School Press, 1982.

Frame, John M. *The Doctrine of the Christian Life.* Phillipsburg, NJ: Presbyterian and Reformed, 2008.

———. *The Doctrine of the Word of God.* Phillipsburg: Presbyterian and Reformed, 2010.

Gaffin, Richard B. *By Faith, Not by Sight: Paul and the Order of Salvation.* Milton Keynes: Paternoster, 2006).

———. *Lectures on Hebrews.* Audio lectures on Westminster Theological Seminary's i-Tunes page.

Garcia, Mark A. *Life in Christ: Union with Christ and Twofold Grace in Calvin's Theology*. Colorado Springs: Paternoster, 2008.

Garret, Duane A. "Meredith Kline on Suzerainty, Circumcision, and Baptism." In Thomas R. Schreiner & Shawn D. Wright (eds.), *Believers Baptism: Sign of the New Covenant in Christ*, 257–84. Nashville, B&H, 2006.

Griffith, Howard. "'The First Title of the Spirit': Adoption in Calvin's Soteriology." *Evangelical Quarterly* 73.2 (2001): 135-53.

Horton, Michael S. *Covenant and Eschatology: The Divine Drama*. Louisville: Westminster/John Knox, 2002.

———. *Lord and Servant: A Covenant Christology*. Louisville: Westminster/John Knox, 2005.

———. *Covenant and Salvation: Union with Christ*. Louisville: Westminster/John Knox, 2007.

———. *People and Place: A Covenant Ecclesiology*. Louisville: Westminster/John Knox, 2008.

———. *The Christian Faith*. Grand Rapids: Zondervan, 2011.

Jeremias, Joachim. *The Origins of Infant Baptism*. Eugene: Wipf and Stock, 2004.

Jordan, James B. "Thoughts on Sovereign Grace and Regeneration." Biblical Horizons Occasional Paper, 2003.

Kline, Meredith G. *By Oath Consigned*. Grand Rapids: Eerdmans, 1968.

Lane, Anthony N.S. "Did the Apostolic Church Baptize Babies? A Seismological Approach." *Tyndale Bulletin* 55.1 (2004): 109–30.

Leithart, Peter J. *The Priesthood of the Plebs: A Theology of Baptism*. Eugene, OR: Wipf and Stock, 2003.

———. "Trinitarian Anthropology: Toward a Trinitarian Re-casting of

Reformed Theology" in E. Calvin Beisner (ed.), *The Auburn Avenue Theology*. Fort Lauderdale: Knox Theological Seminary, 2004.

———. *The Baptized Body*. Moscow: Canon, 2007.

———. Pacific Northwest Presbytery written examination. Available at http://www.federal-vision.com/pdf/pacific_nw_leithart.pdf.

Lillback, Peter A. *The Binding of God: Calvin's Role in the Development of Covenant Theology*. Grand Rapids: Baker, 2001.

Lusk, Rich. "Baptismal Efficacy and Baptismal Latency: A Sacramental Dialogue." *Presbyterion* (2005).

———. "God of My Youth: Infant Faith in the Psalter." In Gregg Strawbridge (ed.), *The Case for Covenant Communion*, 89–110. Monroe: Athanasius Press, 2006.

MacGregor, Geddes. *Corpus Christi: The Nature of the Church According to the Reformed Tradition*. Philadelphia: The Westminster Press, 1958.

Marshall, I. Howard. "Acts." In G.K. Beale & D.A. Carson (eds.), *Commentary on the New Testament Use of the Old Testament*, 513–606. Grand Rapids: Baker, 2007.

Morgan, Edmund S. *Visible Saints: The History of a Puritan Idea*. New York: The New York University Press, 1963.

Muller, Richard A. *Post Reformation Reformed Dogmatics Vol. 3: The Divine Essence and Attributes*. Grand Rapids: Baker, 2003.

Murray, John. *Christian Baptism*. Phillipsburg, NJ: Presbyterian and Reformed, 1980.

Piper, John. "Are There Two Wills in God?" In Thomas R. Schreiner and Bruce A. Ware (eds.), *Still Sovereign*, 107–31. Grand Rapids: Baker, 2000.

Poythress, Vern S. "Indifferentism and Rigorism in the Church: With Implications for Baptizing Small Children." *Westminster Theological Journal*

59.1 (1997): 13-29.

———. "Linking Small Children with Infants in the Theology of Baptizing." *Westminster Theological Journal* 59.2 (1997): 143-58.

Pratt, Richard L. "Infant Baptism in the New Covenant." In Greg Strawbridge (ed.), *The Case for Covenantal Infant Baptism*, 156–74. Phillipsburg, NJ: Presbyterian and Reformed, 2003.

Ridderbos, Herman. *Paul: An Outline of His Theology*. Grand Rapids: Eerdmans, 1975.

Ross, Mark E. "Baptism and Circumcision as Signs and Seals." In Gregg Strawbridge (ed.), *The Case for Covenantal Infant Baptism*, 85–111. Phillipsburg, NJ: Presbyterian and Reformed, 2003.

Schouls, C.A. *The Covenant of Grace: Its Scripture Origins and Development in Continental Theology*. Vineland: Niagara Ligonier Study Center, 1996.

Schreiner, Thomas R. & Ardel B. Caneday. *The Race Set Before Us: A Biblical Theology of Perseverance and Assurance*. Downers Grove: InterVarsity Press, 2001.

Schumacher, William W. *Who Do I Say That You Are?* Eugene: Wipf & Stock, 2010.

Seifrid, Mark A. *Christ Our Righteousness: Paul's Theology of Justification*. Downers Grove, IL: InterVarsity Press, 2000.

Shedd, William G.T. *Dogmatic Theology*. Philipsburg, NJ: Presbyterian & Reformed, 2003.

Smith, James K.A. *Desiring the Kingdom*. Grand Rapids: Baker, 2009.

Taylor, Charles. *Sources of the Self*. Cambridge, MA: Harvard University Press, 1989.

———. *A Secular Age*. Cambridge: Harvard University Press, 2007.

Trigg, Jonathan D. *Baptism in the Theology of Martin Luther*. Leiden: Brill, 1994.

Turretin, Francis. *Institutes of Elenctic Theology*, 3 vols. Phillipsburg, NJ: Presbyterian and Reformed, 1992.

Van Drunen, David. *Living in God's Two Kingdoms*. Wheaton: Crossway, 2010.

Vanhoozer, Kevin J. *First Theology: God, Scripture & Hermeneutics*. Downers Grove, IL: InterVarsity Press, 2002.

———. *Remythologizing Theology: Divine Action, Passion and Authorship* (New York: Cambridge University Press, 2010.

Webb, Stephen H. *The Divine Voice: Christian Proclamation and the Theology of Sound*. Grand Rapids: Brazos, 2004.

Williamson, Paul R. *Sealed With an Oath*. Downers Grove, IL: InterVarsity Press, 2007.

Wilson, Douglas. "Baptism and Children: Their Place in the Old and New Testaments." In Gregg Strawbridge (ed.), *The Case for Covenantal Infant Baptism*, 286–302. Phillipsburg, NJ: Presbyterian and Reformed, 2003.

Witsius, Herman. *The Economy of the Covenants Between God and Man*. Escondido, CA: del Dulk Christian Foundation, 1990.

Yarbrough, Robert W. *1-3 John*. Grand Rapids: Baker, 2008.

ABOUT THE DAVENANT TRUST

The Davenant Trust aims to equip evangelical and Reformed Christians today for church leadership, civic participation, and faithful discipleship in other vocations as responsible citizens, by encouraging scholarly research into the time-tested resources of early Protestant theology, philosophy, ethics, civics, and jurisprudence, and by putting these resources at the disposal of the contemporary church.

We are a nonprofit organization supported by your tax-deductible gifts. Learn more about us, and donate, at www.davenanttrust.org.

Made in the USA
Lexington, KY
07 November 2014

Theory of Optimal Search

Second Edition

Other ORSA Books:

Artificial Intelligence for Military Applications, by Barry J. Silverman and Williams P. Hutzler
Budgeting for Sustainability, edited by John C. Honig
Cost Analysis, Edited by Gerald R. McNichols
Force-on-Force Attrition Modelling, by James G. Taylor
Lanchester Models of Warfare, Vols. I and II, by James G. Taylor
Publishing Guide for Engineering Sciences, by Haluk Bekirogulu and Kip Becker
Search and Detection, by Alan R. Washburn
Simulating Violators, by Chanoch Jacobsen and Richard Bronson
System Dynamics and Modeling, by Rolf Clark

ORSA Books
c/o Ketron, Inc.
1700 N. Moore St.
Arlington, VA 22309

Theory of Optimal Search

LAWRENCE D. STONE

Metron, Inc.
McLean, Virginia

Military Applications Section
Operations Research Society of America

Second Edition

1989

COPYRIGHT ©, BY LAWRENCE D. STONE
ALL RIGHTS RESERVED
NO PART OF THIS PUBLICATION MAY BE REPRODUCED OR
TRANSMITTED IN ANY FORM OR BY ANY MEANS, ELECTRONIC
OR MECHANICAL, INCLUDING PHOTOGRAPHY, RECORDING, OR ANY
INFORMATION STORAGE AND RETRIEVAL SYSTEM, WITHOUT PERMISSION
IN WRITING FROM THE PUBLISHER.

ORSA BOOKS
c/o Ketron, Inc., 1700 N. Moore St., Arlington, Virginia 22209

Previous Edition Copyright © 1975
ACADEMIC PRESS

Library of Congress Catalog Number: 89-60873

ISBN 1-877640-00-X

PRINTED IN THE UNITED STATES OF AMERICA